LOUIS OWENS

American Indian Literature and Critical Studies Series
Gerald Vizenor, General Editor

Louis Owens, 1999. Photograph courtesy of Jacquelyn Kilpatrick.

LOUIS OWENS

Literary Reflections on His Life and Work

Edited by
JACQUELYN KILPATRICK

UNIVERSITY OF OKLAHOMA PRESS : NORMAN

Also by Jacquelyn Kilpatrick
Celluloid Indians: Native Americans and Film (Lincoln, 1999)

Chapter 2 appeared in *Atlantic Literary Review* 1.1 (Jul.–Sep. 2000):
135–57. Chapter 3 appeared in *Toward a Native American Critical
Theory* (Lincoln: University of Nebraska Press, © 2003). Chapter 5
appeared in *SAIL* 10.2 (summer 1998): 61–78. Chapter 9 appeared
in *American Indian Quarterly* 24.2 (spring 2000): 247–63, © 2000 by
the University of Nebraska Press.

Library of Congress Cataloging-in-Publication Data

Louis Owens : literary reflections on his life and work / edited by
Jacquelyn Kilpatrick.
 p. cm. — (American Indian literature and critical studies
series ; v. 46)
 Includes index.
 "Works of Louis Owens": p.
 ISBN 0-8061-3587-5 (alk. paper)
 1. Owens, Louis—Criticism and interpretation. 2. Tricksters
in literature. 3. Indians in literature. I. Kilpatrick, Jacquelyn,
1950– II. Series.

PS3565.W567Z77 2004
813'.54—dc22

                                        2003065023

Louis Owens: Literary Reflections on His Life and Work is Volume 46 in
the American Indian Literature and Critical Studies Series.

The paper in this book meets the guidelines for permanence and
durability of the Committee on Production Guidelines for Book
Longevity of the Council on Library Resources, Inc. ∞

1 2 3 4 5 6 7 8 9 10

This book is meant as a tribute to Louis Owens—a remarkable man, a uniquely talented writer and scholar, and a cherished friend of each of the contributors. It is dedicated to the people Louis most loved—Polly, Elizabeth, and Alexandra Owens.

Contents

Louis Owens

Abbreviations

"As If" "As If an Indian Were Really an Indian: Native American
         Voices and Postcolonial Theory"
DR *Dark River: A Novel*
MM *Mixedblood Messages: Literature, Film, Family, Place*
OD *Other Destinies: Understanding the American Indian Novel*
SS *The Sharpest Sight: A Novel*
Train *I Hear the Train: Reflections, Inventions, Refractions*

Introduction

JACQUELYN KILPATRICK

Every work is a different gamble and exploration.
                                        MIXEDBLOOD MESSAGES

*Together, I believe they form a pattern, one turn and twist of
the labyrinth leading to another.*
                                        I HEAR THE TRAIN

A few years ago, I had the honor of introducing Louis Owens
to a conference audience. At the end of the introduction I
turned to him and, feeling very pleased with myself for
remembering a lengthy list of literary and scholarly awards, honors,
and prizes he had received, asked if I had forgotten anything. His
response was, "I'm the former cross-cut saw champion of the Prescott National Forest."

People who knew Louis will say, "That sounds like him," and it
does. It was not that he was trying to be funny, though he was, or
that he was a bit embarrassed about all the fuss made over his
accomplishments, though he might have been. It was a natural

response for him, because he saw so clearly the complexity of patterns in literature, culture, and life—including his own rather remarkable existence—that neat packages were never close enough to honesty for him. Some balancing was necessary.

He spent much of his life teasing apart the meanings that surrounded him, separating the real from the imposed or supposed and putting it all back together in works of literary complexity. His work and his life, his past and his present were intertwined in intricate and sometimes knotty ways—the dirt-poor kid of Mississippi and California, the wilderness ranger of the North Cascades, the university professor and literary theorist coming together in works of fiction and nonfiction that have changed the way readers interpret Native American Literature.

In an essay titled "Blood Trails," he wrote,

> my family as well as the place . . . and its history figure so profoundly in my own work and my understanding of what the term 'mixedblood' means . . . to get at the concept of mixedblood, if one is of mixed bloods, requires negotiating personal as well as critical terrain. . . . I try to tell stories built around characters that I admit have a lot in common with myself. Most often they are mixedbloods with Choctaw and Cherokee and Irish and maybe Cajun roots, and they inhabit complex worlds in which the overwhelming questions are, Who am I? and How do I live in this place and time? . . . [W]hat I try to do with my fiction is to show Indian people—mixedblood or full-blood, Choctaw-Cherokees or others—who face their confusing existences with strength and humor, repudiating the easy roles of victimage and tragedy. (*MM* 142–43, 165)

In his two volumes of essays, *Mixedblood Messages* and *I Hear the Train,* he wrote of family, place, authors, writing, theory, and what it means to be of mixed blood; these are topics that also emerge in powerful ways in each of his five novels—*Wolfsong, The Sharpest Sight, Bone Game, Nightland,* and *Dark River.* What happens in those novels is not always pretty, and in fact they contain a fair amount of violence and brutality, but they are repudiations of victimage and tragedy through strength and humor, and each includes a return to the center. That "center" is not always as recognizable as those of Silko's *Ceremony* or Momaday's *House Made of Dawn,* in which the protagonists return to a cultural community center. Although that does sometimes happen in Owens's books, as when Cole McCurtain returns to Mississippi with his brother's bones, the return for Owens's characters is an *internal* return to a cultural center, a remberance of family and place, as when Will Striker sees faces in the water of his well or when the dying Jake Nashoba "goes home" at the bottom of a hole in the forest floor. Physical motion is a quality Owens associates with mixedbloods, which means his protagonists must find their cultural center by finding themselves at home in their own skins and with their own mixedblood identities, though their bodies may be moving through time and space or settled in a place far from their cultural homeland(s).

Of his own life in motion, Owens wrote:

> I do not know how to write autobiography, and memory is the most unreliable narrator, so perhaps I should begin by at least trying to get a few things straight: I was born in prison. I grew up in Mississippi and California. I have lived a great deal in the outdoors. I am not a real Indian. I have eight brothers and sisters. My mother walked barefoot across half of Texas. My father killed and ate another man's pig. The world is dangerously literal. Autobiography contains too many "I's." Were they to read what follows, and undoubtedly they will, my family would surely remember our life differently. But since nothing has been written down, I must put things together from the scraps of stories in my memory and imagination, beginning with Mississippi, where everything begins. (*MM* 167)

Memory, that "most unreliable narrator," is of enormous importance to understanding Owens's work. It is memory, whether "in the blood" or in the oral tradition, that produces the continuity that makes a culture, that gives us place. In *Other Destinies* Owens explains Native American oral traditions, stories held in memory, as having "that ability to 'bring into being' and thus radically enter into reality" (9). That sort of memory is in fact not unreliable at all; rather, it is where the heart of a people or an individual is found. "The world is dangerously literal" indeed, and Owens's work often focuses on memory—Native, mixedblood, or Euramerican—as an important arbiter in dealing with the literal inventions of "Indianness," with memory as foot soldier in what Vizenor has dubbed the "word wars."

Within the paragraph quoted above we find some details that are fleshed out in interesting and very different ways in the stories and essays within *Mixedblood Messages* and *I Hear the Train*. As noted, Owens was born in prison, but only because his father worked there. His mother did walk barefoot across Texas, after having been given away by her mother. He was not a "real Indian" in that he was a mixedblood Native American, not an East Indian, a distinction he makes in discussion of the hyperreal/invented Indian's relation to a not quite "post"-colonial theory. And it did all begin in Mississippi, because that is the place attached to the first of the memories that would beget the stories that would combine with the theory to become a unique and important contribution to American/Native American/world literature, culture, ecology, and philosophy.

Within the essays collected in this volume, the contributing authors have investigated a wide variety of topics in Owens's writing. From violence to myth to critical theory to environmental consciousness, the topics lead to discussions of the complexity and beauty of his work. Although the chapters cover a considerable range, there is obviously no way one volume could address all aspects of so complex a writer and his art; this volume is therefore focused only on Owens's work that fits within the "Native American writing" category. Although necessary, that focus leaves a hole too large to ignore in a discussion of his writing—his critical work in American literature, particularly on John Steinbeck, which I will attempt to describe briefly.

Of Owens's twelve published books, two are about Steinbeck: *The Grapes of Wrath: Trouble in the Promised Land* and *John Steinbeck's*

Re-Vision of America. Of the more than seventy-five critical essays and chapters he wrote, thirty-one were on Steinbeck's work. Of the eighty-five plus invited lectures, workshops, and presentations he gave, twenty-three were on Steinbeck, including his appearance as expert guest on the nationally televised two-hour program "Writings of John Steinbeck" on C-SPAN in April 2002.[1] In short, he began his career with a focus on American literature in general but with a particular interest in Steinbeck, and that interest remained an important part of his entire professional life. Though the majority of Owens's research and each of his novels have as their frames and hearts Native American/mixedblood characters and issues, it is not difficult to see the depth of the influence Steinbeck had on his writing.

His interest in Steinbeck was literary, of course, but the two also shared some fundamental personal traits that I think may have drawn Owens to Steinbeck. The most obvious of these is landscape. Owens spent much of his childhood and adolescence in the Salinas Valley; he knew intimately the terrain of Steinbeck's stories and felt a deep tie to the land. "I remember that place with a feeling I can only define as love—remember the texture of the dry earth and rustle of prickly oak leaves, the heat of summer on wild oats and manzanita, the taste of a spring hillside when the world seemed startled with new grass" (*MM* 172).

In addition to the Salinas Valley, Owens also recognized, with painful familiarity, the Central Valley of California depicted in Steinbeck's *Grapes of Wrath*. He lived there as a very small child, while his father worked in the fields; their house was an A-frame tent with the great luxury of a wooden floor. In 1965 Owens returned to the Central (San Joaquin) Valley to work the fields himself, as he had for several summers before. He describes his experience in "Bracero Summer," an essay that is both humorous and heartrending.

> You arrive in the field early, when everything is still wet from night irrigation and morning fog; you get out of your vehicle and take out the hoe you sharpened at home and look at the

first row for the day. The row lines out toward the horizon, curving away to infinity, and you start chopping weeds or thinning beets, row after row after row after row after row as the day warms and grows hot and becomes a mean flame on your curved back. Crop dusters buzz overhead and sometimes you get nailed when they dust, but you laugh and wipe your eyes. Beside you people sing and talk while bent over. You learn good things to say, usually involving the key word *tu* and often *madre*. *Hijo del puta*, you learn, and *pendejo* and *chingate*. You learn when such words are funny and when they are absolutely not funny. You learn that the name of your town, Atascadero, means "mud hole" in Spanish—not "place of standing waters" as you'd been told—and everyone laughs. More than anything else, you learn to defer all gratification not just to the end of the row or field or day, but to the end of summer, maybe the end of years. (*Train* 19)

When journalist Dixie Reid interviewed him in February 2002, Owens said that as "a boy reading Steinbeck, he recognized the landmarks they both knew and was amazed at how Steinbeck elevated those places to metaphorical landscape. By the time he reached graduate school, he had begun to discover the 'hidden' social, political, and environmental depth of Steinbeck's work" (Reid 4). One could easily say the same about Owens's work, as the short segment quoted above clearly shows.

Both writers wrote resistance literature. In *Grapes of Wrath: Trouble in the Promised Land*, Owens describes the uneven critical response Steinbeck's book received and notes that Steinbeck expected criticism because the book was "revolutionary." "The consensus throughout the first couple of decades of criticism of *The Grapes of Wrath* was that Steinbeck was to be classified as a proletarian, that is, as a writer concerned with the social plight of the worker" (13). Owens's work has at its center Native Americans and mixedbloods, whose issues include those associated with poverty, "brown collar" labor, the social and physical environment, and "otherness"—issues prevalent in Steinbeck's work as well. Owens referred to mixedblood writing as "a powerful literature of resistance, a countervoice to the dominant discourse that would reduce Indians to artifactual commodities useful to tourist industries" (*MM* 159), a "social plight" of a different kind.

Both Steinbeck and Owens can be, and frequently have been, read lightly because of the clarity of their writing and the deceptively straightforward stories they tell. Steinbeck could have been speaking for both himself and Louis Owens when he wrote, "Throughout I've tried to make the reader participate in the actuality, what he takes from it will be scaled entirely on his own depth or hollowness. There are five layers in this book; a reader will find as many as he can and he won't find more than he has in himself" (as quoted in Owens, *Grapes* 11). The essays in this volume represent a recognition of and a peeling back of the multiple layers of meaning in Owens's work, a task he undertook himself with a wide variety of literature, particularly that written by John Steinbeck.

There are interesting similarities between these two authors, but I think the major difference is one of class and perspective. They shared many concerns, but while Steinbeck observed the struggle of oppressed workers and destruction of the environment (among other concerns) from the outside and chose to become involved, Owens was *born* involved and chose to study and write his way to a place where some objectivity was possible and where he could make a difference while making art.

Place has often been noted as an important element in Owens's art, which frequently means an outdoor landscape. The descriptions that Owens gave of forest, desert, swampland, and glacier are stunning in their power and powerful in their authenticity. He seems to do naturally what he admired in Steinbeck, transforming a familiar place into a metaphorical landscape while drawing a picture that is palpably real and shows the familiarity Owens had with those landscapes.

Beginning in 1969, Owens worked seasonally for the U.S. Forest Service for seven years, first in the Glacier Peak Wilderness building trails, then as a wilderness ranger in "the most extravagant beauty the natural world has to offer" (*Train* 61), and finally as a sawyer on a hotshot fire crew in the Prescott National Forest. He spoke of those experiences as some of the best times of his life: "In my dreams I seek out wildfire and search for eagles that soar over granite and glacier. In my next life I will do it all over again, every single thing" (*Train* 63).

In "Motion of Fire and Form," he described going back to the Cascades more than a decade after his wilderness ranger days:

> I began to follow coyote, crossing the steep slope easily, remembering even that it is fun to slide down a glacier. Where coyote leapt across the narrow end of a crevasse, I did the same. Together our tracks emerged onto the rock crest on the other side of the glacier, and as I stood there in a tearing wind and looked out at what seemed a thousand miles of Cascade peaks, I imagined coyote doing the same. Why would he be on a mountain of ice and rock except for the pure pleasure of it? As I cut across a snowfield to finish the high route, the eagle circled endlessly. Alone, as I would continue to be for the next ten days, thousands of miles from the Yazoo and Salinas Rivers, I had never felt so at home in my life. (*MM* 180–81)

All his life, from the swampy darkness of the Yazoo River to the blinding light of the usually dry Salinas, from the high reaches of the Cascades to the high desert of New Mexico, Louis Owens was part of his landscape. He told me once that a friend had said the land was always an important character in his books—he liked that idea. He respected the earth and its creatures (most of them), and while he fought the notion of Native Americans as "natural ecologists," he was an environmentalist of the first water. He knew and understood the out-of-doors, and he depicted that world with loving accuracy.

A discussion of Louis Owens could not be considered a serious one if it did not include references to his humor. Because his novels have been deemed by some "murder mysteries," and because they are often violent, and because they address very serious issues, it would be easy to get the idea that they are seriously unfunny. However, Owens used humor and literary irony masterfully, as both tools and weapons. He built understanding with humor, and he destroyed false boundaries; he used it to cut away the layers and get to the philosophical, human heart of a matter. As literary theorist Mikhail Bakhtin noted, "[Laughter] has a deep and philosophical meaning, it is one of the essential forms of the truth concerning the world as a whole. . . . Certain essential aspects of the world are accessible only to laughter" (*Rabelais*). Take, for instance, Owens's description of his experience on a French talk show during one of his book tours, which is worth quoting at length:

I had been on national television, on *Canal Plus* in Paris, with Shirley MacLaine, men in drag, and life-sized puppets. . . . the publicity department of my wealthy publisher, Albin Michel, had used their considerable clout to get me on prime time with a big Hollywood name. It was a coup of such magnitude that folks at the giant glass publishing offices couldn't believe it. A nobody like me on national television with a great American actress? *Comment?* How had it been accomplished, they asked one another. . . . For me it was stardom qualified by the fact that the night before the show I had to wash my Levi's and best shirt out in the hotel shower and semidry both with intense applications of a hair dryer. Real celebrities didn't do such things, I was certain. As I was being rushed to the television studio in Paris, I kept smelling the mildew aroma of my still-damp clothing while Christine, my publisher's manic, thin, chain-smoking public relations woman was chanting in the taxi, "Open your eyes, Louee. Smile beeg." Being slanty-and-slitty eyed and naturally dour, when I tried to follow her advice I looked like I had been deflowered only moments before and wasn't sure what to make of the experience. Smiles don't come all that easily to anyone in my family. It's a traditional Indian thing, I explained to Christine. Traditionally, she had to understand, Choctaws did not smile for fear of offending various spirits who might become jealous of such happiness. The fear arose, perhaps, from those weeks alone in the woods as an infant. My *shilup* and *shilombish*, inside and outside shadows, might just quarrel right in front of the television cameras, resulting in permanent schizophrenia should I appear too jolly. But I tried.

. . . It was only later . . . that I learned my voice had been translated for the national viewing audience across all of France by a young Vietnamese-French woman. What had I looked like, I wondered later, speaking in the voice of a young Vietnamese-French woman? Coyote would have relished the moment, would have continued speaking in the voice of a young Vietnamese-French woman for the remainder of the trip. *Qu'est-ce que c'est,* Coyote? the French would say. (*Train* 110–11)

In this amazing bit of story, the barefoot boy from the Mississippi and California riverbanks nests rather cozily inside the internationally famous author, the one informing the other and each keeping the other honest. The illusion of naïveté is nicely undercut by the irony of his cultural tease, his use of the Indian-as-artifact in his response to Christine's "Open your eyes, Louee." Coyote is indeed speaking in France.

While talking with a class for a telecourse on contemporary Native American authors, Owens said, "Every writer is a trickster. Every writer *should* be a trickster. . . . The role of trickster is to test us—to challenge every value, law, every more we hold dear" (Kilpatrick, "Contemporary"). A laugh is one of trickster's tools, and examples of trickster humor are plentiful in all of Owens's books. As an example, take this little vignette from his first novel, *Wolfsong,* in which "Ab Masingale, the inventor, sat in a chair away from the bar so that his legs in their stiff twin casts could jut out before him." It seems that he had tried to build a helicopter, but "'[m]istake was them tin blades,' Ab said loudly. 'Too damned thin. Damned things got to going around.' He flailed a circle with one arm, and a portly old man with a bowler hat shoved his chair back with a mild look of alarm. 'Got to going around and started bending ever which way till they come off and took to flying by theirselves.'" Ab decides to make the next ones out of the hoods of old Chevrolets, because "[t]here ain't no stronger metal than them old Chevies" (98). This little scene is a minor detail in the story of a young Native American man just home from the university, confronting a clash of cultures in his hometown and his own heart. Its value is that, like a colorful shell on a rotten egg, it surrounds a discussion in the Red Dog bar in which the local Natives are referred to as "woods niggers." The comedy, in close proximity to a tragic turn of mind and phrase, creates a tension that whets the knife-edge of Owens's critique of unthinking racism.

In *The Sharpest Sight* we meet two unforgettable characters, Onatima (or Old Lady Blue Wood) and Uncle Luther, two ancient Choctaws living in the swampland of the Yazoo River. They are hilarious, but they are also two of the most serious characters in the book. An example of this is Luther's attempt to teach his nephew about the value—or rather, the lack of value—of revenge. He tells him about the Choctaw version of a duel, in which the two duelists are accompanied by their seconds. Luther says, "Then when it's time, each second kills his friend. Don't nobody survive a Choctaw duel. . . . That kind of dueling kept a town pretty peaceful" (96). Luther finds humor in almost every situation; by doing so, he makes it possible to look at what would otherwise be too painful to see clearly. As Willie Sypher has noted, "To be able to laugh at evil and error means that we have surmounted them. . . . Whenever we become aware that this is not the best of possible worlds, we need the help of the comedian to meet the insuperable defects of actuality" (246–47). And for a Native American character or a mixedblood author, actuality has a great many defects.

Sypher would no doubt say that Owens was a resistance fighter, someone who "refuses to make . . . concessions in a permanent resistance movement, or rebellion, within the frontiers of human experience" (246–47). Humor allowed Owens to examine the flaws in the fabric of the world without conceding to those flaws. Laughter contextualizes Native Americans' existence and marks them as members of a group to which the dominant society is the Other—in short, it plots the course toward the cultural center and overpowers evil or error by placing it in the realm of the humorous.

Owens's humor often has long, sharp claws. *Dark River* is intensely violent and makes serious critical commentary on a myriad of issues, many of which are dealt with in essays in this volume, but it is also intensely comic. In an interview with John Purdy, Owens said, "I wanted to overturn . . . conventions in this novel, disrupt stereotypes in comic and violent ways, with the emphasis upon the comic. . . . There is quite a bit of violence in the novel, but I like to think it has an almost slapstick quality to it, disturbing and comic at the same time" (Purdy "Clear Waters").

That a ghost in wolf's clothing pops in and out with one-liners is entertaining but, as Owens noted, disturbing in many ways. Other characters also offer something to chuckle over—Avrum, the Jewish anthropologist from New York who is more Indian than his Apache friends, for example. His idea to change the reservation into a theme park is hilarious, but his reasons are serious—he wants to preserve a lifestyle that he finds valuable. He is a positive character whom the Apaches in the novel respect, but it is obvious that the time-frozen nature of his ideas on what "Indian" might be has little to do with the late twentieth-century people he is trying to help. *Dark River* is a dark novel; the issues with which it deals, Native and non-Native, are complex and not at all funny, but like many other novels by Native Americans, it can make a reader laugh out loud. For novels to be active participants in Native American "survivance," it seems that moments of comic tone are very nearly a necessity.

His humor, his understanding of the multiple layers of identity we each carry, his unswervingly ethical honesty, his intellect, and of course his remarkable talent were all important elements in making Louis Owens an outstanding ranger, author, and university professor, but he always said his success was something of a surprise to him—that it just sort of happened. While that is no doubt the way it seemed to him, it was obviously the result of a great deal of hard work. He was only the second person in his extended family to receive a high-school diploma and was the only one to go on to college, but he attained a Ph.D. from UC Davis as a University of

California Regents Fellow before leaving for Italy on a Fulbright Fellowship, and it was only eight years after receiving his doctorate that Owens was made a full professor in the UC system. Over his two decades as a university professor he won many literary and academic awards, but more important than those are the many ways he touched the lives of his students and his colleagues and the impact his work has had and will continue to have on Native Americans, mixedbloods, and Others.

• • •

The writings that follow vary widely in topic, scope, and point of view. Owens's work allows for remarkable diversity in analysis largely because of its brilliant complexity and remarkable style, as the following essays clearly show. However, the first two entries are not essays at all—the first, "5 Canadas," is a poem written by Neil Harrison for Louis Owens.

The second, "Outside Shadow: A Conversation with Louis Owens," by A. Robert Lee, is the last interview Owens gave before his death. I have placed it at the beginning because it is important, I think, to hear his voice. It was originally planned as the first in a series of interviews, and therefore the questions refer primarily to the first part of his life, but his responses resonate insightfully throughout the whole of his too-brief existence.

My essay, "Taking Back the Bones: Louis Owens's 'Post'-Colonial Fiction," uses the theory that Owens developed most clearly in "As If an Indian Were Really an Indian" to illuminate some "post"-colonial aspects of his fiction, specifically within *The Sharpest Sight*.

Elvira Pulitano's essay, "Crossreading Texts, Crossreading Identity: Hybridity, Diaspora, and Transculturation in Louis Owens's *Mixedblood Messages*," discusses Owens's celebration of mixed heritages, pointing to *Mixedblood Messages* as an important achievement in the field of Native American literary theory.

Susan Bernardin's "Moving in Place: *Dark River* and the 'New' Indian Novel" is an exploration of movement, "transmotion," and—Owens's coined term—"indigenous motion" in *Dark River*.

Linda Lizut Helstern's "Re-storying the West: Race, Gender, and Genre in *Nightland*" examines Owens's interrogation of the American national myth and associated race and gender stereotypes in his novel *Nightland*.

Gretchen Ronnow takes a decidedly different point of view in "Secularizing Mythological Space in Louis Owens's *Dark River*," contending that the book is structured by myths and ritual but that it is about language and the monstrous doubles whose complicated existences parallel the infinite redoubling of language and interpretation.

Renny Christopher's essay, "Louis Owens's Representations of Working-Class Consciousness," looks at Owens's writing in the light of the relatively new field of Working-Class Studies.

John Purdy's essay, "*Wolfsong* and Pacific Refrains," speaks of the "intermingling voices" of people, places, and other authors in Owens's fiction; the breadth of Owens's work; and the way it relates to the physical place in which *Wolfsong* was spawned—the Pacific Northwest.

David Brande's essay, "Not the Call of the Wild: The Idea of Wilderness in Louis Owens's *Wolfsong* and *Mixedblood Messages*," explores Owens's treatment of the idea of "wilderness." Brande notes that alongside Owens's critique of the idea of wilderness is a discussion of the epistemological and political status of Native representations and Native attitudes toward the land.

Paul Beekman Taylor scans narrative violence in Owens's novels in his essay, "The Ludic Violence of Louis Owens's *The Sharpest Sight*."

Jesse Peters's essay, the last in the volume, was placed there because it is both a literary analysis of *I Hear the Train* and a personal narrative of a fishing trip with Louis Owens, thereby contextualizing Owens the author and Owens the man. In some ways "'You Got To Fish Ever Goddamn Day': The Importance of Hunting and Fishing Through *I Hear the Train*" does what Owens himself was doing in both *I Hear the Train* and *Mixedblood Messages*—Peters crossreads and crosswrites, cutting neatly between the analytical and the personal. The result is an image of Louis Owens that is easily recognizable by his friends, family, and scholars around the world.

NOTES

1. These numbers are taken from Owens's curriculum vitae. I believe there are some entries missing from that list, so the numbers may actually be higher. Also not included in these numbers are the thirty or more nonfiction essays he published in nonrefereed national publications.

WORKS CITED

Bakhtin, Mikhail. *Rabelais and His World*. Trans. Helene Iswolsky. Bloomington: Indiana UP, 1964.

Kilpatrick, Jacquelyn. "Contemporary Native American Authors." Telecourse by Governors State U, 1996. Segment 3.

Martin, Glen. "Unmasking Suicide." *San Francisco Chronicle* October 6, 2002: E1–5.

Purdy, John. "Clear Waters: A Conversation with Louis Owens." *Studies in American Indian Literatures* 10.2 (summer 1998): 6–22.

Reid, Dixie. "Vintage Steinbeck." *The Sacramento Bee* February 27, 2002.

5 CANADAS

(for Louis)

If I told you one day my brother and I
saw five greater Canadas south of the river
would you see them as we did then
up close for the first time
in living black and gray and white

wing spans as wide as we were tall
my brother and I thirteen and eleven
struck dumb by the sudden clamor
coming off a wrinkled patch of water
in the late September afternoon

five geese in motion so slow
it now seems they will be forever
climbing into an endless sky
and we below them ankle-deep
in tepid shallows south of the Elkhorn

the animal-vegetable-mineral broth
in this flooded meadow so full of tannin
bled from the grass and leaves on the bottom
the water coats our canvas shoes
in warm varnish as we stare open-mouthed

a taste like rust at the back of our throats
old and wild as the fear of knowing
deep in the blood and the father's blood
and the grandfather's blood
what must come next—

    If I told you we were hunting
    carrying guns
    my brother and I thirteen and eleven
    would it mean more
    or less to you

*"Then my brother, two years older, and I both acquired .22
rifles, and we hunted rabbits, putting to use the skills we had
honed on small birds. . . . He who loves this world is, in heart,
a hunter and tracker, can be nothing else."*
LOUIS OWENS, "THE HUNTER'S DANCE,"
I Hear the Train

NEIL HARRISON

CHAPTER ONE

OUTSIDE SHADOW

A Conversation with Louis Owens

A. ROBERT LEE

Out there, in Indian Country, anything could happen. A person might never get home.

LOUIS OWENS, "FINDING GENE,"
I HEAR THE TRAIN

In the light of his death in July 2002, it may well seem an oddity, untoward even, to recall that Louis Owens once said of our proposed book of interviews, *Outside Shadow*—its title taken from a Choctaw phrase he much favored—that it was helping give him a sharper sense than ever of his life.

The exchange that follows was meant to be the opening chapter, which we had provisionally called "Life Studies." Next came "Social Studies," a discussion of Native politics covering tribal sovereignty, land rights, education and welfare, casinos, and issues of mixed-blood identity and essentialism, but which was left unfinished at his death. That would be followed by "Literary Studies," given over to the role of the Native writer, controversies about genre and subject of the kind associated with Elizabeth Cook-Lynn, and his own career and reception as novelist, critic, and essayist. Thereafter we were to go through each of his principal books, their vision and styling of imagination.

Little could I have anticipated that the project we launched in 2001, and which on my own part was meant as timely recognition of his place not just in the literary firmament of Native America but America at large, would end in so abrupt, so simply disastrous, a manner. Like others who knew him far more closely, I mourn him and feel for his family. I could also slap him about the chops. His self-loss was all our loss, untimely to a fault.

Others in this collection will speak more directly to his literary achievement. It was large, consequential, a sustained effort of rendering experience into word and pattern. An irony that will not escape anyone familiar with Louis Owens or his work lies in the fact that, in his early fifties, he had truly begun to win a position of eminence, having an oeuvre that included the half-dozen novels begun with *Wolfsong,* the discursive work gathered in *Mixedblood Messages* and *I Hear the Train,* the literary-critical landmark *Other Destinies,* and the Steinbeck scholarship of his early academic career.

That reputation extends beyond his own country. It may well be symptomatic—I hope so—that I come from a British background in American literary and cultural studies, for Louis had won his following in Italy, France, Germany, indeed across Europe, and certainly in the United Kingdom. In literary-academic forums that have taken me to Japan, China, India, and yet others in Asia, his work has been a frequent reference point—the fiction in a context that invokes the likes of Momaday, Vizenor, Silko, Welch, and Erdrich, along with his criticism and essay output.

He had a profound interest in indigenous cultures across the globe, from Brazil to the Sami people, Australia, and New Zealand. If growing up provincially can often prompt a taste for the international, he embodied it, as the students and scholars who sought him out from all these locales bear witness. In that, as in the teaching, lecturing, and creative writing classes he did in California and New Mexico and in venues across America, he bequeaths a legacy to honor. It will take us time, and intelligence, to see fully what has been lost and yet what, unquestionably, remains.

A. ROBERT LEE: Let's begin, Louis, with your memoir "Motion of Fire and Form" where, not a little startlingly, you write, "I was born in prison." How did that come about?

LOUIS OWENS: My father was an army paratrooper in World War II. His parents, who were sharecroppers along the Yazoo River in Mississippi, both came down with pneumonia at the same time, and he applied for emergency leave to go home and take care of them. When he was denied the leave, he simply went home anyway and took care of his parents for a short while before returning. What he hadn't known was that the Normandy invasion was going to happen and that was why he'd been denied leave. Thus he missed the invasion and was also labeled as AWOL. His punishment by a strangely understanding military was to be made a military police-man and sent to be a guard in the military prison near Lompoc, Cal-ifornia. That was how I came to be born in California and in an army prison hospital during the brief time my father was stationed there. When I was little I heard something of this story and would tell peo-ple I'd been born in prison, much to my mother's consternation.

ARL: Which brings us on to family, a large one of Owenses. "My mother walked across half of Texas" you also say in that memoir. Who was she?

LO: My mother was born in Palestine, Texas, just across the Oklahoma border. Her mother was born in Muldrow, Oklahoma, and was Cherokee and Irish, like many other folks in that part of Oklahoma. Her father, who abandoned his family and had almost no place in her life, was Irish and apparently "no damn good." My mother liked to tell stories, including vignettes about her childhood, intriguing snatches of things like going out to find a lightning-struck tree for special kindling each year or dreaming of the little people who came to warn her of someone's death. Many of those stories involved pretty harsh things, like being given away by her mother at a country dance when she was a child, and being abused by the mixedblood sharecropper she was given to, until his sudden death from snakebite—what the little people had foretold. Her stories make up a kind of puzzle, each vignette a piece, and the pieces don't fit together very neatly because I was never able to grasp the boundaries or outline of the whole. One of those stories was of spending a winter walking across part of Texas toward home in Oklahoma. I have rather surrealistic images from that story of living in the woods, struggling to build fires on frozen ground, and stealing from gardens to feed her little brother and sister as they traveled, of walking on the snow and frozen earth without shoes, living for a brief and luxurious time in an abandoned boxcar somewhere on the journey. It's a strange story that recapitulates in my imagination the Cherokees' Trail of Tears. Of course, her story of that harsh winter was warped and woven through many intense years of her life, and now her telling is warped through the pattern of my own life as I tell it, so it would have to be a strange and surreal remembrance.

ARL: Did she ever feel defeated by her life?

LO: A crucial point to make here, Robert, is that in recounting for us these discrete moments in her life, there was never a trace of self-pity. She told these stories because she knew they were interesting and important to us, her children, not because she wanted to relive the suffering or feel sorry for herself. Never do I recall any hint of that kind of self-victimization in her (the kind of confessional celebration of suffering so profitable in publishing today). She clearly loved life even when it was extraordinarily hard, and the truth is it never did become easy for her right up to her death. I think having eleven children (two died at birth or in infancy) was emblematic of her absolute love of life and life-giving at the same time that, of course, so many children just made the practical aspects of life that much harder.

I've written a few times, perhaps elliptically, about my mother's difficult childhood. I reflect on it in amazement, how she came through so much without bitterness. Even when she was living with seven children in a tent encampment outside of Delano in California's Central Valley, where my father was working in the fields and we kids would go out to glean potatoes, I recall that she tried never to let us kids see that life was too hard or unhappy.

Her stories also included moving out to California with her mother, brother, and sister during the Dust Bowl along with all those countless "Okies," of going to work in the shipyards in southern California eventually, and so on. Photographs indicate that she was very pretty when she was young—with beautiful brown eyes, black hair, and a bright smile—but I never knew her as anything but old and in ill health, even when she must have still been a young mother. She contracted tuberculosis as a child in Oklahoma and lived with it all her life, having to register as a "carrier" of the disease wherever we lived, and she developed cancer early on and eventually died of cancer and emphysema before her sixtieth birthday.

She was a remarkable woman, the most compassionate person I've ever known, and a lover of words and stories and people. She could read and write, though she never got farther than third grade in any kind of school, and she was proud that one of her children actually went to college.

ARL: Did she ever see anything of your writing?

LO: She died while I was writing *The Sharpest Sight*, and though she had been in the early drafts of that novel, as one of the central characters, I found that I had to write around her in the book after her death, and, perhaps more strangely, around all those children she had, my brothers and sisters. In the finished novel, the mother is gone and there are only two children, essentially my older brother and myself, and a father. Still, she would have recognized everything in that book, and I think she would have liked it. She was the one who taught us about owls, witches, little people, the force of dreams, of dream-sending, and which wild plants to gather. She was the one who conveyed the real power of stories to form the world, and it was she who came to one of my brothers, one of my sisters, and me in dreams on the night she died to say good-bye, appearing to each of us identically many hundreds of miles apart.

A few years after my mother's death, I wrote the novel *Nightland* for my aunt—my mother's sister—determined to write a Cherokee novel for her while she was still alive. I dedicated the book to her and was able to place the novel in her hands a few months before she died. Aunt Betty read it and said in surprise that I wrote "Just like a real writer." My mother had raised her little sister, and they were extremely close.

ARL: And your father, Hoey Louis Owens?

LO: My father was born along the Yazoo River in Mississippi, one of four children of Choctaw-Irish-Cajun sharecroppers. His mother was Choctaw and Cajun French from what's called the Choctaw Strip just on the Louisiana side of the Mississippi River, in Catahoula Parish. His father was Irish and Choctaw, though his father's family preferred to hide the Indian portion. I have a wonderful photograph of my father's grandfather, who looks like a stiff-backed, mustachioed Irishman with a fiddle, and my great-grandmother, who looks simply Choctaw.

My father and his brother grew up running wild along the Yazoo. His older brother, Uncle Bill, was apparently determined to get an education and used to walk long miles to go to school. Uncle Bill was an earnest and likable fellow who would be bayoneted on Iwo Jima in World War II and survive only to die in an unsolved homicide when I was in my teens. He made it as far as fifth grade. Like my mother's, however, my father's education stopped at the third grade, and he worked in the fields along the Yazoo until he ran away from home to enlist in the army at fifteen. Whereas my mother was always interested in and proud of being part Cherokee, my father has never really made much of being Choctaw. It's simply part of who he is, and if you ask him if he's Choctaw he'll say "of course," but it's not something he's ever felt it necessary to talk about. Even when he was fired from a job in California by a foreman who called him a "goddamned Indian," he simply reported the event to my mother, not knowing that my brother and I heard, but said nothing more about it. Apparently he did punch the foreman, however.

ARL: What kind of life did he lead?

LO: I've always thought that my father is the only person I've ever known who could be dropped into a wilderness with nothing but a rifle and knife and who would not only survive but enjoy the experience. He knows how to do anything in the woods, how to fish with his hands or gather vegetation, how to trap animals, what a person can eat and cannot eat. He likes solitude and loves the natural world the way a predator loves it. As a young child in Mississippi I used to watch him get ready to go hunting at night, putting his carbide headlamp on—which stank to high heaven—and going out into the frightful woods and swamps by himself. At the time it was both awful and awe inspiring to my young imagination that a man could go out into those woods by himself at night, woods full of snakes and alligators and panthers and much worse to my mind. His vanishing into the night like that left an indelible impression that has certainly colored my own vision of the world and my writing. As an adult I've spent a great deal of time in what some call wilderness by myself, and I've walked many times alone through forests at night, but still I am amazed by that night journey my father made again and again. When one night a panther followed him out of the swamps and jumped onto the roof of our cabin, it felt like a very frightening part of the night itself had come home with him to threaten us. That cat has haunted my dreams and my writing ever since.

While my mother loved words and stories, my father has always been silent. He can do absolutely anything with his hands, from dressing out a deer to rebuilding a motor or building a barn or house, but he does not talk unless forced to. Though he is a deeply flawed man, like most of us I suppose, I've never known anyone to work as hard or do a job more thoroughly, and I learned a great deal by fishing and hunting and working with him and beside him. It may be that I also learned to value words in the shadow of my father's silence. Some of my most cherished memories are of walking at daybreak with my father and brother across wild-oat hills, deer rifles cradled in our arms.

ARL: And the story of the pig he killed?

LO: The pig story is in some ways a fine metaphor for how I understand my father and the world into which he was born, a world that seems immeasurably distant and unknowable to me today. It happened when we were living in Mississippi, in a two-room cabin up on log rounds to protect it from the Yazoo's occasional high water.

We'd been to visit my grandparents somewhere up a long dirt road near the river, and on the way back the big boar ran out of the trees and under the front wheels of the heavy, ancient car we were all piled into. I was very young, maybe four or five, and the memory has quite a hallucinatory quality, all darkness and dim headlights and towering woods. I recall that he wasted no time at all in bleeding the pig and hoisting it into the trunk of the car. I recall also the rich smell of blood that permeated everything.

Then there was the very strange experience of the pig being roasted over a hole dug behind our cabin, and neighbors materializing from the woods miraculously to help eat the pig before the night ended. I guess everyone knew whose pig it was and wanted the evidence gone as quickly as possible. The memory is one of light and shadow, fire and people moving quickly and confusingly, all impression and sensation. In many respects my memories of Mississippi are all like that: disjointed, impressionistic, strange, delightful, and disturbing. It seems a long time ago and far away now.

ARL: What of your siblings? You mention all eight of them with greatest affection, especially your eldest brother Gene. What was family life like?

LO: Family life was a kind of free chaos. At first there were seven of us kids, and then when my youngest brother and sister were born there were nine. We usually lived in the country or on the edge of town, except for a brief spell in a county housing project for underprivileged sorts, and the outdoors figured heavily in everything we did. If we'd all decided to stay indoors, there wouldn't have been enough room. As it was, we often slept two or three or even four to a bed, especially as there were often two or three cousins living with us. The house was always open, and people came and went unannounced and ate whenever and whatever they wanted and could find something to eat. Once a woman no one seemed to know spent two weeks with us, and none of us questioned why she was there or where she came from. It was a kind of maelstrom of kids and adults, but at the center was always our mother, holding that chaos together as best she could and trying to figure out how to feed everyone.

ARL: What about income, cash?

LO: We were of course dreadfully poor, living much of the time on what we brought home from hunting and fishing combined with federal commodities. There was always a hundred-pound sack of pinto beans in a corner of the kitchen because one of my uncles was a bean farmer, and there were big blocks of butter and cheese and cans of peanut butter and bags of sugar and rolled oats from the welfare folks, and there were disturbing cans just labeled "meat." A pot of beans seemed to be cooking at all times of the day, every day. It seems clichéd to recount it now, but there was frequently no money for things like shoes or winter coats, and sometimes simply no food when the commodities ran out. My brother and I would go hunting sometimes to bring home a rabbit or quail or squirrels just for a snack. A man with a third-grade education like my father could work as hard and as long as he possibly could and still not support a family of nine kids. As a father now I think back to that time and realize how dreadful it must have been for my parents to know they couldn't really provide for their children. I can't imagine many things more painful. But they just kept on, not always doing very well but trying.

ARL: Did this lead to family tensions or conflicts?

LO: In talking with friends over the years, I've come to think my family was unusual in one respect: we never argued or fought. Voices were almost never raised in our house, and no one ever hit anyone else. This had the bizarre effect upon me of making me take any harsh word from others very seriously, even when that word was meant as a joke or bit of irony. I had to learn verbal irony as an adolescent and adult, but I emerged from my family as a dangerously literal and naïve sort, as I suppose my brothers and sisters did also. I still do not like arguments of any kind and prefer to walk away from them, though I've learned I cannot always do that.

I feel in some ways absurdly lucky in life. I learned to work hard very early, in the bean fields and chicken houses of our part of California, and to complete tasks. I managed somehow to graduate from high school and even college. Of my eight brothers and sisters, only my older brother also graduated from high school. He was the first in the history of my family on both sides to receive a high-school diploma, and I was the second and last. The remainder of my five sisters and three brothers have lived difficult lives as best they can, some having a more difficult time of it than others. I've sat in the visiting room of a state penitentiary with one brother and worried greatly about other members of my family at frequent intervals. But regardless of the kinds of troubles shared by countless others in this country, they are a generous-hearted and decent group of people. They've accepted my anomalous life with charitable understanding for which I'm grateful, and they even read my writings.

Large families tend to compartmentalize, and my older brother, Gene, and I spent a lot of time together roaming the hills, hunting or fishing or working on cars when we got older. Thus I've always felt especially close to Gene, even when separated for many years. He was a great older brother to have when we were growing up, a role model even when I understood we were as different as night and day from one another.

ARL: It was a family of Native, Celtic, and Cajun origins. Would you say a bit more about these.

LO: Both my mother and father come from mixed lineages or ancestors. That creates a kind of fluid self-perception, perhaps. Irishmen, it seems, were in every woodpile in the South, and Irishmen very frequently married Native women. So an extremely large number of people like my mother come from Irish and Indian backgrounds. In my mother's case, the Irish part never seemed to mean anything significant, other than that she was "white." She was more conscious of being Cherokee, though she was long removed from Cherokee culture in any formal sense. When I was young I heard my mother saying that a group of Cherokees had approached her to join them in a court case over a land claim, but she refused. She didn't trust government or law, and I suspect she figured she would suffer from too much contact with either.

On my father's side, there was the same Irish mixture. Even though Owens is a name of Welsh extraction, my father's family always identified as Irish. As I mentioned, the Choctaw came through my father's mother, who was descended from Choctaw people who had moved across the Mississippi River into Louisiana in the nineteenth century in search of better hunting. She was also Cajun French, a common element in that part of the country. My grandfather was both Irish and Choctaw—what percentage of the latter, I have no idea. But he did not identify as "Indian" at all, and was, I believe, resentful of being thought to be Indian.

ARL: So when you say, again in "Motion of Fire and Form," "I'm not a real Indian," what, as you grew up, did that appear to make you?

LO: All of this has led to a kind of extreme consciousness of hybridity on my part. I was always conscious of being Indian when I was growing up, but my only real contact with Indianness was ephemeral. In Mississippi we didn't live close to the Choctaw reservation (created shortly before my birth) and had no contact with that sort of cultural center. Being a child, I was always trying to figure out who I was and who my parents were, and I had to piece together bits of the mystery from knowledge of my grandparents and the bits of story coming from my mother. Because we were so extraordinarily different from everyone else in California, once we moved there permanently, I tried to comprehend that difference by putting together what I knew of family history. The result was a kind of constantly shifting story of self. "Indian" meant, as far as I could tell, that we were outsiders, different, destined to be poor, living in a house that embarrassed me every day, and living in a manner unlike anyone else. Other people hunted—it was a popular pastime where we lived—but other people didn't hunt every day, often illegally, as a matter of survival. Other people's fathers didn't bring deer home in the middle of the night and have it in the freezer and refrigerator before daylight. Other people didn't have deer hanging in the room off the kitchen so they could cut pieces off to fry any time of the day or night. Other people didn't catch four hundred bluegill in one day and clean and freeze them all the same day.

"Indian," therefore, seemed more a matter of unconscious lifestyle than consciousness. As I've written elsewhere, I didn't realize that some of the things we did—fishing (illegally) with crushed black walnuts or going out to gather wild plants with our mother—were traditionally "Indian" things to do. They were just things we did unselfconsciously.

ARL: How, since, has the idea of "Indian" evolved in your mind?

LO: When I wrote "I'm not a real Indian," I was trying to get at a complex of ideas. First, I'm not what the world defines as "Indian." As Gerald Vizenor has said eloquently, that creature called Indian is a figment of the Europeanized imagination. There are no real "Indians" in that sense. But at the same time, I'm conscious that I am not "real" in the sense of having been produced within a coherent Native community or culture, whatever that coherence might be. I have never defined myself as "Indian," but rather as a mixed-blood, someone of diverse identity and background. Thus, when I hear a prominent Native writer, speaking on National Public Radio, dismiss my writing because I've never lived on a reservation or in an Indian community, as I did a year or so ago, I understand to some extent what that person is saying. It's true that while I've spent time on reservations and have good friends from reservations, I haven't lived in a reservation community, and that's a world I know only secondhand. I'm not like a Luci Tapahonso or Simon Ortiz or Kimberly Blaeser, because I was not produced in an environment in which anything identifiable as a Native American culture predominated. I'm not enrolled in any tribe, so I have no card testifying to my "Indianness." To pretend otherwise would be absurd, and I've tried to make this as clear as I can in my writing, both fiction and nonfiction. I always try to make it as clear as possible that I do not represent myself as a spokesperson for Native Americans (a dangerous thing for anyone to do, I believe), and I never identify myself as "Indian" but rather as a person who has Native antecedents and influences as well as other inheritances. At the same time, I was quite conscious as a child of my grandmothers on both sides, and therefore my parents, being something called "Indian" in their very different ways, and of my parents' inheritances in both story and everyday behavior, and that is my heritage too.

Growing up I was mostly conscious of being painfully different from everyone outside of my family. No child wants to be different, and every child probably struggles to deny or overcome that difference, because difference makes us vulnerable in the precarious world of childhood and, especially, adolescence. I associated that disturbing difference with being "part Indian." I knew I couldn't deny being that, yet it wasn't something I could turn to my advantage either. So I lived with an uncomfortable, indeterminate sense of self and with an overwhelming sense of wishing I were just one thing or another, anything absolute. Only as an adult did I come to realize how rich that unstable life was.

It may be that as the U.S. becomes more and more a truly multicultural place, with interracial and multicultural families proliferating, the nation will undergo something of this kind of crisis of self. The results will be fascinating to watch, I think. Recently a friend whose father is from Iran and whose mother is from the hills of Tennessee told me that he found himself reflected in my own stories and essays. He realized, he said, that he'd been battling his own mixed identity all of his life. There are countless numbers of us, Native American or other, who find ourselves between comfortable, essential self-consciousnesses, and that portion of America is growing rapidly.

ARL: Yazoo country, Mississippi, was the site of your earliest years. What most persists in memory?

LO: Mississippi is in many ways a kind of phantasmagoria in my memory, a fantastic wealth of images and impressions. We didn't live there steadily but actually made a couple of moves back and forth between Mississippi and California, but all of my earliest memories are of that Yazoo country. Our cabin was very close to the river. We couldn't see the water because of thick, junglelike woods between us and the river, but my brother and I were allowed to run wild in those woods all day long as soon as we could walk. We would swing on the muscadine vines, climb trees, catch snakes, sneak into the wire-sided cotton trailers to jump until chased out, and do whatever we wanted from daylight to dark. There were no neighbors close enough to play with, so it was always just the two of us. The world was rich with smells, from the dense odor of fermenting mud and dead fish along the river to the kerosene and carbide in our cabin. The river itself was deep and dark, impenetrable to sight, with a hungry current, or many currents. There were alligators that we'd sometimes see and always hear at night, along with snapping turtles and water moccasins and catfish reputed to devour careless dogs and children. Across that bottomless, dangerous water we played and fished alongside was an even stranger world of thicker, blacker woods and swamps. Our father would go across the river sometimes to hunt at night, and to my childish mind everything over there was associated with a kind of perilous unknown.

Mississippi must have been unbearably hard for our mother out there in the middle of nowhere with no electricity, running water, or much of anything except too many children. At one point, in what was undoubtedly a terrible desperation, she tacked up tar paper inside the cabin to keep the wind from coming through the cracks in the board walls. As a result, we lived in a home of looming black walls, and I remember the strange light cast on those dark paper walls by kerosene lanterns at bedtime. When she couldn't stand it any more, she forced our father to move the family back to California in an old wreck of a car carrying canvas water bags from every projection.

ARL: How, then, do you think of childhood in this context?

LO: For my brother and me, Mississippi was a happy time. We were quite poor, but when we rode the bus along many miles of dirt road to school, there were more desperately poor kids sitting beside us, kids who never had shoes and who hid at lunchtime so no one would see them with nothing to eat. Those kids would materialize out of the woods, white or Indian or black, from mysterious places, and when the bus brought us back they would vanish into the same woods. Beside those kids we felt pretty fortunate, even wealthy, for we at least had shoes.

Sometimes I picked cotton with the mostly black field-workers, but it was play-work for me. My grandmother made a small sack like the huge cotton sacks the black pickers dragged behind them, and I would work along with the laughing and singing men and women until I grew too tired. I do recall weighing my sack along with theirs, however, and eagerly waiting for the pennies or nickel I might receive. I also remember with delight helping my grandmother deliver alligator sandwiches to the cotton pickers and the cases of Nehi punch that would be there as well. The illegal sandwiches, I understand these many years later, came from some of those hunting trips my father made at night.

ARL: What do you remember of the houses you grew up in?

LO: Of buildings in Mississippi, I remember only our bare-wood cabin, with its rain barrel on the porch, and the house my grandparents lived in several miles away, a house that had at one time been a tiny church. Neither home had electricity, and water came from a hand pump on the back porch of each, and much further back was an outhouse. I cannot recall any other houses or buildings except those we would pass miles away on the school bus during the long morning and afternoon rides.

Thus, Mississippi to me was a world comprised of a little cabin on short legs, a shed where coon skins were nailed up, cotton fields on three sides bordered by tall, dark woods, and on the fourth side a narrow, junglelike forest that opened to the deep, black Yazoo River. No people beyond my parents, grandparents, and brothers and sisters make significant appearances in those memories. There was a black holy-roller church somewhere along the dirt road where in passing I would sometimes hear beautiful, wild singing, and sometimes people materialized out of the woods in one form or another, but those people are all just shadows of memory.

For a brief time in Mississippi we lived on a hog farm a few miles from the original cabin, but my entire memory of that time consists of a single image of a mule on a rain-streaked gray day, the poor animal slumped in front of a bleak barn wall as water pelted its gaunt sides. I recall no hogs, but in my family that residence is known as the hog farm.

I suppose Mississippi and the Yazoo have come to symbolize a part of myself that I do not know. It's a remote, disjointed, intriguing place of darkness and light. In the process of writing my second novel, *The Sharpest Sight*, that Yazoo country came very quickly to be a kind of balance against the bright, white world of California's Salinas River valley. The two worlds seem opposite poles, opposite sides of any possible reality one could imagine.

ARL: There was then the move to California at a very young age. What were those first years in the West like?

LO: I was actually born in California, and we moved back and forth more than once, spending time in the West before inevitably heading back to Mississippi in a crowded, rattling car. But we settled finally in California for good when I was about seven. And the primary impression I remember was feeling extraordinarily different from everyone around me. I lived in California almost constantly from age seven through college, and that feeling never really left, even as I also lost the vestiges of Mississippi childhood. It was in effect like losing one sense of self, for the most part a quite happy one, and finding nothing to replace it except uncertainty. Although I came to love deeply the oak trees and oat hills and dry creeks of California, I never adjusted to the people there, always felt myself and my family to be outsiders just barely tolerated on the edges of a society very satisfied with itself. I found myself trying to hide Mississippi and what my family represented from new friends in California whenever possible, deeply embarrassed as I grew older by the palpable signs of our poverty and ignorance and difference from everything that seemed to be valued by Californians. California was a place of insecurity and paradoxical warmth, of perpetual imbalance and nurturing oak trees and wild oats into which a child could disappear. The outer darkness of Mississippi was exchanged for an inner darkness in California, the inner light of the Yazoo country traded for the externally sunlit hills of the Salinas Valley.

ARL: You worked in your teens in the "bracero" program. Why did that leave so strong an impression?

LO: I give an account of this in "Bracero Summer" in *I Hear the Train*. I started working in the fields of California when I was about nine, beginning by hoeing beans. From that time on, field work was a pretty regular experience all the way through high school, though I had other jobs during summers and after school as well. While hoeing beans or sugar beets, it wasn't unusual to work with men and women who were part of the "bracero" program, which brought workers from Mexico into California's fields. So I was well acquainted with the people called "braceros" and felt comfortable working alongside Mexicans and Mexican Americans.

That work made a powerful impression on me, or perhaps many powerful impressions. The deepest may have been the realization that one could do intensely uncomfortable and painful labor for a long time without quitting—that a person could simply endure. The fact that others were working just as long and just as hard in the next row on either side made endurance more possible, day after day and week after week. I suppose that time also laid the foundation for an understanding that much of what we term "race" in this country is really class. Economics determine social strata far more than race does, though of course the two are at times difficult to separate. I know I felt that I had much more in common with the braceros I worked beside, talking about their families back in Mexico, than I did with the children of doctors and engineers I knew in school.

For part of one summer I actually lived in a former bracero camp with several hundred young black men, in California's Central Valley, and worked in the tomato fields near Merced. That interlude had the impact any intense, exciting, frightening, utterly alien experience would have on a sixteen year old.

ARL: "I have lived a great deal of my life outdoors," yet another observation in "Motion of Fire and Form," seems almost an understatement for someone who has been a huntsman, forester, firefighter, and wilderness ranger. Take us through some of this career.

LO: My earliest memories all take place outside, in forests, beside rivers, on hillsides, in canyons and dry creek beds, whether in Mississippi or California. The textures and smells and hues of the outdoors are more familiar to me than any other aspects of the physical world, and I'm at home there. I imagine that I would feel the same way about pavement and brick and steel and the sounds and smells of traffic had I been raised in Manhattan or the Chicago Loop.

I learned to hunt and fish very early in life, and those activities teach us to interact with nature in particular ways. When one is hunting, he is alert to color and texture—the way the hue of a rabbit or deer's fur stands out amidst brush when only a tiny fragment can be seen in shadow, for example—or sound or smell. One learns to tell which animal is moving in a brush thicket by sound alone, or which bird is stirring the air in a particular way with its wing beat. I no longer hunt, but I'm glad I grew up that way because I learned the world of animals through hunting more thoroughly and intimately than I could have any other way. I do still love to fish, though now I use artificial flies rather than bait or spinners (or black walnuts), and I still love to study the intricacies of a stream, just the way I did as a boy.

I've written a bit here and there about being a wilderness ranger, working on trail crew, and being a sawyer on a hotshot fire crew for the U.S. Forest Service, so I won't repeat myself here. Each of those jobs—or lifestyles—was the most wonderful experience I can imagine. As a child, once we settled permanently in California, I always longed for running water. I wanted a stream nearby where my brother and I could fish and hang out. When it rained and the dry creeks ran, we would rush down and build small dams, trying to imagine a real stream, and when we lived close to Atascadero Creek for a while, I fished and probed every shadow and corner of that stream for many miles. I also dreamed about real mountains like those in books such as Heidi. I roamed the Coast Range in California, but I wanted to be in the Alps, which I'd seen in pictures. When I went to work for the Forest Service in the North Cascades, I actually found that fantastic world I'd yearned for, a world of rivers and streams and glaciers and miles and miles of alpine meadow.

For two years, during college summers, I worked on trail crews in the Cascades, maintaining and building trail. Four of us on each crew spent ten days camped in the Glacier Peak Wilderness, packed in by mule string, and then had four days off to raise very limited hell in Seattle. The work was very hard, with crosscut saws, axes, and hazel hoes, and it was all wonderful. The guys I worked with remain my friends these many years later. One of them introduced me to the poetry of Gary Snyder while out on trail, and now I find myself in a university office three doors from the office of Gary Snyder and having lunch with a poet we all thought of back then as a kind of literary deity. I know, incidentally, that it's thought proper in Native circles to disparage Gary Snyder as something like a white shaman, as Leslie Silko has done, but I don't agree at all with such petty territorialism. Sometimes art rises above such things, and I believe Snyder's has done so.

ARL: And your life as a ranger?

LO: After two years I left trail crew and became a wilderness ranger, and those days and weeks alone in the Cascade Mountains were the most amazing times of my life. I spent a great deal of time outdoors alone as a youth, often hunting or fishing or just walking in the hills by myself, but I didn't learn to be truly alone with myself until I worked as a wilderness ranger. When you backpack alone for days or even weeks at a time without encountering another person, you learn to hear the world differently, without the echo of human voices one can never escape otherwise. You also see the world differently, because in silence you walk into the natural world and not only take it by surprise but fit yourself into it more easily. Animals that might flee unseen from the sound of a human voice will sneak over a ridge to see what kind of feet are making sounds on a trail and peer down or across at you. And different kinds of winds create different sounds in disparate stands of trees. At first I wasn't comfortable alone in the alpine country or rain forest, but once I adjusted it seemed the only way to be there. I have taken my daughters backpacking with me since each was five years old, as often as I can, hoping to help them feel at home out there. But unless I'm with my daughters, I always try to backpack or hike alone. Solitude seems the most appropriate way to approach mountains or what the Western world calls wilderness.

ARL: And your experiences as a firefighter?

LO: Although I'd fought fires numerous times in the Cascades, and I was part of a sixty-person fire-fighting crew in the Sierra Nevada of California, being on the Prescott National Forest Hotshot Crew in Arizona was the supreme fire experience of my life. I've written about that in an essay called "In the Service of Forests." I wouldn't exchange the adrenaline excitement and joy of the hotshot experience for anything. Running a chainsaw, cutting a line through timber or brush into the mouth of a racing wildfire, is an astonishing and stupendous thing to do.

I think this long, intimate involvement with the outside world has had a strong effect on my writing. I cannot imagine a story without the physical, natural world of which the story is a part, and the rocks and trees and, perhaps above all, waters of that world always inform the story deeply. Stories, it seems to me, come out of the earth, and every culture's stories reflect the natural world within which that culture was formed. Perhaps, in fact, that is too obvious a point to be worth making.

ARL: Eventually came college, a B.A. and M.A. from UC Santa Barbara and then the Ph.D. from Davis, a campus to which you have recently returned after a spell teaching at the University of New Mexico. You were the only one of the family to go through college. How did that come about?

LO: You know, Robert, even my own brothers and sisters have asked me this question. How in the world did I end up graduating from high school when they didn't, and not just going to college but completing a Ph.D.? And I really don't have an answer for them, or for anyone. In some ways I believe I was just lucky. I could have gone in a different direction a hundred times. I was a worse delinquent than any of my brothers or sisters when I was young, but I was never caught. Things could have gone horribly wrong on many occasions, as they did for others in my family and for friends of mine, but somehow I escaped unscathed. Looking back, it seems as if I was exempted in some miraculous way, totally undeserved. That sense of being saved without merit can leave a blemish like survivor's guilt on one's soul.

School, at least the reading and writing part, was always easy for me, and I was fortunate to have a few good teachers. In high school I was tracked through the shops—wood shop, metal shop, auto shop— and apparently wasn't considered college material, since no one ever advised me to even consider going to college. Even when I received the second highest score in the school on the SAT or ACT exam—I can't remember which at this point—no counselor or teacher mentioned college to me—a fact I'm a little bitter about when I think back upon it. They knew my family, I suppose, and didn't see college in my future. I didn't either, but now I wonder how many kids go nowhere because no adult suggests to them that they have a future. I liked writing, and I even used summer field-work money to buy a portable typewriter from a neighbor, a horrible thing made by Singer, a typewriter that thought it was a sewing machine. But writing was something I did for myself, not for school, and I planned to enlist in the military right after high school the way my brother had. I even thought a military career was what I wanted. Certainly not college.

College came about by accident, really. After high school I moved to Hayward in the Bay Area, where my family had relocated a year before (moving secretly to escape creditors while I was on a backpacking trip, so that I came home to find an empty house). I got a job working swing shift for United Can Company, making cans that were then filled next door in a tomato cannery. The job paid an incredible wage, something like three dollars an hour, and left me crippled after each shift, but I thought I was just killing time until my best friend, a year younger, graduated from high school and we enlisted on what they called the "Buddy System."

When I couldn't take the can factory any longer, despite how much fun it was to be in the Teamsters Union and go to their loud, beery meetings, friends convinced me to try junior college for a while until I could enlist. So I enrolled at Cuesta College, near San Luis Obispo, with no intention of going beyond one year. I'll foreshorten the rest of the story: A wonderful English teacher convinced me I could write and that I should write for the student newspaper. I got hooked on it, staying a second year and becoming the school newspaper's editor, winning a statewide editorial-writing award and getting to interview Ronald Reagan when he was governor, a man who even then stood for everything I detested. My journalism advisor encouraged me to apply to a four-year school and suggested the University of California at Santa Barbara because it was fairly close, even getting the application forms and helping me fill them out.

When I received a letter from UCSB telling me I was admitted and would receive a whole bunch of money as an Educational Opportunity Program student, I threw the letter away along with the necessary forms. I assumed the money was a loan, and having seen my parents dodge creditors all my life, I wasn't going to fall into the trap. My journalism advisor, a tremendous human being, roared when I told him and called the school to get more forms, sitting beside me while I filled out and signed everything. Thus I transferred to UCSB in my junior year and ended up with a college degree. The numerous accidents and false steps that finally led to a Ph.D. from UC Davis make too long a story to tell, but I can confess that I was a reluctant graduate student the whole way, dropping out several times to return to working for the Forest Service.

In short, I was lucky and I got good advice and help from generous people. By all rights I should be running a gas station or logging or doing ranch work, certainly not teaching in a university.

ARL: Let me ask you, Louis, about the 1960s—civil rights, Vietnam, and beyond. How political were you in these years?

LO: I transferred from junior college into UC Santa Barbara in the fall of 1968, and there could not have been a better time to land at UCSB. I had been convinced not to enlist and rush off to Vietnam, and I had somehow evolved as a political liberal, despising Ronald Reagan, Richard Nixon, and the whole right wing of America even in high school. I'd written a scathing editorial about Reagan in my junior-college newspaper, and by 1968 several guys I went through grade school and high school with, including a very close friend who was a tiny human being who could never have passed an army physical, had been killed in Vietnam. Others had come home crippled and bitter. But still I really wasn't very politicized.

That changed rapidly as the campus became radicalized. I attended SDS meetings—the radical Students for a Democratic Society—but withdrew from SDS because I didn't like the single-mindedness of those folks, petitioned against the war, marched carrying signs that said "Don't fight the bankers' wars; burn the banks at home," like students all over the country. After the Cambodian invasion, Isla Vista erupted in riots, the Los Angeles tac squad was brought in to subdue students and nonstudents alike, the National Guard came in by busloads, and Molotov cocktails were flying. My roommate at the time was a Vietnam vet who had been in Vietnam as a Special Forces "adviser" from 1959 through 1962, and he was bitterly antiwar and furthered my education in a major way.

I was inside the Bank of America when it was burned in Isla Vista, not engaged in burning it but determined to see everything that happened and nearly getting killed by a falling ceiling girder. A day or so later I saw a student get shot through the heart and killed by a police sniper. The Bank of America had brought a trailer in and set it up on the site of the burned bank, a symbolic gesture to show that they couldn't be forced out, and people marched on the trailer. A misguided group of fraternity boys went to stand on the steps of the trailer to protect it against the mob, and apparently the sniper, using an infrared scope, mistook the frat guys for rioters trying to burn this token bank. The shooting was ruled an accidental discharge, of course, and the police sniper wasn't charged.

They were intense times, times I wouldn't have missed for the world. One thing they taught me was that our government is quite willing to shoot its own citizens to protect property rights. I believe the U.S. could easily have had its own Tiananmen Square massacre in the early seventies. Certainly the willingness was there on the part of the government, as Kent State made unmistakably clear.

ARL: Were you, at that time, aware of—or indeed involved in—Native American politics?

LO: When I arrived at UCSB, I was recruited by the Native American Students Association and went to some meetings, but I never joined. My reasons were at least twofold. In the first place I've always been made uneasy by any kind of group; I don't join groups and actually very seldom attend social gatherings or conferences. I've been to quite a few powwows over the years and even helped organize a couple when I taught at Cal State Northridge, but that many people in one place make me very nervous. The second reason was that I basically did not trust the guy who was the president of the Native students association there at the time. He struck me as a huckster. In fact I partially modeled a character in *Wolfsong* on him. Perhaps oddly, I ended up much closer to people in MECHA, the Chicano student association, and in the Asian American student association.

For similar reasons, although I thought AIM was doing important things politically in the seventies, and I believed in much of what was going on, I couldn't warm up to the leadership in the movement. Frankly, too many of them struck me as the same kinds of punks I'd grown up with; they seemed very familiar. A lot of personal aggrandizement and posturing were going on—the kind of thing Gerald Vizenor has lampooned brilliantly in his writing, like the cartridge belts with ammo that doesn't match the caliber of rifle an Aimster is holding. Russell Means, for example, just this week was charged with domestic violence in New Mexico, not for the first time, at the same time that he's talking about running for governor of the state. That kind of stuff was much too familiar to me when I was growing up. If you live with or close to alcoholics, like my uncle and grandmother for example, you recognize the manipulation and opportunism that are central to that life.

So I stayed on the margins and paid attention. Sometimes I've regretted that, not going to Wounded Knee for example, just as I've regretted not going to Vietnam while my brother was serving three tours of duty there. But at the time I didn't feel that I could do anything but what I did. I guess you could say that I believed in the cause but I didn't believe many of the people in the cause.

ARL: You've taught in the California State University system, the University of California, and the University of New Mexico. How did those appointments come about? What, mainly, were you teaching?

LO: My first tenure-track teaching appointment was at California State University, Northridge. I'd probably applied for a hundred jobs, after coming back from my Fulbright year in Italy, before I got that offer. I remember getting a purple mimeographed rejection letter from Cal State Sacramento. The purple ink had run, and I had a hard time reading the letter telling me I wasn't wanted. Those were grim times for job seekers in the profession, but ultimately I had offers from the University of Hawaii and Northridge. Hawaii paid about enough to survive on if you didn't have to eat or wear shoes, and they pointed out in their letter that many people didn't wear shoes there, so I took the job at Northridge.

Cal State Northridge was a wonderful place to teach. I was the only nontenured faculty member in Humanities there at the time, and I received tremendous support. I couldn't have asked for better colleagues, and I was immediately made faculty advisor for the Native American Students Association, which I enjoyed a great deal. The only dark spot was living in the San Fernando Valley, paying half of my salary for an apartment on what seemed like a freeway, dusting soot from traffic off the furniture every day despite closed windows. Our first daughter, Elizabeth, was born on my first day of classes, so I was in the hospital with Polly while my students were in class alone.

I loved the school and both Polly and I loathed the place, so much so that after one year I decided to leave teaching and go back to the Forest Service for life. I applied for admission to a Masters in Forestry program at Utah State University and was accepted. But before we could pack up and leave academia forever, I received a phone call from the University of New Mexico. They had an opening, and because an old grad-school friend had made the phone call I flew to Albuquerque for an interview, still determined to return to the Forest Service anyway. The short part of the story is that I loved New Mexico and Albuquerque, accepted the job, and started teaching at the University of New Mexico in 1984.

From the very first I taught American literature, Native American literature, and writing, the same courses I've continued to teach at New Mexico, the University of California at Santa Cruz, and, now, UC Davis. Over the years I've also regularly taught courses on John Steinbeck, a writer whom I believe to be intensely underestimated in academia, and a course I call Theory of Fiction, as well as others, but my focus has always been in those three areas. I think being a three-for has made me more attractive to universities and also kept me a bit more sane. I cannot imagine teaching only creative writing or only Native American literature.

I've worked pretty hard and published regularly, but again I feel just plain lucky in my teaching career. Somehow I managed to move from graduate student within the UC system to full professor within the same system in only eight years, which, according to my dissertation director, James Woodruss, no one else had ever done. I'm proud of that fact, especially coming from my family's distinctly nonintellectual background. I enjoy the classes I teach, and I like the way students keep me on my toes as I try not to let them realize they know more than I do. Sometimes, when I think about it, I'm amazed that I get paid to walk into a room and talk with young, and not-so-young, people about literature. What a great job.

ARL: Italy and France have been way stations in your career as writer-professor. What were your experiences there?

LO: Both were intense in different ways. My wife, Polly, and I went to Italy in August of 1980 when I had a Fulbright fellowship to teach at the University of Pisa, and we stayed through the summer of 1981. Italy was an extraordinary experience. I had never been outside the U.S. before and was dazzled by everything every minute of the day or night. To walk through the streets of Rome or Florence, sit at sidewalk cafes, and hear all those people speaking a foreign language kept me dizzy with pleasure. Polly had been abroad with her family more than once and was far more sophisticated than I, so she took it a bit more in stride. But for me, right off the metaphorical sharecropper's farm, it was all wonderful. It seemed to me that Italians were all beautiful, even if the whole country functioned with a kind of hilarity I'd never experienced. Everything seemed to work in spite of itself. Somehow the mail was delivered and checks were cashed and trains were usually more or less on time, but it was impossible to see any order to it all.

The only darkness in Italy was the land itself. The earth felt used up to me, sad and tired. Every stream was vilely polluted and stank, the brush along the banks shrouded in torn plastic waste. Garbage was everywhere. There seemed to simply be no consciousness at that time of the earth as something valuable, worth caring for. I had much free time and ran many miles through the Italian countryside each day, and I got to see the land up close. I even bought a bicycle and rode up into the mountains and learned that even the beautiful high villages, with streams cascading out of the forests and through the towns, were foully polluted. Polly could not ride with me, because the man who owned the bicycle shop refused to sell a racing bike to a woman; it wasn't proper, he explained flatly.

But there were the Sistine Chapel, the Pietá, the David, and so much more around every corner. I'd never seen great art except in photographs, and I was shaken by it. With an art degree from Berkeley, Polly was able to educate me liberally until I looked in terror at each new museum I was expected to conquer with her. Even today, nothing exhausts me like walking miles through museums on hard marble floors.

The year in Italy allowed us to see Greece, Scandinavia, the Netherlands, Austria, France, Germany, and Spain. It opened my eyes, clouded as they were by an utterly rural upbringing. Until Italy, the can factory in Hayward had been the pinnacle of my exposure to the big world. Santa Barbara hardly counted. More than two decades later, it seems like magic.

ARL: And France?

LO: France was different. I spent a couple of wonderful weeks in Paris with Polly in the spring of 1981, but I didn't get to know France even a little bit until I began going there to promote my novels in the mid-nineties. After *The Sharpest Sight* was published in France and won the Roman Noir Prize in 1995, I began to make fairly regular trips to plug that novel and subsequent ones as they were translated. Because I've written about those trips in *I Hear the Train*, I won't go into detail, but I can say that if Italy was a kind of hypercarnival, France was a kind of intense madness for a "Native American" writer on tour. The French have a great love for the American Indian, and they also have profound collective knowledge of what constitutes a "red Indian." That definition is founded primarily in the nineteenth century and Disney, just as it is for most Americans and the rest of the world. But when one tours in France to promote a novel billed as an "Indian" novel, one confronts daily the manufactured Indian artifact one is expected to be. It was hard; it was maddening. It was also wonderful, of course, for no city can be as beautiful as Paris, and the French countryside is hard to match for random perfection. Unlike Italy in 1980, France seems clean, the earth cared for once you are outside the cities. And while the French can be insanity inducing when telling you who you are supposed to be or putting you on stage with clowns and dancing poodles, they can also be wonderfully generous and gracious hosts. All over France I met splendid, kind, and helpful people, beginning with Francis, my editor at the Albin Michel publishing house. In the little town of Audincourt in eastern France, I encountered one delightful person after another and stood for an hour watching rainbow trout balance in the perfect clarity of the river running through the town's center. In Rennes and St. Maló it was the same, from the mayor on down.

Appearing with dancing dogs and clarinet-playing clowns—or being on national television with a famous American actress, a man in drag, and giant puppets—made France trying and left me laughing in my solitary hotel rooms. But France also taught me much about both the kindness of strangers and the artifactuality of that thing called "Indian."

ARL: You now have a family and offspring of your own. Who are they?

LO: Polly and I met in the fall of 1970 and were married in 1975. I suppose she and I were about as different as two people could be. She comes from very distinguished stock (her ancestor Robert owned the first White House, for example, and two of her ancestors signed the Declaration of Independence), while, as I've suggested, my ancestors were a combination of displaced Native Americans and perhaps equally displaced and rough-edged Irishmen and Frenchmen. Education was taken for granted in her family and considered nearly impossible in mine. On the day she came coasting up to a French I class on her bicycle, a few days before her eighteenth birthday, I fell in love with her. I spent the next five years trying to convince her to marry me, even while wandering the high country of the North Cascades by myself and writing long, mournful letters, and finally I succeeded. In the meantime, Polly graduated from UC Berkeley with a degree in art.

Clearly I wasn't someone with great prospects, as Polly's father recognized immediately and never forgot. But here we are, more than thirty years later in the Manzano Mountains of New Mexico, with two extraordinary daughters, a cat, two dogs, two goldfish, and a frog. Our older daughter, Elizabeth, is now in college, and Alexandra, four years younger, is in the midst of high school. Elizabeth is a writer, with more natural ability than her father could have ever claimed, and Alexandra is an artist like her mother. They are the light of my life, people I love, like, and admire. They've been backpacking with me since each was five years old, and I'm proud of how comfortable they are in the outdoors.

ARL: Within all of this came your emerging life as a writer. When did it begin? With what?

LO: I always liked to write, even felt compelled to do so. That desire to do something with language probably originated with my mother's constant stories and the strange, rich words she used from that other world she was born into. The love of words flourished, I think, because of my older sister, Betty, who read endless stories to us kids as we looked over her shoulder. She would read whatever was available, so I listened to fairy tales and bible stories and Nancy Drew mysteries, making little distinction between them all. We had no television back then, so her reading sessions were important entertainment. I recall sitting with her one day as she was reading, when I suddenly realized I could read the words on the page as she said them. That was some time before I started school, so I was probably between four and five years old, and that was my first realization that I could read. I guess I'd just absorbed the ability through something like osmosis.

The first thing I remember writing that drew attention and gave me an inkling of pride of craft was an assignment in freshman English in junior college. Paul McGill, an inspiring, superb teacher, told us to describe the place where we lived, and I wrote about the landscape around Atascadero. He gave it back to me and told me I could be a writer. No one had ever suggested such a thing, and it was a shock to me. He also suggested that I work on the student newspaper. I was so much in awe of McGill that I did exactly as he said and began writing for the newspaper, becoming the editor as I mentioned before.

I think my desire to actually be a writer began with those words in my first junior-college English class. From that time on I began to try writing stories, even attempting a novel that today I recall as being pretty damned awful, very romantic and turgid and full of stream-of-consciousness nonsense. When I transferred to UCSB, I began to write serious essays for English classes, consciously imitating the things I read in scholastic journals, and the assignments were always well received, but I'd given up on the idea of being a novelist by that time and had decided to be a journalist. At that point I simply liked writing words down on paper or typing them, any kind of words, whether an analysis of a Yeats poem or a campus newspaper article about SDS. One day I read in the Santa Barbara paper that a professor at UCSB had won a Pulitzer Prize and that he was an "Indian" writer.

ARL: We're talking about Scott Momaday?

LO: Yes—I hadn't known there was an Indian professor on campus, and I asked friends in the Native American Students Association if they'd known, but no one I knew seemed aware that there was an Indian in the English Department. So I persuaded the student newspaper to send me to interview Momaday about the Pulitzer Prize, and I went to his office, petrified, and introduced myself. We talked about his writing a bit, but we spent a lot of time talking about being "part-Indian," about being mixedbloods, though I don't believe we used that word. Momaday was patient, generous, and kind, and he made a deep impression.

I'd never had a chance to talk with anyone about who I was or where I came from, and I'd certainly never met anyone who had actually thought about such questions with anything like intellectual depth. I'd never met anyone who, with generosity and tact, seemed to take my own mixed ancestry with any degree of seriousness or interest, and I'd definitely never met a famous writer before. Scott Momaday left a sharp mark on my young soul, reminding me of a brilliant, educated version of my father, a version that didn't mind talking. After *House Made of Dawn,* I began to read everything I could find by Native American writers, especially novels, because Momaday had reignited my desire to one day write a novel.

That was the beginning of my long quest to know as much as I could about writing by and about Native Americans, and that desire was especially whetted once I discovered that so much of this writing dealt with people who came from an often conflicted mixture of worlds or backgrounds. I had had no idea this was an issue for anyone except myself. Because these works were never taught in college classrooms, of course, I had to make this particular literary journey on my own, becoming something of an autodidact in this area as I followed the trail all the way through a doctoral degree without ever once being able to take a course in the subject.

ARL: And your own novel writing?

LO: The novel I had long wanted to write began to take form in the North Cascades in the mid-seventies. One fall I stayed on late rather than return to school. Driven out of the high country by snow,

I did odd jobs around the district ranger station in Darrington, Washington, living alone in the attic of the station bunkhouse. That was when I began writing the novel that became *Wolfsong,* a book not published for nearly fifteen years, by which time it had mutated considerably. *Wolfsong* began with the sound of rain on the bunkhouse roof, and it became a very wet novel, a story built out of rain, filled with rain, singing with the sound of rain in a dense forest. Only gradually did the human characters take form in the midst of that drumming rain, and as they came to life they seemed to emerge out of the cycle of water that made up that world. At first it was all impression and sensation, but gradually the story emerged around a very real copper corporation's determination to desecrate and destroy land sacred to Native peoples.

I put that novel away for a long time and only picked it up again in 1980, when I became bored with writing my doctoral dissertation on John Steinbeck. I completed a draft of the book and showed it to someone for the first time, taking it to the office of Jack Hicks, director of creative writing at UC Davis. Rather shocked that I should show up with a novel, Jack dutifully read it and passed it along to Bill Kittredge, a visiting writer at Davis that year. Bill then sent the novel along to his agent, and eventually it found its way to Gary Fisketjohn, who was, if I remember correctly, with Random House at the time. Fisketjohn wrote to tell me he liked it and was sure they would publish it. By then having begun my first teaching job at Cal State Northridge, I was ecstatic and thought this writing game was a lot easier than people pretended. Of course Random House turned the book down, Fisketjohn nominated it for the Pushcart Press book editor's prize, which it did not win, my writer's heart was broken, and I put the book away again for several years. Meanwhile, however, I began working on a second novel closer to my heart and closer to my family, a book that became *The Sharpest Sight*. Eventually both novels were published, though not in New York and not by Random House, and I kept writing, turning out freelance articles on all kinds of subjects, critical essays and books, and a few stories as well as novels. For every novel there must be another novel about how it was written, but I'll forego those stories for the moment, only saying that each novel for me has been an experiment and fun.

ARL: Yet writing can be, some say must be, a lonely, or at the very least alone, activity?

LO: I've stopped writing on several occasions out of utter despair, believing that whatever comes after the writing is futile, hopeless, too painful. At one point I put into the trash every word I'd ever written, except a novel manuscript (*Wolfsong*) which I'd forgotten that my agent still had in New York. I was never going to write another word. But of course I did write other words, because I couldn't help it. On those rare occasions when my students ask me for honest advice about the large question of writing or not writing, I tell them to only write if they cannot help it. It's a heartbreaking thing to stake one's life on, but of course it's also the most joyous thing in the world once you understand that only the writing matters, and once you understand that you cannot stop.

CHAPTER TWO

TAKING BACK THE BONES

Louis Owens's "Post"-Colonial Fiction

JACQUELYN KILPATRICK

In contemporary Native American literature, a recurring central motif is the search for identity, or more correctly, the return to an identity that has become distant, subsumed into the identities provided by the dominant culture. In writing novels with protagonists in search of a Native identity, these authors frequently involve themselves in what can be thought of as postcolonial writing. However, I must add Louis Owens's point that the United States itself is *not* postcolonial, and therefore "writing back to the center" takes on a different hue for Native American writers. Owens states:

> America does not participate on this continent in what is sometimes termed the "colonial aftermath" or postcolonial condition. . . . [T]he American Revolution was not truly a war to throw off the yoke of colonization as is popularly imagined, but rather a family squabble among the colonizers to determine who would be in charge of the colonization of North America, who would control the land and the lives of the indigenous inhabitants. America never became postcolonial. ("As If" 21)

In short, the colonizers never left. Complicating this notion is the reality that the "Indian" is, as Gerald Vizenor has noted, a Euramerican invention, "a simulation and loan word of dominance. . . . The simulation of the *indian* is the absence of the native, and that absence is a presence of the other" (*Fugitive Poses* 35, 37).

Writing the "real" Native back into America's consciousness is what contemporary Native American writing is largely about, and these narratives and the corresponding critical study of them are changing the landscape of Indian Territory in American literature. Louis Owens is one of the most prolific and innovative of these authors. It is well worth looking at his critical work—what he says about Native American writing—and placing those ideas in perspective with a reading of his novels—looking at what he actually does as he writes. This chapter explores some of the connections between Owens's critical work and his fiction; in the interest of time, space, and coherence, I have confined my comments on his fiction to one novel, *The Sharpest Sight*.

In writing novels, Owens and other Native writers must tell a story, but they must also *un*-tell a story. The idea of what an "Indian" is, was, or could be has been constructed through five centuries of misunderstanding, cultural and racial bias, and appropriation of Native life, land, and identity. What most of Euramerica knows about Native Americans has much to do with stereotypes developed politically, cinematically, or in literature and little to do with the actual people. Both fiction and nonfiction by Native American authors must address this wall of misinformation. Owens is very clear about this: "It is the artifactualization, the stereotyping, the damningly *hyperreal* 'Indian' that makes it so difficult for actual living Indian people to comprehend survival, and to adapt and change while holding to cultural identities, amidst the still-colonialist, dominant Euramerican societies of the Americas" (*MM* 18). Many Native American writers belong to the postcolonial set, not because America is postcolonial but because they—like authors from India, Africa, or the Caribbean—produce narratives that take an active role in the construction or reconstruction of culture and knowledge, rewriting the Native presence in Euramerican history and mythology. Owens and other Native authors write stories and characters recognizable by Native Americans themselves, and "use the colonizer's language . . . to articulate our own worlds and find ourselves whole" (*MM* xiii).

This is a difficult task. To understand a Native story one must understand a great deal about Native cultures. In his essay "Beads and Buckskins," Owens describes what is, what must be, expected of readers of Native American literature.

> [C]ontemporary Native American authors are requiring that readers cross over the conceptual horizon into an Indian world. In addition to Roman and Greek mythology, today it helps a great deal if a reader knows Choctaw, Chippewa, Navajo, or Blackfoot mythologies in order to read Native American works. In addition to the history of ancient Rome, the reader must know the history of Native America. A different kind of sophistication is being required and expected. To cite an example with which I am intimately familiar, a reader should know something about both European and Choctaw mythologies and cultures to understand what to make of a mixedblood character significantly named Attis McCurtain who, while spinning in a black river, encounters tribal bone pickers in my second novel, *The Sharpest Sight*. In a multicultural world both the name Attis and the traditional bone pickers have significance. If we miss one, we miss the whole. (*MM* 20)

Native American writers live in two worlds that fold into each other, overlapping and merging while remaining separate entities. This gives Native American writing a richness and texture that is deeply layered and complex, with levels of meaning that challenge readers to make connections. Mixedbloods like Owens are particularly multilayered and complex, with ancestry from both sides of the colonial line. In his essay "As If An Indian Were Really an Indian," in the collection *I Hear the Train*, Owens carefully explains his position in regard to the subject of his fiction or, as he quotes Edward Said, his "strategic location." He is a mixedblood, with Choctaw and

Cherokee ancestors but also Irish and Cajun French ancestry. He refers to himself as "an American of deeply mixed heritage and somewhat unique upbringing". He has also earned a doctorate and holds the position of full professor at the University of California Davis. He therefore describes his position as a writer as "a complicated and contingent one." He goes on to say, "My strategic location, therefore, may be found in what I think of as a kind of frontier zone, which elsewhere I have referred to as "always unstable, multidirectional, hybridized, characterized by heteroglossia, and indeterminate." He then explains his use of this highly charged term.

> Because the term "frontier" carries with it such a heavy burden of colonial discourse, it can only be conceived of as a space of extreme contestation. . . . In taking such a position, I am arguing for an appropriation, inversion, and transvaluation of this deadly cliché of colonialism—for appropriation, inversion, and abrogation of authority are always trickster's strategies. . . . The very act of appropriating the colonizer's discourse and making it one's own is obviously collaborative and conjunctural. We have long since entered, inescapably, what Pratt terms a "contact zone" and what I prefer to call a "frontier," in James Clifton's definition, "a culturally defined place where peoples with different culturally expressed identities meet and deal with each other." (*MM* 26–27, 52)

It is in this contact zone where important interactions take place in Owens's fiction. In *Other Destinies: Understanding the American Indian Novel,* Owens notes that almost every novel written by a Native American "describes a circular journey toward home and identity. For some protagonists too much has been lost for the journey to be completed; for those who succeed, the key is remembrance" (191). In *The Sharpest Sight* we see a protagonist who is struggling to come to terms with loss, gain remembrance, and recover an identity. It is a superbly subversive, tricksterish text that elegantly "writes back" to the center. It is a murder mystery, but that is far too simple a way to look at Owens's achievement. It appropriates the genre and uses it as a vehicle for reclaiming history, for examining that frontier zone, and for inviting readers into a different way of knowing. Owens has stated that the "murder mystery" is, in fact, entirely appropriate for this kind of novel, one which represents the search for missing bones (history), for the person, and for solutions (personal communication, 12 July 2000).

The protagonist, Cole McCurtain, completes a circular journey toward identity such as Owens described. This journey is an unsettling race through a labyrinth of alienation, cultural dismemberment, sex, violence, and muted boundaries between time and space, life and death. The reclamation of identity is not an easy one, and remembrance for the displaced, isolated McCurtain mixedbloods would seem virtually unattainable except for their cultural ace in the hole—the center point of the novel—Uncle Luther. Luther is a Mississippi Choctaw who is drawn into and begins to gently steer the story that is being told. When we are first introduced to Luther, the description is that of an owl, the bird we come to associate with him and whose cultural signifiers inform the character. "His hands and forearms, fragile and hollow looking as the bones of a bird, rested on his lap, and only his head turned as the eyes searched for something in the margins of the room. . . . he heard the horned owl— *ishkitini*—and he nodded his head" (*SS* 7). Like the owl of European and Euramerican myth, Luther has significant wisdom as, like the owl of the Choctaw stories, he has an understanding of death and the power to enter the world beyond what we recognize as life and to return. He has, in fact, just completed a journey through time and space, where he has followed *nalusachito*, soul-eater, to the Salinas Valley in California, and he has brought the "outer shadow," the *shilombish*, of his murdered great-nephew home with him. In creating Uncle Luther, Owens has created a repository of Choctaw culture, a sort of living safety-deposit box, and a challenge to the non-Native reader. He holds a key to reclamation of culture for his great-nephew and for the readers of the novel as well. As he gently guides Cole back onto the "Indian road," Luther also gives the reader much of what he or she needs to know in order to navigate the text.

Luther has been accused of witchcraft, which gives him a bit of perverse pleasure, but his substantive power is a positive power. As his old friend Onatima says, "He never hurts anything" (155), and he acts with knowledgeable respect and dignity when the occasion demands it. After bringing his grand-nephew's outer shadow back to Mississippi, he sits on the bed, tired from the effort, and Owens has some fun deconstructing the stereotype of the wise old Indian elder. His language starts with the kind of tragic stoicism one would expect from an ancient but terribly wise chief in a Hollywood movie.

> "It is time." The old man spoke with his eyes downcast, in a voice of sadness and dignity. "You must go now. Be brave, grandson. The other has gone before, and he has not found the bright path. It will be difficult for you." He seated himself again and folded his hands in his lap. "Don't worry. We will find them."

But Luther is real, and he is also Trickster—and things do not always go along perfectly for a trickster.

> He looked up again, and this time there was a note of irritation in his voice when he said, "It is time, grandson." The shadow stood unmoving in the corner. "Shit," the old man said, "Goddamnit." It wasn't supposed to happen that way. (*SS* 7–8)

Luther and Onatima, or Old Lady Blue Wood, are wonderfully live representations of the original beings familiar in Native American stories, particularly Blackfoot stories, as Old Man and Old Woman. In *Other Destinies* Owens described the way James Welch presented this pair in *Winter in the Blood*. "Together, Old Man and Old Woman design the people, with Old Man having the first say and Old Woman second, and Old Man playing the trickster role in the process . . . the repeated use of the names 'Old Woman' and 'Old Man' . . . [is] an appropriate association since it is from the pair that the narrator inherits identity and authenticity" (*OD* 143). Although Old Man and Old Woman are not Choctaw figures, Onatima and Luther resonate on the same frequency as Welch's couple and have commonalities with beings from other Native cultures, such as the First Man and First Woman of the Cherokee, Kanati and Selu. They are the "wedded contraries" that do indeed provide an identity for the McCurtain men, have considerable say in the way the story within the novel moves along, and—like traditional tricksters—provide opportunities for gaining insight as well as adding considerable humor.

In addition to her role as Old Woman, Onatima's identity is made of webs of meaning. She is the novel's symbolic Spider Woman or Thought Woman, the "feminine creative principle and form for thought or reason" (*OD* 169). She is well tuned to that which exists beyond words and physical form, she is a caretaker of the earth, and she knows the stories that make the world.

> Cole thought about the coon skins Uncle Luther had taken to Jobe's store.
>
> "The animals understand," the old lady said.
>
> Cole looked at her in surprise and she smiled kindly. "Choctaw people have been living right here for at least two thousand years according to the books," she said. "If we had not respected this world and treated it with care, we would have long ago destroyed it. You see what white people have done in only a few hundred years?" (*SS* 115)

The books to which she refers are of great importance to Onatima. She is well educated in both cultures, and she sees the power stories wield in both worlds. In this way she is much like Owens, and her purpose in the novel is much like Owens's purpose as a novelist. She gives Luther books to read so that he will understand the discourse of the other, dominant and oppressive culture, and when Luther says, "Lucky thing most of us Indians wasn't reading their stories," she responds, "Lucky thing some of us were" (*SS* 216). But Luther is also an excellent reader, largely because he believes in the *power* of the story.

> "Us Choctaws made up stories that told us about these things, stories like soul-eater, so we could have words for such things

and watch them carefully. If we didn't have the stories we couldn't live in this world. . . . it takes stories to keep the balance." (*SS* 97)

Even with the assistance of Luther and Onatima, finding an identity that is solid and centered is not easy for the mixedbloods of this novel. They are in an uphill battle against a system of definitions embraced by the dominant culture. As Onatima and Luther repeatedly point out, those definitions are dangerous and they are printed in black and white. Luther is somewhat disgusted but also highly amused by a historian's grossly romanticized description of the Choctaw. He tells Cole, tongue firmly planted in cheek, "This is a good book. Tells us all about ourselves." He thumbs through and then reads:

> "The Choctaw warrior, as I knew him in his native Mississippi forest, was as fine a specimen of manly perfection as I have ever beheld." He looked up with a grin. "He seemed to be as perfect as the human form could be. Tall, beautiful in symmetry of form and face, graceful, active, straight, fleet, with lofty and independent bearing, he seemed worthy of saying, as he of Juan Fernandez fame: 'I am monarch of all I survey.' His black piercing eye seemed to penetrate and read the very thoughts of the heart, while his firm step proclaimed a feeling sense of his manly independence". . . . The old man paused and looked at Cole with a wide grin. . . . "Now there's a man that hit the nail on the head." (*SS* 88)

In less than one page of text, Owens has deconstructed the image of the Noble Savage, commented on the writing *about* Indians, removed the Native elder from the Wise Old Chief stereotype, made the "mystic" Indian who "reads the very thought of the heart" sound rather silly, defused the past-tense verb by having a live and lively Choctaw reading the passage, and placed all that ridiculousness into a context that is surmountable by allowing us to laugh at it. Owens noted, "If a fear of inauthenticity is the burden of postmodernity, as has been suggested by David Harvey in *The Condition of Postmodernity* among others, it is particularly the burden not only of the Euramerican seeking merely his self-reflection, but even more so that of the indigenous American in the face of this hyperreal 'Indian'" ("As If" 218). Laughter is then an appropriate response for Luther, because it is through knowledgeable laughter that such silliness and misrepresentation can be put into perspective. Laughter, or a mischievous grin, is an important tool in Luther's—Owens's— "ethnographical salvage operation."

In "As If an Indian Were Really an Indian," Owens writes at length about the images of Native Americans that have been produced and reproduced in books like the one mentioned above, which is an actual text found in libraries around the world. Owens states:

> European America holds a mirror and a mask up to the Native American. The tricky mirror is that Other presence that reflects the Euramerican consciousness back at itself, but the side of the mirror turned toward the Native is transparent, letting the Native see not his or her own reflection but the face of the Euramerican beyond the mirror. For the dominant culture, the Euramerican controlling this surveillance, the reflection provides merely a self-recognition that results in a kind of being-for-itself and, ultimately, as Fanon suggests, an utter absence of certainty of self. The Native, in turn, finds no reflection directed back from the center, no recognition of "being" from that direction. ("As If" 217)

Luther and Onatima, of course, do see through the mask and the mirror. They are firmly in control of their own existences and possess a firm conception of their own identities. They have not become what Vine Deloria calls "the Indian of [Euramerica's] dreams" (xv). This is not an easy task, for the old people or for the authors who are "writing back."

If the *reader* is expected to understand Choctaw, Cherokee, Blackfoot or any other Native mythology and tradition, then it behooves the author to get it right—and also to know what has been presented from the other side, to recognize the mask, and to look through the mirror. This leads to an interesting conundrum. The Native author finds himself or herself having to go to the university library to read about his or her own people. It is an obviously frustrating experience for these authors, and Owens makes his frustration very clear.

> Are we not caught up in a Borges-like maze of contradictory signifiers when an Indian author must go to white writings about Indians to find out who he or she is or where he or she comes from and then "write back" against the dominant culture? To write "authentically" the "Indian" author must consult constructions of "Indianness" by the dominant non-Indian culture that has always controlled printed discourse. It is enough to drive one mad. (*MM* 19)

In *The Sharpest Sight* Luther and Onatima provide an entertaining and decisive perspective on traditional stories and stories told by the dominant culture. Through them, it becomes apparent that the story is the bearer of culture, a strategy of survivance.

Owens has stated that "The complex webs of language called stories become ceremonial acts performed in order to maintain the world as both knowable and inhabitable." In addition, stories act as conveyors of identity and, as Michel Foucault suggests, they have "the duty of providing immortality" (*OD* 169). By preserving continuity between past and present, by preventing a loss of self, the stories told by the Old Man and the Old Woman allow Hoey and Cole McCurtain a way to imagine that a future could exist.

The order preserved by the stories is very fragile, and a single generation of unarticulated continuity can produce enormous damage. Stories must be remembered and passed to the next generation if a culture is to survive. Although Hoey is trying somewhat desperately to remember, to regain what he learned from his Uncle Luther as a child on the Yazoo River, he has forgotten much. He has bent the chain, and his sons are in danger of a total break from their cultural anchorage, unless he can regain what has been lost.

Early in the novel, Hoey's younger son, Cole, notes that his father "seemed to be more and more Indian every day, and the more Indian he became the stranger he seemed" (*SS* 13). Being Indian is something Cole cannot imagine, and it is something on which Hoey has a very loose grip. When Cole sights in on a rabbit but instead of pulling the trigger says "bang," Hoey scoffs, "Indians don't yell 'bang' when they go after meat" (14). However, later on in the story, when Hoey has learned more about what "being an Indian" might be, he sights in on the shoulder blades of his enemy, the man he has been quietly hunting, and says, "bang." Again, Owens has turned the tricky mirror back on itself, setting up the Euramerican expectation/assumption (how Indians hunt) and working through ideas about what it is to be not only "Indian" but *Choctaw,* that leads to a very different understanding of "Indianness."

Hoey has perhaps remembered more than he realizes, even at the novel's beginning. He at least has a sense of the past and a need to understand. As Cole points out, Hoey takes much pleasure "in the little things," but "the bigger things, like history, seemed to torment him" (18). He has an abiding hatred for Andrew Jackson and Thomas Jefferson for their roles in the history of Native Americans, and Hoey longs for a sense of identity, for a sense of place. He says:

> "Us Indians are a mixed-up bunch. It's like somebody took a big stick and stirred us all up. . . . You know, I read about some tribes, like the Navajo and them others in Arizona and New Mexico, the Hopi and some others, that's still living where they always lived. Some of them people live in houses a thousand years old, maybe ten thousand. You imagine how that must feel?" (19)

In *Other Destinies* Owens explores the idea of identity's relation to place. To hold a sense of identity is "to be removed from the experience of ephemerality, fragmentation, and deracination that characterizes the modern predicament and, most significantly, to be defined according to eternal, immutable values arising from a profound integration with place" (*OD* 95).

The "place" in *The Sharpest Sight* is depicted by the Yazoo River swampland of the McCurtains' birth, but the location of much of the story's action is on another river, the Salinas in California. Like the McCurtain blood, which runs both Native and Euramerican, the rivers each represent a possibility for identity. One of the novel's questions is which to choose—or can both be chosen?

Choosing both seems a reasonable response for a mixedblood character and a mixedblood author such as Owens. In response to Pratt's idea that autoethnographic texts are responses to "metropolitan representation," Owens states that "inhabiting both sides of the frontier plus the middle, the mixed-blood text also writes back to itself" (*MM* 40). The waters run contrary to each other, parallel with one another, and sometimes the waters merge.

In an autobiographical essay, *Water Witch*, Owens describes the Salinas Valley and his father as he witched for water.

> A displaced Mississippi Choctaw, half-breed, squat and reddish, blind in one eye, he'd spit tobacco juice at the stick or cairn and turn back toward the house, feeling maybe the stirring of Yazoo mud from the river of his birth as if the water he never merely discovered, but drew all that way from a darker, damper world. Within a few days he'd be back with his boss and they'd drill a well at the spot he'd marked. Not once did the water fail, but always it was hidden and secret, for that was the way of water in our part of California. (Riley 274)

It seems that Owens is doing much the same thing in *The Sharpest Sight*, drawing all the way from a darker, damper world to the hidden and secret world of Amarga, California. The two rivers are dangerous and require proper navigation, but they are also symbols of fertility and life, and they are connected in an eternal, immutable, timeless and spaceless reality. The melding of the two is underlined when Cole dreams, "his mind drifting away from the cabin clearing, the river and swamp.... He imagined the push of the current in that other river, shifting, spinning, uncovering things, and his whole life was a singular journey to this moment in a clearing in a place he didn't know" (*SS* 67).

Writing as a mixedblood presents some interesting challenges, but it also allows for interesting possibilities. With a foot in each world (though one perhaps more firmly planted than the other), the mixedblood author has enormous responsibility but also an exhilarating freedom. Owens writes, "the mixedblood is not a cultural broker but a cultural breaker, break-dancing trickster-fashion through all signs, fracturing the self-reflexive mirror of the dominant center, deconstructing rigid borders, slipping between the seams, embodying contradictions, and contradancing across every boundary" (*MM* 41).

In *The Sharpest Sight* borders of many types are muted or deconstructed and boundaries are crossed, even the seemingly indisputable line between life and death. In fact, some of the novel's most active participants are—technically—dead. These characters are not symbolic or metaphoric; they simply represent elements not usual to Western thought but natural and accepted in many Native American traditions. The Native ideas are given a sense of normalcy here that definitely privileges the Other audience and challenges the dominant culture to deal with them. In this novel's world ghosts talk to the living or otherwise influence events by the presence of their spectral shapes, natural and supernatural in syncretic bonding. The reader is gently moved into what N. Scott Momaday calls "the realization of the imaginative experience" (168).

These ghosts function in the story in a variety of ways. The first nonliving consciousness we see is that of Cole's brother, who has been murdered just before the time the novel begins.

Attis McCurtain spun in the river, riding the black flood, aware of the branches that trailed over his face and touched his body, spinning in the current of the night toward something he could feel coming closer, rising up to meet him. He knew he was dead, and in death an ancient memory had awakened, a stirring in his stilled blood, moving with him and around him on the flood. (8)

Attis was drafted for a horrific tour of duty in Vietnam and later shipped to a mental hospital for murdering his girlfriend in what was mis-termed a "sex crime." His chance for recovering his lost identity has been cut short, but the memory in his blood is a Choctaw memory. As he floats in the torrent, he hears "'*Chahta yakni.*' The words echoed as if he had spoken them. '*Chahta isht ia,*' a voice answered back" (9). Attis has said *Chahta isht ia* (Choctaw blood) before—in the hospital, to his friend Mundo Morales. At that time Mundo had no way to respond to him, and Attis lapsed into silence. But when Attis calls out in Choctaw after his death, his answer comes. He becomes a Choctaw ghost with two parts, *shilombish,* the outside shadow, and *shilup,* the inner shadow. (In significant ways, the bifurcation of the Choctaw spirit is an excellent metaphor for the mixedblood author. Each is important, and it is necessary that they correspond with each other without becoming each other.)

It is Attis's outside shadow that has gone to Mississippi with Luther to await reunification with its bones. Without the bones, it cannot go on. It will fall to Cole to find his brother's bones, return them to Mississippi, and complete the ritual, finding his own sense of identity and place in the process. In this way Attis works as a catalyst for this and all other stories in the novel, and taking back his bones is a powerful metaphor. Attis's bones, his Choctaw bones, are finally reclaimed by the novel's end, after a dismembering and a "re-membering," to use Paula Gunn Allen's term. Attis has died because of the horrors he faced in Vietnam and the resulting psychological trauma he and those around him experienced. He lost the ability to see himself, became lost in the mirror, and separated from his bones long before he died. In important ways he represents the Native American whom Owens describes as,

> put[ting] on the constructed mask provided by the colonizer, and the mask is not merely a mirror but more crucially a static death mask, fashioned beforehand, to which the living person is expected to conform. He or she who steps behind the mask becomes the Vanishing American, a savage/noble, mystical,

pitiable, romantic fabrication of the Euramerican psyche fated to play out the epic role defined by Mikhail Bakhtin: "The epic and tragic hero," Bakhtin writes, "is the hero who by his very nature must perish. . . . Outside his destiny the epic and tragic hero is nothing; he is, therefore, a function of the plot fate assigns him; he cannot become the hero of another destiny or another plot" (*Dialogic Imagination* 36). While the "Indian" holds a special and crucial place within the American narrative, the Native who looks beyond his or her immediate community and culture for recognition finds primarily irrelevance and absurdity. ("As If" 218)

Nor is death a release for Attis. Cole worries about him, wondering if those who do murder in war can go on the bright road. He fears his brother may be going down the dark river, where those who do bad things must go. Given the description of Attis in the beginning of the novel, the reader will wonder the same thing. It is Cole's taking back of the bones that will assure Attis's re-membering, as it re-constructs a Choctaw identity for his brother.

The *viejo* is a different kind of ghost, a non-Native ghost. He is the grandfather of Mundo Morales, Attis's best friend and the deputy sheriff who must first prove his friend has been killed and then find his murderer. The *viejo* talks to Mundo on a regular basis, helping him as he makes his way through the story and toward a realization of his own identity and place in the world. Unlike Attis, who is divided and mute after his acceptance of death, the *viejo* is talkative, enjoys the idea of sex almost as much as he enjoyed the real thing while he was alive, and is very proud of his suit. He is a strange entity to Luther, who sees him but does not at first understand his existence, although he admits he dresses well. Luther later realizes that the *viejo* is undivided and able to function as he does because he is not a Choctaw ghost but a Catholic ghost, a very different thing. Again, Owens points to the division in worldview and makes a bridge between them without melting one into the other.

The *viejo*'s function in this novel is much like Luther's. He gives his grandson good advice, generally, and—with the aid of two other personalities in the spiritual neutral zone, the Mondragon sisters—provides identity, complete with a family tree that goes all the way back to Adelita, the Native American slave girl whom the family patriarch made a progenitor of the Morales family. It seems that Mundo is a mixedblood as well. Mundo is one of the most positive characters in the novel, and as the story proceeds, he (and the reader) begin to unwind his family history, in the process uncovering layers of colonialism—Spanish and Euramerican. His ancestor, Adelita the Indian slave, takes Mundo's bloodline deeper into the California earth, and his Spanish ancestors represent a colonizing of that blood. These layers are now buried under the heavier weight of the later Euramerican colonization of the California coast. Mundo's family tree is a road map of California cultural/colonial history.

Mundo has only a vague idea of his family background, but at least he knows that his family once owned most of the land around Amarga. Cole McCurtain, on the other hand, has fragments that seem constantly to contradict each other. The first time we meet Cole, he is going through a precisely spoken recitation of his ethnic makeup. He has started with the sentiment on the back of his brother's flight jacket, which he wears: "I shall fear no evil, for I am . . ." He then proceeds with the percentages of Cherokee and Choctaw in the family line, ending with "Let's say I'm nearly a half-breed, whatever that means. Hoey McCurtain knows, but what I know from books in school and those old TV movies is that a half-breed can't be trusted, is a killer, a betrayer, a breed." He smiles and then finishes the sentence on the jacket: "the meanest motherfucker in the valley" (*SS* 10–11). Later, Cole and we find that he is indeed a warrior and that it has nothing to do with being the *meanest* anything. He will eventually come to terms with his mixed heritage and make a choice to accept his Choctaw blood, but at the novel's start he has a powerful if vague need to explain himself to himself. As Gayatri Spivak has noted, "the desire to explain might be a symptom of the desire to have a self that can control knowledge and a world that can be known" (Ashcroft et al. 104).

Attis is, on the surface, largely what the Euramerican literature about mixedbloods would lead one to expect. He has been in the mental hospital for killing his girlfriend due to what we would now recognize as post-traumatic stress syndrome. The killing was tragic and bloody, and that leads others in the novel, particularly the FBI agent who comes to investigate Attis's disappearance, to conclude that he is the stereotypical "breed." As Owens writes, this stereotype,

> the tortured and torturing "breed" has served as a matrix for the conflicted terror of Euramerica, the horror of liminality that is the particular trauma of the colonial mind. In the narratives of the dominant, colonial culture . . . the mixedblood is a mirror that gives back a self-image with disturbing implications, like the reflecting forest of Hawthorne's darkest fiction. (*MM* 26)

And Attis *is* disturbing. As we get to know him through his brother's and his friend's memories, we see him not as a pathological killer but as a gentle, intelligent, and sensitive young man traumatized by war. In unraveling Attis's personality and history, Owens effectively deconstructs the stereotype of the mixedblood or "breed."

Mundo Morales experiences another kind of stereotyping—a recognizable mask/mirror. He is constantly reminded, by the sheriff, by the town's "leading citizen," and even by a federal agent from outside, that he has the job of deputy sheriff because it was given to him, implying that it is not an earned position. It is part of the function of the mask/mirror that expectations for Native Americans, or mixedbloods like the McCurtains and Mundo Morales, be contained. As Owens notes, "for Native Americans the only burden of expectation is that he or she put on the constructed mask provided by the colonizer" ("As If" 218).

Mundo Morales's very name means moral world, a blazing clue that Mundo, more than anyone, is perfectly suited for attending to justice. But even more striking than the "gift" of the job is the constant reference to the position he held before, that of janitor at the local high school. "'Evening, Morales,' the sheriff said. 'How you like being a full-time deputy? Beats hell out of cleaning toilets, don't you think?'" (*SS* 39). After a few references like that one, it becomes very clear that the authority figures in the novel are using language as an exercise of power and perhaps to remind themselves that they have that power. These people expect Mundo to respond with the language of victimization and what Rey Chow has called "self-sub-alternization," but he steadfastly refuses. In fact, no mixedbloods in the novel ever engage in "aesthetic victimry," to use Vizenor's term, but they seem always to be expected to do so. This provides for an interesting duality in conversations, as though Owens is allowing us to hear the words spoken while whispering in our ears that it is only the surface.

Even Mundo's service in Vietnam is degraded by the Euramericans in the story. The federal agent, who has come to investigate Attis's disappearance, has done some checking on Mundo. He says "with a record like yours I don't see how you got in the military in the first place. . . . Of course we were in a war and they needed everybody they could get for the body counts, even a Mexican" (85). Mundo is not even surprised by Lee Scott's words; they must not be new to him.

Lee Scott is the epitome of everything negative the dominant culture's authority structure has to offer. He repeatedly mentions that he has "studied" Indians because they fascinate him, which— besides reducing Indians to specimens—has done absolutely nothing to alleviate his incredible ignorance of anything Native American. He would almost be a humorous character if he were not so painfully recognizable. As Owens has noted,

> [Native Americans] are the Others who must be both subsumed and erased in a strange dance of repulsion and desire that has given rise to both one of the longest sustained histories of genocide and ethnocide in the world as well as a fascinating drama in which the colonizer attempts to empty out and reoccupy not merely the geographical terrain but the constructed space of the indigenous other. ("As If" 216–17)

This emptying out and reoccupying of the Other is exactly what Lee Scott is all about. Everything he knows about Native America is cliché at best, but it fits his inner view of himself as a warrior, something he actually has no way of understanding. Scott was also in Vietnam, something he never tires of telling people:

> Special Forces advisor from '60 to '62. Led ARVN patrols. Jungle all the time, the whole three years. Had an Indian as point man, a young brave from one of the pueblos in New Mexico. I've always been fascinated by Indians. Made a study of their traditions when I was younger. They're raised not to show pain, you know. It's a shame they're all vanishing. A noble way of life goes with them, something valuable and essential in all of us. This one was a short, quiet fellow, good with a knife, like most of them. (86–86)

This short paragraph is a Native American nightmare. The clichés start with the Native American as point man. Attis wrote Cole about that: "You know what they do with Indians? They put us on point. The stupid bastards think Indians can see at night, that we don't make any noise" (20). Then Scott follows with the prevalent and rather insulting idea that Indians are a "vanishing breed," which of course negates any kind of accretive dynamism. He throws in the romanticized and hyperbolized cliché of "valuable and essential in all of us" before proceeding with more stereotypical ideas: they do not show pain, they are short, most are good with a knife, and they are, of course, quiet—preferably very quiet. Scott is also guilty of attempting to appropriate an Indian identity: "Had a pet praying mantis, carried it with me everywhere in a little wicker cage. Everybody said I was nuts, but it was like a totem, you know—a helper like you Indians used to have. I think it saved my life" (167). Cole's reaction is "Who *are* you? [emphasis mine]." The reader is left with the uncomfortable notion that perhaps "who he is" is not far from what really exists in the world of defining "Indianness" according to the dominant culture.[1] As Owens has noted, "the same operative strategy of desire that for a very long time governed representation of other minority cultures clearly still controls Euramerican discourse representing the Native American Indian" ("As If" 223–24). Native Americans are different from the other minorities in America in a number of ways, two of the most important of which are the assumed knowledge of Native Americans and the assumption of Indian identity by Euramericans. The fact that those assuming the identities generally consider it a compliment tends to make the issue even more complex and difficult.

Scott says to Cole, "Native Americans, you know, the red brothers. . . . You see, I've always been fascinated by Indians. Made a hobby of Indians when I was a boy. Collected arrowheads and stuff. It was like I was trying to find out who I was, and those things could tell me." But if he is really trying to usurp an Indian identity, it might also have involved a death wish, because he says, "Back then I didn't know there were any Indians left alive. I thought you'd all vanished like dinosaurs" (168).

Owens has made the point that the dominant culture has no way of knowing the Other. Like Scott, its magnified representative in *The Sharpest Sight*, it is not "capable of sincerely questioning the epistemological foundations of the dominant cultural center" and "simply cannot comprehend that 'other' way of knowing" (*OD* 82). The result is a negation of existence by "the ones who would insist upon the Indian as victim, those who insist upon the 'vanishing American' image of the Indian as incapable of change and invariably defeated" (*OD* 188). At the same time the Native American is an integral part of Euramerica's idea of itself. As Owens has said, "[i]n imagining the Indian, America imagines itself" ("As If" 214). This presents a difficult milieu in which the Native American author must write. Owens asserts, however, that the Native Americans who people the novels by mixedblood authors are generally not defeated. These authors, including Owens himself, "almost invariably create protagonists who are poised . . . at the dividing point . . . they would send their characters—in nearly every case a mixedblood—down the Indian road and away from the American Dream . . . the quest will be the same: a search for Indian identity and order in the chaos between worlds" (*OD* 77–78).

It is the search for and the attainment of identity that provides the pulse which shows the mixedblood heart is alive and well. Louise Erdrich writes that "One of the characteristics of being a mixed blood is searching. You look back and say, 'Who am I from?' You must question. You must make certain choices" (as quoted in *OD*, 194). The choices made by the characters in *The Sharpest Sight* ultimately lead to the attainment of identity, but the "Indian road" is not an easy one to travel for a mixedblood with a sketchily drawn road map.

As I have noted, Hoey McCurtain has a bit of a head start in the novel. He has had the benefit of growing up with Luther, but that was long ago, and the memory has dimmed. At the beginning of the novel he is looking for the missing pieces in books, and we have already seen what the books have to offer. He tells Cole, "You know, I guess I don't understand how to be Indian anymore. . . . I've been reading books and remembering how it was back then and trying to figure out how to act and think. But books can't tell you things like that." His information is incomplete and his experiences not all positive, but Hoey is trying, and that is the important element in the final success of his and also his son's search. Even at this point he has come to an important conclusion, one that Onatima will echo— "What it boils down to is respecting your world, every little piece of it" (*SS* 57).

Hoey has choices to make. His father made one when he had Hoey's ethnicity listed as "white" on his birth certificate, and Hoey decides he has just as much right to choose to be Indian. He does not ignore the fact that he is a mixedblood, however, and when Cole asks, "Why do you have to be just one thing or the other?" he responds that he thought there was a better way of living his life. He was trying to remember the things Uncle Luther told him, but he says that if he were in Ireland, he might choose the Irish way (*SS* 59–60). Hoey chooses to imagine himself Choctaw.

Momaday says, "We are what we imagine. Our very existence consists in our imagination of ourselves. Our best destiny is to imagine, at least, completely, who and what and that we are" ("Man Made of Words" 44). Hoey gives the same message to Cole—"You are what you think you are." Cole says that "Hoey McCurtain thought he was Choctaw, not just Indian but Choctaw" (*SS* 15). He is imagining himself into existence, and in having him so do, Owens is performing an act of subversion.

Imagining himself is no longer an option for Attis, which makes him the most tragic character in *The Sharpest Sight*. If "the greatest tragedy that can befall us is to go unimagined," as Momaday says, then Attis's death is a double loss. Like a traditional culture hero taken one step too far, Attis has "suffered . . . to the point of annihilation" (*OD* 174). From the time he returns from the war, he is unable to cope with his past experiences, think about a future, or even exist in the present. He cannot imagine that he exists, and so, in a very real sense, he does not exist. Jessard Deal, the local tavern owner and highly intelligent misanthrope, says that "Attis didn't have a clue" (*SS* 81). He suffers from what Fanon might call an utter absence of certainty of self.

Attis has only his Euramerican name, but Cole also has a Choctaw name, *Taska mikushi humma*, which—if Luther remembers right—means Little-chief-warrior Red. Luther gave the name to Cole when he was small because he "was bleeding all over but . . . was brave like a warrior" (*SS* 75). As the adult Cole listens to Luther tell about his naming, he runs his thumb along a small leather bag containing two arrowheads and a small, carved doll made of stone.

He thought about what Uncle Luther had said. A long time before, men had sat on a hillside in California and made the two points in the bag, chipping an idea of who they were into obsidian and flint, and somewhere nearby someone had picked up a white stone and imagined the figure in the bag. And now his old uncle was telling Cole that he had an Indian name, a Choctaw name. A name that had come to him through an act of his brother's, but a name that set him forever apart from Attis, as though he were stone shaped by the old man's words. "Little-chief-warrior Red," he thought to himself, if that was right. (75)

Attis recognizes the warrior in Cole as well. He knows, "his brother was stronger than him, a warrior who could give him strength" (93). It is too late for Attis, but Cole is beginning to understand what imagining means and what a warrior might be. He is beginning the "re-membering" of his Native self. Like the ancient men he imagines, he is fashioning an idea of who he is that is independent of the dominant culture.

Owens takes us step by step through Cole's quest and his opening into consciousness. From the beginning Cole shows an awareness of the definitions placed on him, as when he recites what he has learned of "breeds" from books and TV, and Mundo says, "Cole wasn't like most guys his age. Sometimes he reminded Mundo of one of the spaced-out priests they used to find walking the roads in Nam. Or one of those guys that lived on the island with the one they called the Coconut Monk" (44). Just as Luther saw the warrior in the little boy, Mundo sees another kind of potential in the young man. But Owens never lets us forget that Cole is a mixedblood. Immediately after thinking of Cole as a "spaced-out priest," Mundo notices that he is the only one of the McCurtains who would look directly into another person's eyes. He thinks, "Maybe you had to be less than half to make eye contact" (4). Making contact is a good metaphor for what the mixedblood author does as well, and perhaps it is having roots in each world that allows Owens and other mixedblood authors to construct and deconstruct the world of dual cultures so carefully. Not only do they "convey the spirit that is one's own," they do so in a language that is at once that of the Other and their own because they are part of both worlds—a unique and interesting position.

Cole is perched on that knife's edge, yearning for an Indian identity but resisting it as well. As he watches Luther, he thinks, "the old uncle was Choctaw, really Choctaw, what he, Cole McCurtain, could never be" (65). He rocks back and forth on that dividing point, sensing the truth—"'You think this panther is *nalusachito?*' He felt himself begin to shiver again, remembering the river, the shadows down there," but he immediately rocks back to "'*Nalusachito*'s a myth . . . , an old superstition.' The Choctaw word was rough and heavy on his tongue" (71). The word does not come naturally to him yet, but that he is able to articulate it is an important step. However, Cole tries to rationalize and deny the truth that he is beginning to see.

> Abruptly the distance his father had traveled was sad, tragic, and he knew all at once what his father must have known for many years. They'd all gone too far, and Attis had been right. None of them, not even Hoey McCurtain, could ever go back. It was more than a mix of blood. . . The panther that haunted the cabin wasn't *nalusachito*. The soul-eater came from inside. The cat was only what Cole had already imagined it to be, a genetic accident that had come to this place only to be angered by a white man who, like Cole, knew what it really was. (72)

Owens is touching on what must be a deep seated fear of all colonized people, the fear of truly losing one's cultural heritage, one's cultural self. But in this story, there is a return, a taking back of bones. *Nalusachito,* the soul-eater, can be read as the eater of the cultural soul, the loss of connection, and it is more than a "genetic" accident. It can also be defeated—or more correctly, put back in place. That requires re-membering, taking back the bones, writing a people back into the history constructed by another. In this way *The Sharpest Sight* functions beautifully. By mimicking and manipulating the genre of the murder mystery, Owens has produced the kind of text described by Leela Gandhi as a "sly weapon of anti-colonial civility, an ambivalent mixture of deference and disobedience," which "inaugurates the process of anti-colonial self-differentiation. . . . . the paradigmatic moment of anti-colonial counter-texuality [that] is seen to begin with the first indecorous mixing of Western genres with local content" (Ghandi 149–50).

This story will end with Cole's finding, cleaning, and finally taking back his brother's bones, an action Cole could not have imagined in the novel's beginning, when he had very little understanding of what "taking back the bones" could mean. "Hoey McCurtain, Choctaw from Mississippi, with chiefs in his family, or so he often said after a few beers. Cole had read about Choctaws, and sometimes he thought that it was just as likely his ancestors had been bone-pickers, growing their fingernails long for their task" (*SS* 11). If so, it is an honorable family history, as he comes to see. Picking the bones was a great honor in the old Choctaw culture, and bone-pickers were held in high esteem for the honor they did the dead. So it is with the author who would take back the bones of the culture, keep them safe, and allow life to go on. At the end of *The Sharpest Sight,* Lee Scott calls the ritual of cleaning and placing the bones "primitive," but Cole quietly, firmly, and with a loaded gun refuses to turn over his brother's remains. After the agent leaves, Cole "took two blue sheets, which he partially opened on either side of the jacket. Then he began to clean his brother's bones" (254). This is a fair metaphor for Owens's work—quietly, firmly, and with a loaded pen, he writes back to the center and takes back the cultural bones.

NOTES

1. See Philip Deloria's *Playing Indian* (New Haven: Yale UP, 1998), which gives an insightful, chronological look at appropriations of Native American identity.

WORKS CITED

Ashcroft, Bill, and Gareth Griffiths and Helen Tiffin, eds. *The Post-Colonial Studies Reader.* New York: Routledge, 1997.

Bakhtin, Mikhail. *The Dialogic Imagination: Four Essays.* Trans. Caryl Emerson and Michael Holquist. Ed. Michael Holquist. Austin: U of Texas P, 1981.

———. *Rabelais and His World.* Trans. Helene Iswolsky. Bloomington: Indiana UP, 1964.

Deloria, Vine. "American Fantasy." *The Pretend Indians: Images of Native Americans in the Movies.* Ed. Gretchen Bataille and Charles L. P. Silet. Ames: Iowa UP, 1980.

Fanon, Frantz. *The Wretched of the Earth.* New York: Grove Press, 1967.

Ghandi, Leela. *Postcolonial Theory: A Critical Introduction.* New York: Columbia UP, 1998.

Momaday, N. Scott. "A Man Made of Words." *The Names: A Memoir.* Tucson: U of Arizona P, 1976.

Vizenor, Gerald. *Fugitive Poses.* Lincoln: U of Nebraska P, 1998.

CHAPTER THREE

CROSSREADING TEXTS, CROSSREADING IDENTITY

Hybridity, Diaspora, and Transculturation in Louis Owens's Mixedblood Messages

ELVIRA PULITANO

An appreciation for the boundless capacity of language that, through storytelling, brings us together, despite great distances between cultures, despite great distances in time.

LESLIE SILKO

I/i can be I or i, you and me both involved. We sometimes includes, other times excludes me . . . you may stand on the other side of the hill once in a while, but you may also be me, while remaining what you are and what i am not.

TRINH T. MINH-HA

In his pivotal work on the poetics of Native American oral traditions, Dell Hymes reinterprets a Chinook story that he first analyzed in 1968. In this story a woman stubbornly refuses to listen to her daughter, who has been trying to tell her unsettling but crucial news concerning their future. In the event the daughter can only remonstrate: "In vain I tried to tell you." As he reflects on his methodology, on his successes and failures in using anthropological philology and structural linguistics in the attempt to bring the Chinook text to life, restoring voice to oral texts that have been little more than museum specimens, Hymes writes: "If we refuse to consider and interpret the surprising facts of device, design, and performance inherent in the worlds of the texts, the Indians who made the texts, and those who preserved what they made, will have worked in vain. We will be telling the texts not to speak. We will mistake, perhaps, to our costs, the nature of which they speak" (5–6). While coming from the specific field of ethnopoetics, Hymes's observations "speak" perfectly well to the subject of this chapter—crossreading and crosscultural communication as ways of opening up ideas while exploring other cultural positions. As critics involved in reading texts originating in differing epistemologies, in the narratives of Native American oral traditions, even when these same texts are heavily hybridized within Western discursive paradigms, we might, Hymes suggests, listen carefully to what these narratives have to say; we might consider accurately both our and their different viewpoints and ultimately learn to see things in new ways. As readers and critics of something called Native American literature, our primary responsibility is to make sure that these texts will not speak "in vain."

In *Mixedblood Messages: Literature, Film, Family, Place,* Louis Owens explores the way in which people read across cultures and what the aims and consequences of these readings can and should be. Crucial to Owens is the idea of dialogue within and between people in order to expose boundaries that shape and constitute different cultural and personal worlds. Elaborating on Bakhtin's formulations, Owens applies concepts such as *dialogism* and *heteroglossia* to the idea of reading across lines of cultural identity, overcoming rigid binary oppositions between Western and Native perspectives and constructing a criticism that challenges old ways of theorizing. Unlike those critics who argue for an authentic tradition of Indian intellectualism founded on the categories of nationhood and sovereignty, Owens argues for a hybridized, multidirectional and multigenre discursive mode, one that encompasses his mixedblood, hybrid identity and ultimately redefines the authoritative discourse of Eurocentric theory. While acknowledging the fact that an authentic "Indian perspective" is problematic and all the more contradictory, especially in light of his own as well as many other Native American authors' strategic location within the discourse of mainstream academia, he conceives of writing within and outside the metropolitan center as a powerfully subversive tool, a tricksterish subversion through which Native Americans can survive as Indigenous people and living human beings. In terms similar to those elaborated in the oral tradition of tribal cultures, in which words have the power to create and transform reality, Owens turns to language as the most powerful tool with which to ensure the life and vitality of Native writing and identity, in opposition to the stasis and entrapment created by the stereotypes and clichés of Euramerican discourse. As a critic deeply committed to a discourse on hybridity and dialogism, Owens intends to explore new creative avenues in language through which Native people can constantly reimagine themselves in new terms. Writing from a notion of identity that, as Stuart Hall notices, is always in the making, a matter of "becoming" rather than "being" ("Cultural Identity" 225), Owens produces a hybrid, multivoiced text in which different discourses crisscross one another while significantly challenging Western ways of doing theory. Paralleling Trinh T. Minh-ha's idea of theory as a "form of creativity" ("The Undone Interval" 4), Owens blends autobiography, criticism, film commentary, and environmental reflections, while suggesting a different way in which Native American scholars can enter the theoretical debate of the Western academy. To those critics who continue to resist "theory" within Native American studies, considering it merely a further instrument of Western ideological imperialism, Owens's text represents a perfect example of how Native American scholars can and should engage themselves in the current critical dialogue in order to challenge the monolithic discourse of Eurocentric theory itself. While focusing mainly on *Mixedblood Messages*, the following discussion will also consider Owens's essay "As If an Indian Were Really an Indian: Native

American Voices and Postcolonial Theory" (published in *I Hear the Train*), in order to illustrate the author's position within current debates on postcolonial discourse.

In *Mixedblood Messages* Owens's subversion of conventional Western theoretical strategies begins in his refusal to subscribe to objective methods by bringing into the text the identity of the critic and submitting the same identity to a severe scrutiny. Exploring the significance of his mixed heritage as opposed to essentialist notions of Indian authenticity, Owens produces a text that borders at the junctures of various critical discourses, shuttling back and forth between scholarly argument and personal narrative. He writes:

> In *Mixedblood Messages,* I wanted to put together a book that looked at mixed identity and the construction of Indianness from as many angles as possible. Thus I included essays on literature, film, and environment. However, I also wanted to foreground the subjectivity of the critical posture, to write a book in which the critic is the subject as much as the subject is criticized. It becomes, then, a kind of metacriticism in which the usual subject position of the godlike critic is interrogated. In that sense, the criticism criticizes the critic, . . . as well as the critic (writer) criticizing (analyzing) the subject. (Personal communication, 13 March 2001)

Owens begins his critical journey into "mixed messages" and crosscultural readings with "Crow Love," a personal childhood memory but also a story that symbolically reflects the colonial situation. As a child, Owens writes, he was friends with a boy whose father had made him believe that "to make crows speak human words it was necessary to split their tongues with a sharp knife" (xii). As painful as this story now sounds in Owens's memories, he writes that in a similar pose, the colonizer "performs his surgery," "desperate to give his words to the 'other,' so that the whole world will ultimately give back the reflected self" (xii). For more than five hundred years, the tongues of Native American people have been split, dismembered, reduced to "inarticulatedness," a condition that

N. Scott Momaday's novel *House Made of Dawn* conveys brilliantly. When Europeans arrived in the New World, they did not hear the Natives' speech since, as Owens relates in "Columbus Had It Coming," one of the admiral's first gestures was to ship a group of Taino Natives back to Spain so that "they might be taught to speak" (211). Language as a conquering and silencing/erasing tool has been used by the colonizers for more than five hundred years on the American continent, with the only purpose to subsume indigenous people into the manifest destiny of what Owens calls "Euramerica."

Nevertheless, Owens posits, despite this ongoing project of physical and cultural annihilation, despite more than five hundred years of being uprooted, relocated, and even terminated, Native people have, astonishingly, survived. And their stories have been crucial in the act of cultural reappropriation and liberation. Using the language of Bill Ashcroft et al. in *The Empire Writes Back,* Owens writes: "The people he [Columbus] mistakenly and unrepentantly called 'Indians' have indeed 'learned to speak,' appropriating the master discourse—including the utterance 'Indian'—abrogating its authority, making the invaders' language our language, english with a lower case e, and turning it against the center" (4). From the outset, then, Owens situates the experience of Native American people within a postcolonial discursive mode, anticipating the rather complicated issue of how appropriate or even legitimate it is to use the category "postcolonial" in relation to the Native American condition, an issue that he explores in detail in "As If an Indian Were Really an Indian," to which I will return.

The proliferation in the past few decades of texts by Native American authors is, according to Owens, an extraordinary sign of the "subversive survival" of indigenous people. Produced in English by mostly highly educated mixedblood authors, these works nonetheless come from what D'Arcy McNickle has termed a "different map of the mind" and Owens, following McNickle, calls a different "conceptual horizon" (*MM* 4). As works that attempt to convey in writing the world of the oral tradition, a world in which myths and ceremonies are indistinguishable from everyday reality, these works produce an "other" literature that nonetheless, Owens argues, "participates profoundly in the discourse we call American and World Literature" (56). By appropriating a language other than the written and incorporating it within the structures of the colonizer's discursive modes, Native American writers accomplish what Owens terms an act of "crosswriting," a subversive maneuver that significantly challenges readers to reconsider their beliefs and worldviews. Parallel to crosswriting is, then, the act of "crossreading"—that is, crossing our own "conceptual horizons" in the attempt to understand different epistemologies. Owens writes: "More and more we will be required to read across lines of cultural identity around us and within us. It is not easy but it is necessary, and the rewards are immeasurable" (11).

While primarily referring to works of fiction, Owens clearly implies that the act of "crossreading" can be profitably applied to any kind of literary discourse, including a theoretical one. A text such as *Mixedblood Messages* might at first unsettle readers' expectations if they are not willing to cross over their own "theoretical horizons" to explore the differing cultural codes of the author's background. While heavily and inevitably drawing on Western hermeneutical discourse, Owens's book brings to our attention elements from Choctaw-Cherokee epistemology, particularly the belief that individuals can "alter the world for good or bad with language, even with thought" (209). In a subtle example of his own "crossreading," Owens writes how at an early age he learned the importance of stories and their inextricable relationship with the world we inhabit:

> I happen to be descended from a mix of Choctaw, Cherokee, Irish, and Cajun ancestors. Within all these cultures the oral tradition runs strong. Stories, I learned very early, make the world knowable and inhabitable. Stories make the world, period. Whether they tell of Raven or Coyote imagining the world into complex being or start by telling us that in the beginning was the word and the word was with God, stories arise from that essential and most human need—what the poet Wallace Stevens called that blessed rage for order, the Maker's

rage to order words of the sea. Stories also arise out of our inescapable need to feel ourselves related to what John Steinbeck and Edward F. Ricketts . . . called "the whole thing, known and unknowable." (*MM* 210)

By translating an old but seemingly universal belief into a contemporary context, Owens posits that the only way for our global community to live is to turn to language and the power inherent in human discourse in order to alter reality as a way to read across lines of cultural identity. In the case of Native Americans, it means to go past the stereotypes and clichés of an artifact called "indian" in order finally to recognize the presence of Natives always reinventing themselves in new stories. It is with this idea of cross-cultural encounter that Owens invites us to approach Native American Literature. He urges us to come to terms with the fact that Native American writers are demanding that

> the world must enter into dialogue with that literature and make it profoundly a part of our own modern existence, just as Native Americans have for centuries made European literature a part of Native America. And they are insisting that rather than looking to this literature as a reflection of what they expect to see—their own constructed Indianness—readers must look past their mirroring consciousness to the other side. (23–24)

The essay "Mapping the Mixedblood: Frontier and Territory in Native America" is Owens's response to Euramerica's ongoing attempt to annihilate and erase the Indian, confining him to the safe Territory of its own discourse. Borrowing Mary Louise Pratt's notion of "contact zones," Owens appropriates the term "frontier," which "carries with it such a heavy burden of colonial discourse" (26), thus making the space that it signifies one of extreme contestation, fluidity, and multidirectional hybridization. He writes: "Frontier, I would suggest, is the zone of trickster, a shimmering, always changing zone of multifaceted contact within which every utterance is challenged and interrogated, all referents put into question." As such, frontier for Owens stands in stark contrast to "territory," conceived as a "place of containment, invented to control and subdue the dangerous potentialities of imagined Indians" (26). In the year 1890 Frederick Jackson Turner proclaimed "the death of the frontier," assuming the "Indians" to be either killed in massacres such as Wounded Knee or pushed more and more into the boundaries of the official Indian Territory. Owens insists on the necessity of revitalizing the term *frontier* so that the utterance "Indian," a further version of territory, is symbolically deconstructed. Against deadly stereotypes and clichés that aim at confining the Indian to museum rooms, Owens argues that "Native Americans . . . continue to resist this ideology of containment and to insist upon the freedom to re-imagine themselves within a fluid, always shifting frontier space" (27).

Owens's frontier/territory discourse assumes an all the more significant role in the discussion of Native American literature and literary theory. In the discursive field of Native American studies, it would seem almost legitimate, according to Owens, to avoid this new form of colonial enterprise known as "critical theory." To those critics who insist on an autonomous tradition of Indian intellectualism, Western/Eurocentric theory appears indeed a "French disease," as Arnold Krupat humorously defines the often strong feeling of resistance on the part of traditional humanists against poststructuralism and deconstruction (*For Those Who Come After* xv–xvi). Within the field of Native American studies, fervent representatives of a nationalist approach insist that in order to promote an autonomous "Indian tradition of intellectualism," it is necessary to categorically reject the master's tools and embrace the battle against colonialism with weapons different from those the dominant discourse provides. However, Owens writes, such separatist sentiments are difficult to translate into practice since, whether we like it or not, Native American critics already function within the dominant discourse and "do not have the luxury of simply opting out" (*MM* 52). More importantly, one may argue, such a separatist stance runs the risk of confining the Indian (once again) in the "safe" territory of Euramerican discourse. Instead of participating in the cultural struggle from within, appropriating the master's tongue and obligating the same master to listen to voices other than his own, challenging, thus, the very foundations of his own Ethnocentric discourse, the Indian reverts to a "Nativist" mode. In the safe territory of Indian criticism, the parameters are still, ironically, dictated by Western categories.

In "The Song Is Very Short: Native American Literature and Literary Theory," Owens explores the degree to which Native American authors are implicated in the theoretical discourse of the metropolitan center. In the past few years various critics, including Owens himself, have relied on the instruments of postmodernist and poststructuralist theory to interpret Native American texts. Recently, Owens observes in "As If an Indian Were Really an Indian," critics have found themselves more and more using the language of postcolonialism as a viable tool with which to explicate the hybridization of Native American texts—as well as the diasporic condition of their authors. Beginning with Krupat, it has been argued that the literature produced by Native American authors bears interesting parallels with the ideological perspective of postcolonial literatures (*Turn to Native* 30). Notwithstanding cultural, historical, and geopolitical differences or the crucial fact that the condition of the Native population is one of ongoing colonialism, Native American literature—like other postcolonial literatures—operates within the context of what Krupat, drawing on Talal Asad, has termed "anti-imperial translation" (*Turn to Native* 35), presenting an English powerfully affected by a foreign tongue and adopting Western literary forms to convey, in writing, the rhythms and patterns of the oral tradition. More significantly, I would argue, the concept of identity as permeable and multirelational—resembling the shape-shifting character of trickster as it is conveyed in the work of virtually every contemporary mixedblood author but primarily that of Gerald Vizenor—would seem the most significant point of encounter between Native American literature and postcolonial theory. Yet, Owens points out, distinctions need to be made and questions raised before labeling Native American literary productions "postcolonial." As Krupat reminds us, it is not precisely correct to conceptualize

Native American literature as postcolonial, since there is not yet a "post" to the colonial status of Native Americans: "Call it domestic imperialism or internal colonialism; in either case, a considerable number of Native people exist in conditions of politically sustained subalternity" (*Turn to Native* 30). Owens characterizes the general situation as follows:

> a very real danger faced by the Native American, or any marginalized writer who would assume the role as scholar-critic-theorist, is that of consciously or unconsciously using Eurocentric theory merely as a way of legitimizing his of her voice—picking up the master's tools not to dismantle the master's house but simply to prove that we are tool-using creatures just like him and therefore worthy of intellectual recognition. (*MM* 53)

Particularly dangerous, Owens goes on to suggest, is the attraction of postcolonial theory often conceived as an oppositional discourse.

Both in *Mixedblood Messages* and in "As If an Indian Were Really an Indian," Owens interrogates the significant erasure of Native American voices from postcolonial discourse. With the exception of Trinh, the major representative figures of postcolonial theory ignore the existence of a powerful literature produced by contemporary Native American authors. Owens argues that while referring to other minority voices, critics such as Edward Said and Homi Bhabha constantly overlook "the existence of a resistance literature arising from indigenous, colonized inhabitants of the Americas ("As If an Indian" 210). By applying Dipesh Chakrabarty's concept of the "symmetry of ignorance," in relation to the work of mainstream academic historians, Owens suggests that this absence of reciprocity applies even more to postcolonial theory's ignorance of Native American literature than it does to the First World's ignorance of Third World history. In other words, Owens claims, to be taken seriously, Native American critics are expected to be familiar with the theories of Bhabha, Gayatri Spivak, and so forth, but there is no "symmetry of expectation" as far as the production of Native authors is concerned.

Both in *Mixedblood Messages* and in "As If an Indian Were Really an Indian," Owens takes stances similar to those articulated within the discourse of postcolonialism. More significantly, he even appropriates postcolonial terminology—specifically, the concepts of *mimicry* and *diaspora*—and translates them into a Native American paradigm, a gesture that might at first suggest Spivak's notion of *catachresis*. However, when considered from within a Native epistemological viewpoint, Owens's act of appropriation becomes, ultimately, a tricksterish subversion, as he shows the *ambivalence* of both colonial and postcolonial discourse. Like a trickster straddling worlds and worldviews, his ultimate goal being that of testing ideas and idealogues, Owens's catachrestic maneuver aims at testing/disrupting postcolonial assumptions and predicaments, significantly proving that an "appropriation" of postcolonial theory on the part of Native American scholars and critics is not always just a tactic "worthy of intellectual recognition." Critics might obviously point out that such acts of "translation," regardless of how they are intended, rely, ironically, on the language of an ambivalent discourse of antiresistance, one heavily influenced by Eurocentric discursive modes. The question here is not simple and goes back to Owens's overarching argument that whether we like it or not, Native American authors are already implicated in the dominant discourse of the metropolitan center. Any appeal to a "pure" or "authentic" Native American theory is utopian and absurd. Paralleling Gates's main argument in *Black Literature and Literary Theory*, Owens posits that in the context of a Native American discourse we should ask how it is possible to "produce a signifying [Native] difference" by repeating the paradigms of the mainstream academic discourse, while simultaneously showing the same discourse some of its significant limitations. For Owens, then, the very act of appropriation is the result of a collaborative and conjunctural practice.

When, in 1969, N. Scott Momaday was awarded the Pulitzer Prize for his first novel, *House Made of Dawn*, the Pulitzer jury proudly acknowledged "the arrival on the American literary scene of a matured, sophisticated literary artist from the original Americans"

(Schubnell, as quoted in *MM* 58). In the attempt to understand the significance of this statement, Owens suggests that "these words indicate that an aboriginal writer has finally learned to write like the colonial center that determines legitimate discourse" ("As If an Indian" 224). Elaborating on Bhabha's formulations, Owens claims that Momaday's creative gesture was a superb, impressive act of mimic subversion, one requiring extensive education on the part of its author, without which it would have been impossible to be heard at the center. Having earned a doctorate from Stanford and having skillfully appropriated the literary techniques of Modernist discourse, Momaday acts, Owens posits, as the quintessential "mimic man" of anticolonial resistance, one who turns the "other/slippage" position, to use Bhabha's term, into a powerful weapon of appropriation. While subversively and superbly employing the language of Euramerican Modernism, *House Made of Dawn* relies on an intricate web of elements from the Pueblo and Navajo oral traditions, a complex layering that, although undoubtedly unrecognized by the Pulitzer jury (and, if recognized, probably considered simply a touch of exoticism), places the novel in that shifting, hybridized, and unstable position of anticolonial resistance. Owens writes: "Exoticism packaged in familiar and therefore accessible formulas, carefully managed so as to admit the metropolitan reader while never implying that the painful difficulties illuminated within the text are the responsibility of that reader, clearly *House Made of Dawn* is both 'inside' and 'outside' the West" ("As If an Indian" 225). While recognizing Momaday's brilliant act of subversion, Owens, however, notices how such mimic maneuvers, such negotiations, "are never free of cost" (226). Himself a critic both "inside" and "outside" the metropolitan center, Owens shares with Spivak the sense of a certain complicity with the heritage of imperialism, "the impossible 'no' to a structure which one critiques, yet inhabits intimately" (*Outside* 281). Owens writes:

> Those of us in the field of what we call Native American literature can and undoubtedly will chafe at the ignorance and

erasure of Native American voices within the metropolitan center, and within what at times appears to be the loyal opposition to that center called postcolonial theory. And we can and undoubtedly will continue to try to make our voices heard— "to give voice to the silent," . . . However . . . it seems that a necessary, if difficult, lesson for all of us may well be that in giving voice to the silent we unavoidably give voice to the forces that conspire to effect that silence. ("As If an Indian" 226)

Owens's reflections on the ambivalence of his own subject-speaking position as a writer and critic bring him to examine his mixed identity and complex family history. In the third section of *Mixedblood Messages*, "Autobiographical Reflections, or Mixed Blood and Mixed Messages," Owens explores concepts of "motion" and "diaspora" as a means of understanding his ancestors' liminal experience as well as his own. Looking at family pictures, Owens imagines the life of his ancestors in Indian Territory at the beginning of the twentieth century by creating stories and filling the gaps in the stories already told by the pictures. Photographs assume an important role in this section, and Owens himself seems fascinated by these cultural artifacts. Elsewhere he has written that "all photographs of Native people tell more than one story, open themselves to different possibilities, different inventions" ("Their Shadows Before Them"). For Owens, photographs become a means of keeping, telling, and retelling stories, imagining and rewriting a text that might give him a sense of who he is and where he comes from.

In "The Man Made of Words," Momaday writes: "We are what we imagine. Our own very existence consists in our imagination of ourselves. Our best destiny is to imagine, at least, completely, who and what, and *that* we are. The greatest tragedy that can befall us is to go unimagined" (167). From this act of imagination Momaday wrote *The Way to Rainy Mountain,* a journey into his Kiowa past, into what he calls the "memory in the blood" of his ancestors. Elaborating on Momaday's formulations, Owens writes about his own "blood trails," his own Choctaw and Cherokee roots "sifted through generational storytelling" (150). As he explains, behind the title of the essay lies, of course, "The Trail of Tears," one of the many forced relocations of Native people, this being the one that laid the foundations of the state of Oklahoma. To a certain extent, Owens writes, stories are "another sort of removal most American Indian people have experienced, another kind of trail that winds through generations and locations and finally leaves us sometimes in a kind of suspension. These are the blood trails that we follow back toward a sense of where we come from and who we are" (*MM* 150). The presence of automobiles in most of his family photographs triggers his reflections on what he calls "indigenous motion," a quality that is "genetically encoded in American Indian being" (164) and is clearly reflected in the migration stories of the various tribes, including his Choctaw-Cherokee ancestors. These same stories, Owens further claims, have allowed Indian people to adapt and change to centuries of cultural displacement. Filtered through the veil of memory and imagination, these same stories now surface in Owens's writing to help him to re-create a past while giving meaning and coherence to the present and also help him to read backward and forward simultaneously. Both in form and content, *Mixedblood Messages* conveys Owens's sense of "indigenous motion." By creating a fluid, mixedgenre text, in which different discourses are woven together to give significance to his own liminal experience, Owens illustrates how the syncretic and adaptive nature of the oral tradition finds its way onto the written page, creating a shifting, hybridized space in which tribally based ideas can be creatively and effectively incorporated into a new creation.

In "Motion of Fire and Form" Owens writes: "I conceive of myself today not as an 'Indian,' but as a mixedblood, a person of complex roots and histories. Along with my parents and grandparents, brothers and sisters, I am the product of liminal space, the result of union between desperate individuals on the edges of dispossessed cultures and the marginalized spawn of invaders" (176). Similarly, in "As If an Indian Were Really an Indian," this frontier-zone identity is further elaborated to embrace Hall's notion of diaspora. Hall argues:

The diaspora experience as I intend it here is defined, not by essence or purity, but by the recognition of a necessary heterogeneity and diversity; by a conception of 'identity' which lives with and through, not despite difference; by hybridity. Diaspora identities are those which are constantly producing and reproducing themselves anew, through transformation and difference. ("Cultural Identity," 235)

As a person of "complex roots and histories," raised most of his earliest years in Mississippi Choctaw country, an English Professor with a Ph.D., Owens defines his work, as well as that of other mixed-blood writers, as the production of a migrant living and working in what might be termed the "Native American diaspora." He writes that "today in the U.S., urban centers and academic institutions have come to constitute a kind of diaspora for Native Americans who through many generations of displacement and orchestrated ethnocide are often far from their traditional homelands and cultural communities" ("As If an Indian" 208).

However, much like the contested term "postcolonial," the concept of "diaspora" is never clear of commodification. Contemporary invocations of diaspora have been severely criticized, both politically and intellectually, by those people who claim natural or first-nation sovereignty. Such criticism is most likely inevitable since, as James Clifford points out, the "specific cosmopolitanisms" articulated by diaspora discourses and identities "are in constitutive tension" with nation-state ideologies and indigenous claims to sovereignty ("Diasporas" 308). Tribal assertions of "sovereignty" and "first nationhood," he argues, usually emphasize "continuity of habitation," "aboriginality," and a "natural connection to the land." More importantly, representatives of "tribalist" discourse, in the most extreme cases, aim at recovering a "pure," original past, a precontact time that might legitimate nationalistic claims.

In the specific field of postcolonialism, one has to recall the scathing critique of Aijaz Ahmad, who posits that "people who live in the metropolitan countries for professional reasons . . . use words like 'exile' or 'diaspora'—words which have centuries of pain and dis-possession inscribed in them—to designate what is after all, only personal convenience" (*In Theory* 85). Whether or not we agree with Ahmad's harsh critique, a critique not free from interrogatives of its own, the above-mentioned objections to the concept of diaspora bring us back full circle to the haunting questions Owens himself points out in his discussion of Momaday's mimic subversion. Both "inside" and "outside" the metropolitan center, Native American writers and critics inhabit—whether consciously or unconsciously—the same structure that they forcefully critique; as such, Owens writes, they are "distinctly *migrant* in the sense that [they] possess a mobility denied to [their] less privileged relations" ("As If an Indian" 224). Along the same lines, Rey Chow notices that "diasporic con-sciouness is perhaps not so much a historical accident as it is an intel-lectual reality—the reality of being intellectual" (*Writing Diaspora* 15).

Recent articulations of diaspora inevitably suggest that the term that once described the Jewish, Greek, and Armenian dispersion has now expanded to include a larger, semantic domain to the extent that people who are not *in diaspora* (in the traditional sense) might experience diasporic dimensions. In Owens's case such a diasporic dimension is significantly encoded in his complex, mixedblood identity, in the crucial concept of motion that is, as he puts it, "the matrix from which identity must be forged" (*MM* 165). More sig-nificantly, such a diasporic dimension is inscribed in stories, in those very acts of imagination that he must follow to get a sense of who he is and where he comes from. Within a Native epistemology, it has been argued that stories are, in a sense, maps, whether they convey information about specific trails or, more significantly, make sense of a locale and its importance to the people. It is to such imaginative trails rather than to tribalist assertions of sovereignty and nation-hood that Owens clings in order to come to terms with his mixed-blood identity.

In "Blood Trails," Owens engages in a passionate, often humor-ous exchange with Elizabeth Cook Lynn in order to demystify essen-tialist blood-quantum theories as signifiers of Indianness. The main thrust of Cook Lynn's "American Indian Intellectualism and The New Indian Story" is an attack on the production of mixedblood authors, which she considers "a kind of liberation phenomenon" and a "deconstruction of a tribal-nation past" (69). As products of a university setting, mixedblood authors—a list that includes the names of Wendy Rose, Diane Glancy, Joseph Bruchach, Gerald Vizenor, and Louis Owens among others—express, according to Cook Lynn, the Indian experience in assimilative and mainstream terms, promoting individualistic values that have no stake in First Nation ideology (Cook-Lynn, "American Indian Intellectualism" 69). In response Owens claims, first, that the fiction of mixedblood authors focuses on the recovery of a sense of identity, a recovery dependent on a rediscovered sense of place as well as community. He is even more critical of Cook-Lynn's notion of "tribal realism," a vague concept that ironically suggests Vizenor's notion of the "invented Indian." The authors mentioned by Cook-Lynn, Owens argues, do not live in reservation communities, but they "create art about urban or rural mixedblood experience" (MM 158). They tell stories of who they are today, stories of survival in which the past is constantly reimagined into the present tense, not "frozen" in some distant, entropic time. Owens writes:

> Should the stories of such people, the products of colonial America's five hundred years of cultural wars against indigenous peoples, not be told because they do not fit the definition of what one Lakota critic thinks is tribally "real"? Are their stories not ones that "matter" or have "meaning"? Contrary to what Cook-Lynn asserts, this is a powerful literature of resistance, a countervoice to the dominant discourse that would reduce Indians to artifactual commodities useful to tourist industries. (MM 159)

Owens's critique might be further contextualized upon considering Cook-Lynn's own subject-speaking position in the above-mentioned essay. Quoting the Italian Marxist critic Antonio Gramsci, Cook-Lynn argues that mixedblood authors who have become part

of the elite American university scene are "failed intellectuals because
they have not lived up to the responsibility of transmitting knowledge between certain diverse blocs of society" (Cook-Lynn 70). They
are not, in other words, what Gramsci would term "organic intellectuals," because they often write "in the esoteric language of French
and Russian literary scholars that has overturned the lit/critic scene"
(76). What Cook-Lynn overlooks at this point of her discussion is
Gramsci's unfounded idealism, his faith in how effective the work
of his organic intellectual can ultimately be. Specifically, Cook-Lynn
overlooks Gramsci's complex subjectivity, his coming from Sardinia
(the subaltern/colonized peasantry of Southern Italy), a condition
that accounts for his ambivalence regarding the role of the intellectual as it is articulated in the *Prison Notebooks*. As ironic as it might
seem, Gramsci's ambivalent position resembles the diasporic condition of many contemporary Native American writers and critics
(including Cook-Lynn), people who, from the privileged position of
a university setting, consciously or unconsciously participate in the
construction of the subaltern/Other culture of which they are also
a part. Even more problematic is Cook-Lynn's tendency—shared by
many Third World critics—to patch together out of Gramsci's work
a notion of nationhood that is not necessarily Gramscian but simply
useful to her argument.

The question of how effectively Native American authors working
in the safe space of an academic institution commit themselves to
their Native communities is quite complicated and is one on which
Native writers may not always agree. As Jace Weaver points out,
"today we exist in many different kinds of community—reservation,
rural village, urban, tribal, pan-Indian, traditional, Christian. Many
move back and forth between a variety of these communities. Our
different locations, physical, mental, and spiritual, will inevitably
lead to different conceptions of what survival, liberation, and com-
munitism require" ("Native American" 53–54). Similarly, reflecting
on the "social function of art," Trinh writes: "Commitment as an ideal
is particularly dear to Third World writers" since it helps to alleviate the sense of guilt for being privileged, for joining "the clan of

literates" while the majority of community members "stoop over the tomato fields, bending under the hot sun (a perpetuation of the same privilege)" (*Woman* 10). Commitment, Cook-Lynn argues, should also be the primary concern of Native intellectuals, who should write "in a vocabulary that people can understand" ("American Indian Intellectualism" 75) rather than in the esoteric language of imperialist discourse. However, Trinh reminds us, the search for "clarity" or correct expression can also be "a means of subjection," a quality of official, taught language, since clarity itself "has long been the criterion set forth in the treatises on rhetoric whose aim was to order discourse so as to persuade" (*Woman* 16). Coming from a poststructuralist insight, Trinh's notion of writing is one in which rules are broken down and fixed ideas are continually dismantled.

Similarly, Owens's experimenting with Western literary genres and discourses, while skillfully incorporating elements from the oral tradition of tribal cultures, aims at destabilizing the master's discourse, abrogating its authority, and forcing readers to come to terms with new ways of reading and thinking. While representatives of the nationalist, separatist discourse might continue to critique Owens's work for employing the lexicon of hegemonic theory, Owen's critical strategies still raise interesting questions about the "social" function of Native American intellectuals. Drawing on Robert Young, Owens writes that today Native Americans are helping reposition a "global point of view" (*MM* 4), challenging us to come to terms with the fact that the so-called First World is not always in a privileged position with regard to the Second or Third World. More significantly, Owens posits, Native Americans are repositioning terms such as First, Second, and Third World "to signify not the cultural/historial hegemony of the Western world but rather those paradigmatic, mythic levels that underlie this present world in the origin myths" (*MM* 4). Although Native American intellectuals cannot always speak to the economically, racially, and politically oppressed people on reservations, Owens suggests that they can speak about their dangerous and denigrated positions inside the dominant culture. More importantly, by conceptualizing the reality of indigenous people as something other than Other, Native American intellectuals might help decenter the very essence of (Western) subjectivity.

By demanding that the West begin to "listen" to voices other than its own, Native American intellectuals actively participate in those acts of cross-cultural communication that are necessary, Owens posits, for the global community to survive. Those who argue that such a "cosmopolitan" position inevitably makes Native American intellectuals complicit with colonialist discourse—since it avoids the material and political realities of First Nation ideology—should be reminded that the domain of culture is a primary component in the struggle toward decolonization. Again, Chow's observations will be helpful at this point:

> We need to remember as intellectuals that the battles we fight are battles of words. Those who argue the oppositional standpoint are not *doing* anything different from their enemies and are most certainly not directly changing the downtrodden lives of those who seek their survival in metropolitan and nonmetropolitan spaces alike. What academic intellectuals must confront is thus not *their* "victimization" by society at large (or their victimization-in-solidarity-with-the-oppressed), but the power, wealth, and privilege that ironically accumulate from their "oppositional" viewpoint, and the widening gap between the professed contents of their words and the upward mobility they gain from such words. (17)

By envisioning a "para-sitical intervention," Chow cuts at the heart of the debate concerning how intellectuals struggle against a hegemony that already includes them and can no longer be clearly demarcated into national and transnational spaces. Putting it in Foucauldian terms, Chow raises questions of how intellectuals can resist the forms of power that transform them into its objects and instruments in the sphere of "knowledge," "truth," "consciousness," and "discourse." These same issues are of primary concern to Owens's theoretical approach.

In the fourth section of *Mixedblood Messages*, "Words, Wilderness and Native America," Owens enters the ongoing debate between intellectual activity and political engagement by focusing on environmental issues. The essays collected in this section are, in the author's words, "environmental reflections," inextricably related, however, to the topic of the power of words with which the book began. According to Owens, inherent in Native American writers is a sense of responsibility to use words with care, since "we can form and alter the world for good or bad with language, even with thought" (*MM* 209). Words are inextricably related to the natural world, as the innumerable creation stories out of which Native people derive their sense of identity tell us. Owens writes: "Silence a people's stories and you erase a culture" (*MM* 211), a fact that Euramerica's colonizing impulse knew far too well, considering that the first step toward appropriation and possession of the indigenous people on the North American continent was the silencing of their voices. Since the battles writers/critics fight are battles of words, Owens reminds all of us of the enormous responsibility that we have to use words with care if we intend to alter the world for good. As writers, Owens suggests, it is our responsibility to make people understand that the only way we as humans can survive on this planet is to arrest our self-destructive impulse as far as the environment is concerned.

While the "environmental reflections" of this last section might at first suggest a further reenactment of stereotypes on Indianness, Owens is particularly careful to free his message from any kind of romantic appeal to "Mother Earth," instead bringing Native American epistemology into play in an analysis of First World ideology. Framing his reflections in terms of the current debates surrounding ecocriticism, Owens suggests that the move toward a more bio-centric worldview—extending notions of ethics and broadening conceptions of global community to include nonhuman life-forms and the physical environment—should be made by first listening to the "voice" of the indigenous people, who conceived of their relationship with the environment in terms quite different from those of the Eurocentric West. If, as critics have pointed out, eco-criticism is testing the boundaries of academic discourse, requiring that the voice of the physical environment be heard, Owens, I argue, makes the case for a "transformative ecocriticism," one that employs the perspective and worldview of the indigenous people, who, nonetheless, managed to live on this continent for many thousands of years, developing an ethic of respect for the land.

Titled "Everywhere There Was Life: How Native Americans Can Save the Earth," the last essay in *Mixedblood Messages* (with its rather ironic title) is anything but a romantic tirade on the Indian as an environmentalist or "saver of the earth"—a concept, Owens notices, primarily developed by Euramericans, since "theirs has for five hundred years been the dominant discourse on this continent" (220). Quoting passages from Momaday's *The Way to Rainy Mountain*, McNickle's *Wind from an Enemy Sky*, and Luther Standing Bear's *Land of the Spotted Eagle*, Owens emphasizes the Native American "sophisticated holistic understanding of the ecosystems they inhabited" (225), an understanding in which there was no place for the word "wilderness." Drawing on McNickle, Owens reminds us that "we inhabit a world that is ecosystemic and not egosystemic, a world in which everything is interrelated and humanity is connected with the natural world through social relationship" (227). In order for us to see this interconnectedness, brilliantly conveyed by Silko through the spider's-web metaphor in *Ceremony*, it is imperative, Owens suggests, that we move beyond our current conceptual horizons and embrace the traditional knowledge of indigenous people. Instead of perpetuating the asymmetrical movement whereby members of the dominant culture rarely feel obliged to assimilate the various epistemologies of other cultures, whereas minority cultures are always obliged—in order to survive—to master the hegemonic culture, we should, Owens posits, reverse the nature of this exchange. Only by crossing physical and cultural boundaries can we arrive at the understanding that the rewards of such crossreading acts can, indeed, be immeasurable.

A significant and subtle expression of Owens's own crossreading and crosswriting, *Mixedblood Messages,* merges different discourses and epistemologies in the attempt to find some comfort zone in a universe of what its author calls "conflicted stories." Weaving in and out of the theoretical and the personal, Owens envisions his critical work as another way of telling a story, imagining, as he puts it, "the kinds of fictions a Nabokovian annotator might contrive in order to find his own beloved image in an otherwise alien text, with footnotes" (*Train* xi). A Nabokovian annotator-cum-trickster, Owens, in *Mixedblood Messages,* constructs his own "beloved image," footnoting stories about other stories while significantly challenging Western ways of doing theory.

WORKS CITED

Ajah, Ahmad. In *Theory: Classes, Nations, Literatures.* London: Verso, 1992.

Ashcroft Bill, Gareth Griffiths, and Helen Tiffin. *The Empire Writes Back: Theory and Practice in Post-colonial Literatures.* London and New York: Routledge, 1989.

Chow, Ray. *Writing Diaspora: Tactics of Intervention in Contemporary Cultural Studies.* Bloomington: Indiana UP, 1993.

Cook-Lynn, Elizabeth. "The American Indian Fiction Writers: Cosmopolitanism, Nationalism, the Third World, and First Nation Sovereignty." *Nothing But the Truth: An Anthology on Native American Literature.* Ed. John Purdy and James Ruppert. New Jersey: Prentice Hall, 2001.

———. "American Indian Intellectualism and the New Indian Story." *American Indian Quarterly* 20.1 (1996): 57–76.

Hall, Stuart. "Cultural Identity and Diaspora." *Identity, Community, Culture, Difference.* Ed. Jonathan Rutherdorf. London: Lawrence and Wishart, 1990. 223–37.

Hymes, Dell. *"In Vain I Tried to Tell You": Essays in Native American Ethnopoetics.* Philadelphia: U of Pennsylvania P, 1981.

Krupat, Arnold. *For Those Who Come After: A Study of Native American Autobiography.* Berkeley: U of California P, 1985.

———. *The Turn to the Native: Studies in Criticism and Culture.* Lincoln and London: U of Nebraska P, 1996.

Momaday, N. Scott. "The Man Made of Words." *The Remembered Earth: An Anthology of Contemporary Native American Literature.* Ed. Geary Hobson. Albuquerque: U of New Mexico P, 1981.

Trinh T. Minh-ha. "The Undone Interval: Trinh T. Minh-ha in Conversation with Annamaria Morelli." *The Post-Colonial Question: Common Skies,*

Divided Horizons. Ed. Iain Chambers and Lidia Curti. New York: Routledge, 1996. 3–16.

———. *Woman, Native Other*. Bloomington: Indiana UP, 1989.

Weaver, Jace. "Native American Authors and Their Communities." *Wicazo Sa Review* 12.1 (1997): 47–87.

CHAPTER FOUR

Moving in Place

Dark River *and the "New" Indian Novel*

SUSAN BERNARDIN

In his autobiographical essay "Blood Trails," Louis Owens meditates on a familial legacy of mixedblood migrations—those both forced and voluntary—out of which he writes. Patterned against older stories of tribal migration and newer stories of removals, his family's peripatetic history, he suggests, has imprinted his own fictional exploration of what James Clifford has elsewhere called "roots and routes."[1] Considering this tangle of intertwined histories, Owens identifies mixedbloods as "the products of motion, or what Gerald Vizenor, in *Fugitive Poses*, calls "transmotion" (*MM* 149). At the same time, by recalling the family stories that connected him to a place he never knew growing up—his mother's Cherokee Oklahoma, a place synonymous with forced removal *and* reconstituted homelands—Owens suggests a broader message behind his invocation of motion. In the same essay he writes: "given the almost universal tribal attachment to place, or sacred geography, motion is paradoxically an image associated profoundly with Indian people" (*MM* 150).

Owens's coinage of the term "indigenous motion" (*MM* 164) contrasts sharply with what he regularly describes as an "American metanarrative" of motion, built around the twin engines of restless mobility and individualism, "free of roots and responsibilities to family, community, or the earth itself" (*MM* 162). For Owens, the recognition of indigenous motion erodes the static signifier of "Indianness" while emphasizing the necessary portability of story and memory for "the more than 50 percent of American Indians displaced far from traditional cultural centers" (*MM* 166).

This seeming paradox of motion and rootedness that Owens relates to "the past, present, and present past of Indianness" (*MM* 161) animates all five of his novels. Retracing his own life's migrations, Owens's characters arc in their imaginations and life experiences between Mississippi and California, New Mexico and Oklahoma, California and Washington. Although each of his novels—*Wolfsong, The Sharpest Sight, Bone Game, Nightland,* and *Dark River*—"begins and ends with place itself" (*MM* 181), in between Owens dis-places characters who enlist in forms of imaginative and at times geographical motion to answer questions about identity, home, and belonging. What happens, for example, when the stories of one's homeland are unavailable, as is the case with Tom Joseph in *Wolfsong*? Or what happens when the problem of geographical distance from one's origins intertwines with cultural and familial loss, as for Jacob Nashoba, the mixedblood Choctaw character in Owens's last novel, *Dark River*? In the place of place itself, how might stories bring characters home?

Such questions set into motion *Dark River*, perhaps Owens's most ambitious articulation of indigenous motion, or "transmotion." Through the novel's crosscurrents of rootedness and movement, of Native and non-Native stories, of land and language, Owens stages a sustained encounter between competing epistemologies. Working in concert, the novel's thematic, structural, and theoretical movements refuse narratives of closure, stasis, and immobility that have proved so threatening to American Indian survival. In doing so, the novel can also be viewed as a response to the "word wars" of recent years in American Indian literary studies. Considered by Owens to be his "summa," *Dark River* ultimately provides a metacommentary on ongoing debates about the status, role, and future of American Indian–authored fiction.

Like *Wolfsong, Dark River* roots itself in a precisely imagined, albeit fictionally renamed, place: the White Mountains in eastern Arizona, homelands of the Western Apache. Yet, like Wolfsong's narrative evocation of "liquid air" (*Wolfsong* 18) and the rain-drenched riverine setting of *The Sharpest Sight, Dark River* also works to dissolve boundaries between earth and sky. Its opening declaration that "Thunder flowed" suggests not only a universe in motion but a story in midstream. From the novel's first scene, the sights and sounds of an owl erase the temporal and spatial distance separating the nominal protagonist, Jacob Nashoba, from his origins along the shadowy Yazoo River in Choctaw country. At that moment Nashoba recognizes what he later tells a fellow Vietnam veteran: "there aren't any other times or worlds" (*DR* 167).

This narrative motion of porous borders is belied, however, by Nashoba's investment and entrapment in Euramerican epistemologies that feed off his separation from his roots. Like the characters populating Owens's other novels, Nashoba finds himself in tribal homelands other than his own. Nashoba's geographical displacement has been sculpted by his mother's migration to California during his childhood, his subsequent far-flung journey to Vietnam, and his postwar wanderings across the Southwest. Like Cole McCurtain in *The Sharpest Sight,* Nashoba feels only an attenuated connection with the place of his birth. His sense of distance from his "roots" is measured in the novel's opening pages by his fragmentary relation to Choctaw people, their language and stories, a relation comprised of shards of memories and words whose meanings he only partially remembers.

At the same time, Nashoba strenuously polices the boundaries between himself and his Apache wife's people. His inability—or refusal—to get help for the "ghost sickness" he has inherited from the war eventually compels his wife, Tali, to deposit his belongings outside her door, though not outside her compassionate supervision. By refusing to share the stories of where he comes from but also "unthinkingly will[ing] himself not to learn" about his wife's people, feeling "without the right to know such things" (50), Nashoba persists in being an outsider.

Owens underscores the pathological dimensions of this willed self-separation by linking him to namesakes who spring from American cultural myths of individualism. Over the course of the narrative, Nashoba periodically picks up Hemingway's *The Sun Also Rises*, a novel inhabited by Jake Barnes, a similarly deracinated, emotionally disconnected veteran. Moreover, Nashoba carries with him a nickname from the Black Mountain Apache community that slyly comments on his occupation as game warden. Dubbed the "Lone Ranger" or "LR" by tribal members, Nashoba insists on "going it alone"; in doing so, he offends the community and reinforces his marginal status. Like the black mask donned by the "real" Lone Ranger to hide his identity, Nashoba remains unknown and hence dangerous to residents. Echoing an elder in *Ceremony*, who was addressing a character similarly marginalized within the community, Black Mountain matriarch Mrs. Edwards tells him: "they still don't know who you are" (*DR* 47).

In recognition of this estrangement, the tribe appoints him game warden, a job that aptly requires him to police the U.S. government's boundaries demarcating tribal lands. For years he has patrolled the rugged Dark River canyon, a place for gathering wild plums and a site of Apache resistance to the U.S. military in the previous century but now a place frequented only by this lone ranger. Yet his affinity for the Dark River canyon—an affinity so strong he had felt a sense of homecoming upon his first encounter with it—strengthens his sense of distance from the very people whose stories make the land fully intelligible: "the more he learned about the land, the less he knew about the people" (50). Although he instantly felt that he had "arrived somewhere at last" in the Dark River canyon (51) and that "he knew the country, the creek, and dry streambeds, the creases and secrets of the river canyon, the wide mesas," he concedes that he "knew only the surface" (50).

FROM THE LAND OF SKY BLUE WATERS

Yet Nashoba's ceaseless patrolling of the "wilderness" cannot mask his own immobility in myths of rugged individualism that rely on flawed assumptions about the land. One of the few possessions Nashoba has carried with him to the reservation is a broken electric beer sign, acquired from another Choctaw in a bar in Albuquerque shortly before he arrived at Black Mountain. We have seen this sign before in Owens's novels: in *Wolfsong*, it catches Tom Joseph's attention in the Red Dog bar, while in *The Sharpest Sight* it occupies a central place in Jessard Deal's tavern, watching over the staged rituals of violence that he coaxes out of his customers. So when this shifty, shifting sign appears in *Dark River*, readers should heed the Choctaw's reported comment to Jake that "it's a symbol, Cousin" (12).

Indeed, throughout the first half of the novel Jake repeatedly "studies" the sign framing his office wall, a sign that motions toward the metanarrative of Euramerican occupation of Indian Country. The sign features a lone white man in stasis, forever paddling a canoe. The Theodore Hamm Brewery of St. Paul—legendary for its advertising campaigns, especially from the 1950s through the 1970s—created countless similar signs, accompanied by the slogan, "from the land of sky blue waters." Set amid Minnesota Northwoods lakescapes, Hamm's beer advertisements featured variations of Nashoba's sign, such as a lone canoe resting on a vacant rocky shore lined with pine trees. Such images encapsulate the broader American story that Owens confronts throughout his fiction: the long-cherished notion of finding oneself in the "wilderness," a wilderness suitably emptied of indigenous people save for the moving "sign" of their appropriation, such as an Ojibway canoe.

In his own repetitive turn toward the sign on the wall, Nashoba signals Owens's ongoing concern with discerning "what are our relations with the natural world, with one another, and most crucially, with ourselves?" (*MM* 181). The reader first follows Nashoba's glance at the sign in chapter two and his accompanying observation that "The white man in the canoe didn't move, the waters didn't flow, the grass on the island didn't grow" (12). The language of stasis, infused with an ironic jab at the deceitful rhetoric of treaty discourse, underscores the density of allusions operating here. Echoing the title and movement of Tom King's novel, *Green Grass, Running Water,* the broken sign, like broken treaties, embodies the betrayal of promises of indigenous sovereignty. The "cold plastic" of the lifeless sign acknowledges the lie behind the promise implicit in beer advertising and made explicit in Woody Guthrie's famous refrain: "This land was made for you and me."

Nashoba's own fixation on the sign reveals his absorption in mainstream America's system of signs linking notions of rugged individualism, the wilderness, and masculinity. His friend Jessie, a trickster-dealer in sham vision quests, challenges Nashoba's allegiance to a sign that he claims is fine "just as it is." After offering to fix it, Jessie describes a similar sign he had once seen: "It's got these ripples going all the time, with that guy lifting and dipping his paddle. Drives you nuts trying to figure out where one of those ripples starts and another one ends and how the guy looks like he's moving but he's not. Everything tells you this guy's going somewhere, real lifelike, but it's just illusion" (17). Yet the sign's very stasis draws Nashoba to it, mirroring as it does his own sense of moving in place.

Nashoba once again studies the "motionless sign" in chapter four, wondering "what was it about a man in a boat in constant motion that never went anywhere people found so attractive? He liked the still white man, the eternally raised paddle, the half-risen fish" (48–49). Nashoba's attraction to the sign's predictability and seeming transparency helps to explain the lure of Hemingway's prose for him: "his language . . . doesn't require some kind of action. . . . there's this sense that he's not trying to hide anything, that nothing's going to change" (11). Similarly, Nashoba mistakenly believes of his adopted home that "here the streams were fast and clear, hiding nothing" (50). Preferring the illusion of clarity and the cold comfort of inaction, Nashoba is a poor interpreter of the signs in his midst. The beer sign thus serves as a constant reminder of Jake's emotional and imaginative immobility: moving in place, he cannot seem to move toward any sustained relationship with the community, with his wife, or with the stories peopling the land. When the dead sign suddenly and mysteriously starts working, Nashoba sees "the man in the canoe once again paddling his endless circles, each ripple the same with each electric stroke, beginning and ending simultaneously, never going anywhere. A trout broke the surface of the lake just behind the moving motionless canoe, broke the sparkling blue surface again and again. Action without effect, motion removed from time, a man in unceasing movement going nowhere beautifully. Even alive, the grass didn't grow, the water didn't flow" (93–94). In this scene, the sign comes alive with meaning as Nashoba recognizes his complicity in maintaining a superficial relationship with the world he inhabits. While Mundo Morales in *The Sharpest Sight* could concede that the beer sign depicted "somebody's idea of heaven" (79), Nashoba senses its emblematic relationship to a flawed conception of the land that has served as "the dumping grounds for American dreams" (Bruchac, NPR Tribute). In doing so, he voices one of Owens's main arguments migrating throughout his works: "Whites always came from someplace else and figured they could just keep moving because they owned everything and could leave any mess behind" (*DR* 106).

In this same scene Nashoba also discerns the vital difference between how we move *through* and *in* place. For mainstream America, "Indian Country" has signified a place apart, separate from, "beyond law," enemy territory (106). Nashoba makes the belated discovery that a shared sense of responsibility to and for the land remaining to Indians cuts across tribal boundaries: "there was such a thing as an Indian, something that cut across the lines of Choctaw and Cherokee and Black Mountain and Lakota to make some kind of connection" (106). This crucial insight catalyzes his decision to leave Black Mountain in search of his "real" home back east. Most importantly, he recognizes that he too "had headed west just like white America. And he'd made a mess too" (107). If "motion is the matrix within which identity must be formed" (*MM* 165), Nashoba begins to move in his imagination away from the place assigned to him in Euramerican stories and toward the homeland of his memory in the final chapters of the novel.

Moreover, just as Mundo Morales in *The Sharpest Sight* "imagined a fish breaking the surface of the sky-blue lake, coming unexpectedly out of those reflected depths to rearrange, to change the story" (82), so too does Nashoba break the fixed pattern of his life by finding his adopted granddaughter before he leaves Black Mountain. That move back into Dark River canyon, however, places him in the midst of militia war games spun out of control—the pathological and perverse end of the Puritans' original "errand into the wilderness." By battling contemporary monsters, Nashoba emerges from the edges of Choctaw and Western Apache stories to become a participant in their re-creation. Rather than "going nowhere beautifully," he moves toward integration, so that by the end of the novel and the end of his life, "his body seemed part of the earth" (259). Moreover, by moving toward what Uncle Luther in *The Sharpest Sight* calls "responsibility for everything within us and around us" (134), Nashoba and his story—to paraphrase Shorty Luke—is "honored in the telling and hearing" (207). Rather than standing alone, Nashoba's story becomes part of a larger Apache story. And in the process of becoming part of *that* story, Nashoba is reconnected to his own stories and people.

THIS AIN'T NO THEME PARK

But that is hardly the "END" of the story, as readers confront a narrative whose own riverine motions, like the Dark River, are "ceaselessly changing and moving, but remaining constant" (263). Owens's preoccupation with rivers in all of his fiction, as in his own life, surfaces as the structural design of this novel. The confluence of form and story ably demonstrates the workings of indigenous motion in the text. From the last line of chapter one—"that's what they say" (9)—readers should recognize that Jake Nashoba's story is enfolded within older and larger stories whose strengths emerge from their narrative energy and capaciousness. Indeed, the operating principle is its inclusiveness, both in its uses of Apache and Choctaw oral narratives and in its subversive incorporation of countless referents from U.S. popular and literary culture. A notorious rooster in the novel is named Plymouth Rock; his owner is the formidable Mrs. (John) Edwards, a powerful Apache elder. Moreover, the circulation of signs among all five of Owens's novels, from beer signs to signs of Puritan ideology, suggests the ways in which Owens perceived his entire work—both fiction and nonfiction—as "all one story." Through its seamless movement of form and content, *Dark River* dissolves static and stale conceptions of "Indianness," while emphasizing the "changing same" of the tribal real.

In doing so, the fluid narrative structure itself responds most imaginatively to the sign of the invented Indian. The ringleader for this narrative mayhem is Shorty Luke, "story thief" and Hollywood veteran whose wry comments about being an Indian actor among Italians playing Indians underscore the novel's exuberantly satirical presentation of Indian Country. Shorty's habit of (re)telling the stories of others, along with his relentless debunking of simulations of "Indianness," mirrors Owens's own narrative tricks, such as his sly references to the work of Silko, King, Vizenor, Alexie, and other Native writers. In Shorty's exchanges with Avrum Goldberg, a Jewish anthropologist who has remade himself into *his* image of "the traditional" Apache, Shorty points out the paradox of continuity through change. In a complaint that reflexively nods to the plotline he finds himself in, Goldberg wonders about the appeal of mystery novels: "why read the same story over and over, even if the names change?" Shorty replies by turning to the foundational oral narratives of his people, commenting: "that thing about it always being the same story isn't the problem. We tell the same stories all the time. . . . But nobody ever gets tired of hearing them. It's always like hearing each story for the first time" (257).

Whereas the beer sign only simulated motion, the stories that Goldberg considers fixed and static are kinetic "by nature." Shorty tries to teach him that these stories can take unpredictable turns through the motions of the teller, the listener, and the context: "We know all of the old stories and how they end, but all kinds of little things and even big things can change between beginning and end. And it depends on who's telling and who's listening" (227). Such fluid patterns emerge as Shorty works the story that is the novel: "I've come to that part of the story, but now that part has drifted beyond this moment like one of those leaves you see in a stream that overtakes another and moves on while the other moves around and around. Sometimes stories do that" (270). As Mrs. Edwards reminds us, "words never stop" (270).

As spokesman for the novel's metanarrative on story making and storyteller for Nashoba's movements within the narrative, Shorty Luke represents the extraordinary narrative energy of the text. He also reminds the resident "Indian expert"—the anthropologist—of the obvious: peoples, like language and stories, cannot be freeze framed. In response to the anthropologist's laughable efforts to steer the tribe toward re-creating itself as a grant-funded Apache village, Shorty breaks into song, claiming "this ain't no disco, this ain't no theme park" (209). Riffing off of The Talking Heads' seminal song, "Life During Wartime," Shorty shows that when it comes to survival, "this ain't no fooling around." Entrusted with the novel's last words, which are also words of beginning, Shorty similarly refuses any moves toward narrative containment.

The interplay of the novel's dizzying cast of twenty-odd characters thematically reinforces Shorty's own practice of imaginative indigenous motion. From Shorty to Sandrine Le Bris, Parisian martial-arts expert and vision quester, the characters not only self-consciously view themselves *as* characters in intersecting Hollywood and Apache story lines but even participate in changing the stories they inhabit and the roles scripted for them. Most especially, characters mock, disrupt, and comment on the roles assigned to whites and Indians that have been enshrined by decades of Hollywood films and centuries of U.S. policy and cultural sentiment. Through the latter part of the novel, many of the characters repeatedly call attention to such roles, often interrupting their own "lines" to contest or revise the script they are following. Nashoba's Apache "granddaughter" Allison, for example, complains to the Parisian, "I

don't mean to be rude, but this isn't going to be one of those stories . . . where the white person comes in and saves the Indians"
(222). Like old Apache stories in the process of renewal in the narrative, the characters re-make themselves, deflecting any predictable
turn in the metanarrative of Euramerica and Native Americans. As
Shorty intones, "you got to avoid cleeshayed plots" (212). One might
conclude that the novel simply traffics in postmodern play through
its constant references to staging, role-playing, and scripting. Rather,
the novel's self-reflexivity highlights how Native and non-Native
peoples might differently respond to the ubiquity of cliché and fabrication in non-Native representations of indigenous peoples. More
specifically, the novel both acknowledges and tries itself to resist
reinscribing story lines implicated in the appropriation and invention of Indians. The characters' self-conscious efforts to change such
narrative patterns—much like the fish breaking the fixed pattern of
the beer sign—argue for the necessity of eluding the static roles and
plot scenarios that for so long have dictated relations between
Euramerica and Indian Country.

Consequently, Owens's fluid narrative form, as an enactment of
oral story making, shapes an ending that is anything but over. In the
last few pages, the surviving characters debate how to end the novel,
trying out different takes and re-takes of the ending. When the villain "hopefully" proposes shooting everybody, "the good guys all
dead as hell and the bad guy unpunished," the Parisian dismisses
his version of an Indian story as "too postmodern, . . . or too *noir*"
(282–83). While the "bad guy's" imagined endgame is all too predictable in its extermination of the Native characters, it is also
notable for its invocation of the land: "Camera pans back to take in
the whole scene, pine trees, river, clouds overhead. . . . Very peaceful and ironic. Last frame is me walking away through all this beautiful nature" (283). His vision of "beautiful nature," dependent on
the violent appropriation of the land and slaughter of indigenous
people, serves as a brutal reminder of the history that made possible the seemingly innocuous and placid image of the lone paddler
in Nashoba's beer sign.

Despite his desire to close off other destinies for these characters, the villain does not get to win this one. Nor do other suggested denouements happen, because they do not accord with Apache stories: as Shorty notes, there is "no messing around" with some of the stories. Through its serious play on predictable plots, the "end" of *Dark River* is an end in motion, demonstrating the ceaseless impulse to create and renew the world through story. As Owens related in an interview, "At the end of the novel, I sort of wanted to deconstruct the novel, I suppose, and the whole process of storytelling. Explore what it means to say stories have no ends" (Purdy 13). By offering an ending that is no ending, Owens argues for the power of story in "a world in which endings stalk us and we can only keep inventing ways to both explain and forestall closure" (*Train* xiii).

In its parodic and wry deflection of predictable plots, scenarios, and endings, *Dark River* not only challenges Euramerica's embrace of certain kinds of "Indian stories" but also literary critics' own investment in certain kinds of Indian novels. By enacting, at the level of both form and content, Owens's complex workings of "indigenous motion," *Dark River* responds to a range of debates within contemporary Native American literary studies. In their very excessiveness, the plotlines of *Dark River* call attention to their constructedness: they tell us that we are made up of and made by stories. In his preface to *I Hear the Train*, Owens calls criticism "stories about others' stories" (xi). In its efforts to "loosen the seams"—to use Vizenor's phrasing—of all kinds of "Indian stories" told by non-Natives and even by Natives, *Dark River* sets into motion a sustained consideration of the "role" Native writers are expected to play in relation to different, competing constituencies.

By turning to indigenous motion as an expression of Native sovereignty, what Gerald Vizenor has described as "the right of motion . . . the ability and vision to move in imagination," Owens has traced out in *Dark River* a moving middle ground between two poles of Native literary criticism: metropolitan approaches, such as those offered by postcolonial and poststructural theory, and nation-based approaches anchored in the particular traditions and histories of individual Indian nations. Owens was very critical of postcolonial theory, particularly in its elisions of Native American literature and studies, as shown in his essay, "As If an Indian Were Really an Indian." Yet he was also critical of the dividing lines more recently invoked by Native writers, marking off so-called "real" and mixedblood Indians, for example, and dictating what kinds of Native literature should be written and read and *who* should do it. Most especially, he was addressing some of the work of scholars such as Elizabeth Cook-Lynn and Craig Womack. In varying polemical terms, each has argued for Native American literary studies to (re)turn to the Nation—a nation-based model of literary criticism that defers to the theoretical and critical traditions of distinct Indian nations. In doing so, they challenge the pole of Native literary criticism anchored in the American "metropole," where Euramerican theoretical approaches seem to have little in common with forwarding the varied movements of tribal sovereignty.

Owens's novel inhabits a moving space between these two approaches, pointing the way to a form of the novel that articulates broader pan-tribal concerns within precisely detailed tribal homelands. All of his novels feature deracinated mixedblood characters in search of a solid ground of identity and belonging. Such stories have been critiqued of late because they are not viewed as grounded in specific Indian nations and are themselves seen as "clichéd." Yet Owens's characters, even as they are peripatetic and often far removed from ancestral homelands, are moving in places that are richly storied. For example, novels such as *Nightland* and *Dark River* are firmly situated on specific tribal lands and examine the effects of the "Indian diaspora" on intertribal affiliations. His characters, in their earnest search to find their way home, speak for the power of specific tribal land bases as the source of identity. Nashoba's refusal to learn and listen to the stories of his adopted homeland is shown to be self-destructive and defeating. Yet Owens was also concerned with how his characters, the survivors of centuries of dislocation, disruption, and displacement, might learn from the portability of words that enabled Indian people "to carry with them whole cultures within memory and story" (*MM* 164).

Finally, in its refusal of closure and fluid dissolution of boundaries, *Dark River* suggests the limitations of recent moves in Native literary studies to construct narrowly defined criteria for tribally centered literature and criticism. In a brief commentary, "Part and Whole: Dangerous Bifurcations," published in a special issue of *Paradoxa* devoted to "Native American Literature: Boundaries and Sovereignties," Owens responds, along with several other Native scholars, to the question of the merits of constructing a distinctly Native American theoretical discourse and whether Native scholars can be a part of both dominant and Native nations without "compromising their position in either" ("Wisdom of the Elders" 276). Challenging a move in Native literature that he perceives as essentializing and separatist, he writes: "can we actually imagine that cultures are not formed in dialogue, that transculturation is not the condition of culture formation. . . . How can we peel away the complexity of cultural and intellectual realities that form and inform us to find an essential something that may be endangered by dialogue, both internal and external?" (286–87). Owens also answers these questions throughout his fiction with his signature narrative tactic of bringing in all kinds of "American" stories.

Through his characters' appropriations of all kinds of American stories, from Moby-Dick and Huck Finn to Jonathan Edwards and John Wayne, Owens demonstrates the comic and tragicomic, violent and violating, yet intertwined stories of indigenous peoples and Euramericans. In doing so, the novel travels both old and new ground in its efforts to refuse what Vizenor has famously called "terminal creeds"— those fixed critical, interpretive, or theoretical stances that deny motion, change, and growth. Like *Bone Game*'s Onatima, who linked words and worlds when she held a copy of *Moby-Dick* and said, "that's how they make the world" (20), Owens confronted the story-making choices of writers and critics of Native and American literatures.

In "Homing In," a foundational essay of Native literary studies, William Bevis foregrounds themes of imaginative and physical return that he found operating within several major Native-authored texts. He claims that in stark contrast to classic American novels, many Native American novels feature "homing plots," plots that move the protagonist to a tribally, not individually, defined worldview. Such novels, he argues, imply that "identity" for an American Indian is not as much a matter of finding "oneself" as of finding a "self" that is "transpersonal" and includes a society, a past, and a place.

For his part Owens pondered, in the absence of physical return, other ways of returning home. "Home" is the last word of several of his novels, including *Dark River,* and is the elusive heart of his writing. With *Dark River* Owens asks us to consider not the practicality of "homing in" but rather the possibilities of "homing out." In his essay "Fire and Form," for example, Owens relates a story about following coyote tracks onto a glacier high in the North Cascades. Crossing that frozen water, in an unbounded space of sky and land, Owens writes that despite being "thousands of miles from the Yazoo and Salinas rivers, I had never felt so at home in my life (*MM* 181). Most significantly, he came to realize that "Home had become a much bigger place" (*MM* 181). It seems that Owens was meditating on what it means to belong, to be a part of something larger than oneself, to be at home *in* the world and with the world.

Most importantly, he believed that "stories are what we carry with us through time and across distance" (*MM* 166). Throughout his work, Owens kept spinning stories that told of going home, finding home, and being at home. More specifically, he noted that "We make stories in order to find ourselves at home in a chaos made familiar and comforting through the stories we make" (*Train* xiii). Owens once told me that he regarded *Dark River* as "a reply to [his] first four novels, a summa maybe" (personal communication, 30 June 2000). In its invitation to consider the making of stories as strategies of survival, of homecoming, and of continuity, *Dark River* challenges those of us who might have difficulty seeing past the word "END" as written in bold letters after the last line of his first novel. Owens's return in his final novel to the question of endings and open endings suggests that it is up to "us" to keep the stories going. Will we, then, like Shorty, continue these stories, so that they too may "be honored in the telling and hearing" (207)?

NOTES

1. See, for example, James Clifford, *Routes: Travel and Translation in the Late Twentieth Century* (Cambridge: Harvard UP, 1997), and Paul Gilroy, *The Black Atlantic: Modernity and Double Consciousness* (Cambridge: Harvard UP, 1993).

WORKS CITED

Bevis, William. "Native American Novels: Homing In." *Recovering the Word.* Ed. Brian Swan and Arnold Krupat. Berkeley: U of California P, 1987. 580–620.

Bruchac, Joseph. National Public Radio. Tribute to Louis Owens. Aug. 3, 2002.

Purdy, John. "Clear Waters: A Conversation with Louis Owens." *Studies in American Indian Literatures* 10.2 (summer 1998), 6–22.

Roppelo, Kimberly. "Wisdom of the Elders." *Native American Literature: Boundaries and Sovereignties.* Ed. Kathryn W. Shanley. Spec. issue of *Paradoxa* 15 (2001): 6–22.

CHAPTER FIVE

Re-storying the West

Race, Gender, and Genre in Nightland

LINDA LIZUT HELSTERN

One story of the West—the story of valiant white settlers armed against savagery and wilderness with law, culture, civilization, and guns—has been fixed in the popular imagination by the genre Western. This is the story against which contemporary American Indian identity has been configured, and for many it remains the only story of the West. Signaling a transformation in the title of his fourth novel, *Nightland*, Louis Owens reminds us that westering was never a single story but rather a multiplicity of stories, often conflicting. Offering both older and newer stories that inform the western cultural landscape, Owens, in *Nightland*, interrogates the myth of the Old West and its associated racial and gender stereotypes.

Nightland is the Cherokee ritual term for West, home of the Thunders and home of the dead (Hail "Seven"; Ugvweyuhi 102–03). Confidently appropriating the conventions of the genre Western and juxtaposing them against elements of Cherokee and Pueblo myth and ritual, Owens reconfigures the mythic West of cowboys, Indians, and frontier justice as postcontact Indian Country inhabited by a cultural mix of Anglos, mixedbloods, fullbloods, animals, and ghosts.

Here Indians are not only cowboys, they are distinct individuals with differing perspectives on tribal affiliation and traditions.

Owens's New West, where antelope graze among the twenty-seven dishes of the Very Large Array, is a place where two mixed-blood deer hunters find a big buck turned to big bucks and the Great Thunder of the Cherokees still wielding his ultimate weapon, lightning. In an environment simultaneously secular and spiritual, where Anglos are distinctly marginalized, American Indian anger and American Indian greed—part of the West's postcolonial legacy—meet and clash with traditional American Indian values. The ultimate moral force in this novel is not the law but traditional Cherokee wisdom, often dispensed by a storyteller named Siquani, whose age can only be guessed.

The issue of American Indian identity in *Nightland* is no less complicated than the moral issue on which this tale is hung. Ultimately, the novel suggests that the very idea of a singular, stable identity upon which the formula Western depends is a fiction. The mixedblood hunters Billy Keene and Will Striker are simultaneously heroes and thieves, Indians and settlers, or at least the sons of settlers. Their Cherokee fathers and white mothers had come west from Sequoyah County, Oklahoma, during the Dust Bowl migration, bringing with them Grampa Siquani, whose traditional talents included water witching. Even as Cherokees, this younger mixedblood generation cannot claim to be Native. Their alien status is abundantly clear to Will, who notes, "Compared to the Indians of New Mexico, Cherokees might as well be Norwegians. That's how a lot of other Indians thought of Cherokees anyway" (31). The pattern of Cherokee life in the United States, indeed, bears remarkable similarity to the westering pattern of white Americans. While the Cherokees' forced evacuation from their traditional North Carolina/Tennessee homelands is generally known, it should be remembered that the first tribal moves west, to Missouri, then to Arkansas, and on to Texas, were voluntary (Hail "Cherokees"). Inasmuch as the Chisholm Trail, the route of the first successful cattle drives, was pioneered by the mixedblood Cherokee trader Jesse Chisholm, it might even be suggested that the ultimate symbol of the West, the cowboy, owes its genesis to the Cherokees.

Grampa Siquani holds the hard journey over the Trail of Tears in his personal memory. It was a journey that in 1839 resettled a culture that included wealthy, literate southern plantation owners in alien Indian Territory across the Mississippi. Even when he moved on to New Mexico, Grampa Siquani never left behind, in time or place, his traditional Cherokee values, his pragmatism, or his sense of humor; he knows the old stories and brings them to bear whenever the occasion calls for it. Even his name speaks stories. It contains echoes of Sequoyah, sometimes transliterated Sikwayi, whose invention of the Cherokee syllabary moved his people to literacy in a phenomenally short period of time (Smith, interview; Mooney 531, 108–11 and n.40). Sequoyah may be the ultimate mixedblood role model for the contemporary mixedblood writer, but Siquani more specifically echoes the name of the contemporary Cherokee storyteller Willie Siquani (Owens, interview). His stories were among those collected by Jack and Anna Kilpatrick in *Friends of the Thunder,* where his name is spelled Siquanid'. One of these is the story of a lucky fisherman who saw the famed outlaw Cherokee Bill disappear before his eyes and found and hid the fortune in stolen gold that Bill left behind. The old fisherman never used the money, and though he wanted his sons to have it, they were never able to find the hiding place he revealed to them on his deathbed (176–79). Billy Keene and Will Striker see themselves, first and foremost, as fishermen, and the plot of Siquanid''s story bears memorable similarities to Owens's, right down to the disappearing cash.

Nightland gains moral depth through another of Siquanid''s stories, the tale of "Thunder and the Uk'ten." The Kilpatricks call this story about the choice between good and evil "one of the greatest of all American Indian myths" (*Friends* 51). It is the story of two boys who find a hungry snake while they are out hunting and keep themselves busy feeding it. The snake eventually grows to an enormous size and develops horns. One day, hearing trouble, the boys find the snake coiled around Thunder, who is fighting for his life. They must decide quickly whose side they will take; both opponents appeal to their friendship. The boys ultimately support Thunder, who has reminded them, "I always help you." After they shoot the snake, Thunder, indeed, continues to help them, teaching them how to escape the snake's fumes, which yet have the power to destroy them (53–56). This is a story of the power of reciprocal responsibility. As Thunder tells the boys, "While we live on earth, or until the world ends, we must protect and help each other" (55). Because of these two boys, Thunder has remained the guardian of the Cherokee people, who speak of him always "with the deepest tenderness and reverence" (51).

Billy Keene and Will Striker have been listening to Grampa Siquani's stories all of their lives. Now in their mid-forties and soon old enough to be considered elders in their own right, the two men have always held very different attitudes toward the stories, attitudes that reflect their differing personal feelings about their Cherokee identity. Will has heard Siquani's and his father's stories with great respect and has passed their lessons on to his own children; they are responsible for the very ropes that hold the earth in place, he reminds Holly and Si at the conclusion of the creation story (49). Will has also been taught to respect the classics of English and American literature, his white mother's stories, though his mother herself had always seemed to Will "a permanent visitor in the Indian world of her own home" (24). But these stories came later, and Will always heard them juxtaposed with the landscape of Grampa Siquani's stories, that "Cherokee world in which earth and sky were densely inhabited and one need only recall the right story to know how to act" (24). For the young Will, "Dover Beach" became but a variant of Siquani's stories of the darkening land. One Euramerican story, however, could not be told in the Striker home: *The Last of the Mohicans,* the premiere story of the vanishing Indian race and the prototype, according to Henry Nash Smith, of the genre Western (109–11). Will's father burned this book in anger before he had half finished it. Billy finds Siquani's stories irrelevant in the modern world, the Anglo world where he has somewhat more experience than Will.

From childhood, he has felt that as a mixedblood he could choose his own identity; even as a contestant in American Indian rodeos, Billy never felt Indian (111).

Given his respect for the moral power of stories, it is not surprising that Will Striker should hearken back to Grampa Siquani's wisdom when he and Billy find themselves in the Cibola National Forest with a suitcase full of money that does not belong to them. While Billy, the New Morality man, insists that the money is "a gift from the Great Spirit," Will counters flatly, "It's corpse money. Money a man got a tree through his guts for. We both know where money like this comes from" (5–6). While Billy makes a case for keeping the money no one knows they have, arguing that they can use it to take care of their land, their livelihood, Will continues to make associations between their current dilemma and old Cherokee stories; not only had Billy seen a body fall out of the sky from the West, it looked like a buzzard. If Will ultimately goes along with Billy's version of the story, it is not until after the two men have foiled their armed pursuers to make a successful getaway. Even as they nurture their snake, Will, knowing both the Cherokee and the Euramerican stories, acknowledges his role in perpetrating evil. Tying his handkerchief over his nose and mouth, he becomes an Old West two-gun outlaw, a man who looks, in Billy's words, like he "just stole a million dollars" (14). What Billy has forgotten is that, according to the white story line, outlaws must die in the end.

Billy's very name places him in the lineage of the most famous of all the Western outlaws, American Indian and Euramerican. Grampa Siquani could suggest an alternative to the scenario of violent death lived out by Billy the Kid and Billy Pigeon alike, if only Billy Keene would listen. Since childhood, his life and Will's have been inscribed in the Cherokee myth of the Thunder Boys, the sons of the Great Thunder who live with him in the Nightland. Even their given names, Billy and Will, like *Tso:suwa* and *So:suwa*, are but variants of one another. The morning after their fateful hunting trip, Grampa reminds Billy that his father used to account for his troublemaking penchant by saying he was the wild boy his mama found in the water (41). Like the mythic wild boy, Billy was always the leader his almost-brother followed (Ugvweyuhi 17).

If Billy forgets his Thunder Boy identity and the story told both by his father and Siquani, it is not for want of biographical similarity. Billy himself remembers the time when he and Will peered through the boards of the corn shed, watching Billy's mother performing a ritual of some sort. Billy immediately concluded that she was practicing witchcraft, the same conclusion that the wild boy drew under similar circumstances when his mother Selu was simply bringing forth corn from her own body, as she did before every meal (111; Kilpatrick, *Friends* 129). Will, with the tenacity suggested by his name, holds to his Cherokee identity and his mythic Thunder Boy identity, tending his meager patch of corn through the August drought and respecting the old stories. The Thunder Boys were taught to plant corn by Selu, and Cal Striker had told his son that Cherokee people always plant corn because "corn is our mother" (101).

With that explanation Will's father concluded his story of Selu's creation. She was brought forth as a companion to Kanati, the lone man on earth. What Cal Striker's abbreviated version of the story does not reveal, however, is the reason for Selu's creation. Kanati was bored and, in his boredom, was killing too many animals. This angered the other animals, who complained to the creator. Human sexuality, it would seem, came into the world to restore harmony and ecological balance. If Billy and Will, like the cowboy heroes of the genre Western, seem destined to lead lives without women, it is not for want of advice from Grampa Siquani, who counsels marriage for Billy and marital reconciliation for Will. Knowing Will's heart better than he himself does, Siquani goes so far as to suggest a bit of traditional Cherokee love medicine to secure the return of his straying wife; Siquani's spell promises that a beloved White Woman, lonely in her soul, will find every other man an old crow compared with her sparrow-hawk husband (47–48; Kilpatrick, *Run* 75–76). Siquani explicitly reminds Will of the moral grounding of his advice with a brief allusion to Kanati's story: "A man by himself gets into trouble, like old Kanati," he notes (48). For those who know the story, Siquani's brief allusion speaks volumes, especially when his reminder is followed immediately by a question about whether Will is growing corn in his garden this year.

This story holds special significance for Siquani. In the contemporary version of the Thunder Boys' story, Siquani stands as Kanati, the Great Thunder by another name. He himself makes the connection explicit, confiding to the ghost of Arturo Cruz that when Billy is gone and he is by himself for a long time, he feels like Kanati "all alone on the earth, before First Woman come" (157). That Kanati is but another name for First Man sheds important light on the repeated theme of Siquani's stories—Cherokee death and survivance. His extended conversation with Billy early in the novel, which begins with advice on Billy's sex life, eventually brings Grampa to stories of the winter deaths on the Trail of Tears and the disappearance of traditional Cherokees who refused, some fifty years later, to be recorded on the Dawes rolls, the U.S. government's official list of "real Indians" (42; Smith, interview). These stories are told in the briefest possible form, which is enough for anyone who has heard them before. The logic of Grampa's fragmentary thoughts eludes Billy. He does not even recognize the story of the Trail of Tears. As the conversation continues, however, Billy recognizes an urgency in Siquani's tone that he has never heard before. Siquani adds the missing continuity when he tells the story of the Trail of Tears, not once but twice, to the ghost Arturo, a Pueblo Indian who could not be expected to know Cherokee history. Siquani admits to Arturo that he moved this far west only "for the story to be complete" (92). Knowing that his lineage will come to an end, Siquani, nonetheless, accepts from Awa Usdi the responsibility for remembering everything, assured that a day would come when "Indians and the deer, too, would be strong again" (157). Siquani mourns not only for those who have died but for those like his grandson Billy who "don't remember where they come from or how to talk right," who have stopped listening to the stories (92).

Indeed, Billy cuts off his only extended conversation with Grampa Siquani when he ceases to understand its drift. Of all the Cherokee stories he has just heard, stories of himself as the wild Thunder Boy, of Awa Usdi, of Nightland, the Trail of Tears, and the impact of the allotment act, the only thing that seems to register with Billy is a veiled threat to his white identity. Siquani gets the message. He knows his grandson. In one final story he invokes a vision of identity pasted together from the fixed racial stereotypes of traditional American literature.

"If you was lucky," Siquani teases the confused Billy, "[your] bottom half would be Indian because us Indians is the best lovers. That's why all those white women was always sneaking into our towns, and then when they got caught they'd pretend that they was kidnapped. If you was unlucky, it'd be the top half, because then you'd always be thinking about how Indians got everything stolen. If you was white on top and Indian on the bottom, your top half could steal everybody's money and your bottom half could steal their women." (43)

In Owens's novel, being "white on top" also speaks to a dimension of hybrid cultural identity beyond race. As it happens, the brains behind the drug ring responsible for the cash drop that Billy and Will have found are university-educated fullbloods. They have come to see Indians as victims of the white world, a world constructed through power relations rather than reciprocal relations. Using Anglo logic and following the tradition of the white traders who first brought alcohol into Native communities, Pueblo drug lord Paco Ortega seeks to alter the power dynamic in a way that will put Indians on top. Consumed with ideas of revenge for the genocide committed at Acoma and Wounded Knee and furious with Americans' historic refusal to take moral responsibility for their actions, he thinks he has found the way to make the white world destroy itself—with drugs that whites originally appropriated out of context from Indian cultures.

Paco Ortega ultimately meets his demise at the hands of Odessa Whitehawk, an Apache with a Ph.D. in American Indian law and religion—the ultimate genre Western savage and the ultimate expert on stereotypes about "Indians." She, too, is consumed with a desire for revenge. On the surface Odessa would seem to be the ultimate liberated woman. She no sooner rescues Billy Keene from a barroom brawl with an assured physicality than he takes her home, falls in love, and begins to fantasize that he can rebuild the home and ranch his parents had dreamed about and worked for before their deaths in a lightning fire. Even when it seems that Billy is about to reclaim his American Indian identity through recuperation of genuine sexual desire for Odessa, a certain confusion persists. The name Odessa Whitehawk contains not only the seeds of gender confusion through its cross-connection of male and female elements from Siquani's spell—sparrow hawk and White Woman—but the seeds of racial confusion as well. Reflecting upon the violent acts of another White Hawk, Thomas White Hawk, the gifted Lakota premed student who confessed to committing both murder and rape in the course of a robbery, Gerald Vizenor pondered "links of identity, dissociation, and cultural schizophrenia" (149).

Odessa has been named for the west Texas oil boomtown where she was conceived, a link with natural-resource exploitation and profit rather than the traditional landscape of her Mescalero ancestors. Billy's New Morality meets its match in Odessa; he is, unfortunately, too naïve to recognize the plotline of the Old Western that would make Odessa suspect on two counts. She is not only an Indian but a sexual woman. In a West of moral dualisms, sexuality was most often relegated to the bordello. Occasionally, a sexual woman might be featured as an "Outlaw Girl," a role that comes to fit Odessa Whitehawk clearly enough (Heatherington 79). Odessa is a woman in charge of her own sexuality and fully aware of other women's sexuality. Even as she saves Billy from being cast in the role of jealous lover, she suggests appreciatively that his ex-girlfriend must be "a great fuck" (77). Her machismo stands in sharp contrast to Billy's passive masculinity. He had been ready to crawl out of the local bar to save his skin, and Odessa knows it. If she admires Billy's survival strategy, it is not in Odessa's nature to accept a passive role. Asked by Billy if she is planning an escape as she intently surveys the road that took them to his ranch, Odessa quickly responds, "Maybe I'm planning an attack. I like cowboys" (77).

Billy tries a quick reverse to regain control of the situation. Not entirely sure yet that he wants to develop a relationship, he cannily gives Odessa the chance to opt out, hinting that she, perhaps, should have second thoughts about him. He asks if she knows that most of the real old-time cowboys were queer, citing a scholarly book as his source of information on the subject. Billy's book, *When Men Were Men: The Real History of the West*, is a fiction created by Louis Owens, but Billy's facts largely square with the account of cowboy sexuality offered by Walter L. Williams in *The Spirit and the Flesh: Sexual Diversity in American Indian Culture* (157–60). Far from the ultimate symbol of American masculinity popularized by the Western, the working cowboy in a world without women, according to Williams, lived a predominantly homosexual lifestyle. Billy spins an elaborate yarn about life in the bunkhouse, but Odessa demonstrates a verbal skill to match her physical prowess, maintaining control of the conversation. When Billy attempts to dissociate contemporary cowboys from old-time cowboys, using a logic that equates heterosexual with Indian and homosexual with white, she counters sardonically, "Today you're all real men" (78).

If Odessa's response accommodates sexual liberation on one level, on another it suggests a hidden misanthropy, and Billy does not miss her implication. It is genetically impossible for American Indians to be homosexual, Billy admonishes Odessa, putting heterosexuality in the same category with alcoholism and outdoor acumen—the markers that have fixed Indian identity in the popular mind. Billy just may buy into the stereotypes, but Odessa clearly does not. A reference to her friends at Zuni pushes Billy's assertion to the level of irony, for the most studied of all Native American cross-gendered cross-dressers was the Zuni man-woman We'wha. It is entirely possible to read Owens's gendering in terms of tribal identities. Joyce Dugan, former principal chief of the Eastern Band of Cherokee, notes that the strong leadership role traditionally accorded women in her tribe has, in Native circles, earned the

Cherokees a reputation as a "petticoat tribe" (Dugan). Known for their savagery even to the youngest fans of the television Western, the Apaches would, by contrast, rank at the high end of the macho scale.

His conversation with Odessa is not the first time Billy has introduced the subject of alternative sexualities, however. He has earlier suggested to Will that tabloid personals might be the key to an improved lifestyle. He pitches his argument to Will's Indian identity, insisting that living alone is "not natural. A man needs balance" (66). The balance Billy suggests is not strictly feminine. He seems to want a piece of this "balanced" action himself, advocating for a woman who fantasizes sex with two men at once and a lesbian couple determined to lose their virginity together. What is striking in Billy is not a latent homosexuality but his immature heterosexuality, the chance, perhaps, to relive the most memorable sexual experience of his adolescence—the night he and Will lost their virginity with the Ruiz sisters, one couple in the backseat of Billy's father's car, the other in the front seat (115).

Madelon Heatherington asserts that an arrested adolescent sexuality is the mark of the typical Western hero; when thrown into the company of a woman, Heatherington insists, "the cowboy's panic is not a homosexual panic at all; it is an asexual panic, a terror at the possibility of any kind of full emotional sexuality lurking anywhere" (86–87). Viewed from the perspective of its origins in the romance, where human sexuality provides the ultimate expression of the land's renewed fertility, the cowboy's refusal to make a sexual commitment bodes ill. While he may do everything in his power to save civilization from the scourge that threatens it, he refuses to engage in the only act that will assure its continuance. In the Western, according to Heatherington, the taboo against sexuality seems "designed precisely to keep fertility at bay" (87). Marriage, except for marriage to an Indian woman, "virtually unmans the Western hero, removing him from truly masculine pursuits, which are essentially celibate and therefore perhaps more holy as well as more fun than those accessible to domesticated males" (Heatherington 86).

Until the appearance of Odessa, the American Indian woman who seduces him in his own bed, Billy never risks an emotional commitment despite a string of sexual involvements. He is abandoned by his most recent lover for his sexual indifference. Indeed, at the height of Carla's orgasm, all Billy can think about is trout fishing, in American literature perhaps the most holy and celibate of all the "truly masculine pursuits."

Will, by contrast, has made a long-term sexual commitment, fathering a daughter and a son, but in typical Western fashion, finds himself unmanned by marriage to a white woman. Will's malaise persists until his wife chooses finally to make her life and career elsewhere. Jace Striker recognizes clearly that her husband's fundamental nature is "monastic" (127). What she really means is that Will is thoroughly domesticated. On her unexpected return home, Jace finds his room spotless, the Pendleton blanket on his cot "stretched so taut that not a wrinkle showed" (146). Throughout his marriage, Will had objected to animals in the house. Even after several years of living alone, muddy paw prints on the floor catch his eye instantly. For Will, the old house is filled with family associations, from his mother's books to the dirty cereal bowls that have not stacked up beside the kitchen sink since his children left home. Even in this most feminized of spaces, however, Owens makes it difficult to disentangle issues of race and gender. Although Billy, too, lives on the ranch he has inherited from his parents, he lacks all feeling for house, home, and family until he begins to recoup an American Indian identity through his attraction to Odessa.

Will's estranged wife sees herself clearly enough to recognize that she is a woman who intimidates men (129). Owens frames this perception not in terms of Jace's professional accomplishments as a corporate attorney but in terms of her physical presence—as a woman utterly comfortable with her sexual self. Jace offers a contrast to the other women in *Nightland* in her ability to actualize both her masculine and feminine energies. While Jace has developed her intellectual, rational capabilities and found practical application for them, she continues to listen to her intuitions and never relinquishes her commitment to family relationships. It is a strong intuition of something seriously amiss with Will that leads Jace to call home repeatedly until she makes contact and finally to drive back to the ranch (29, 126). Even Owens's choice of her seemingly androgynous name speaks to this masculine/feminine balance, for Jace shares her name with a well-known Cherokee environmental activist, a male attorney who also holds a doctorate in religion. The connection is significant not only because Jace's return to her husband will be accompanied by the full restoration of fertility to their ranch but because it points to the ultimate instability of all identities.

Owens figures gender and race into the identity equation in yet another way. If Jace Striker practices a profession traditionally closed to women, her law degree positions her with moral women of the genre Western, "the harbingers of law and order enforced by police and courts" (Cawelti, *Adventure* 222). The effeminate Code of Law stood in diametric opposition to the Code of the West, upheld by "real" men. In her new position with the county public defender's office, Jace will, however, play a dual role, standing on the side of the law by standing against it. Applying Billy's race/sex logic to Jace Striker qualifies her as Cherokee if William Bevis is correct that the return to home and culture is the distinguishing feature of the contemporary American Indian novel. Her opposite, Odessa White-hawk, whose ultimate goal is to leave the country, would then find herself categorized white despite her race and her academic training in Indian law and religion.

Owens further complicates the issue of identity by freeing sexuality from the male/female gender norm. The most erotic scene in the novel may be a moment of physical intimacy between Odessa and Jace. The woman who has bartered her sexuality for money like an Old West prostitute has nothing to gain by offering Jace a back rub, but with her touch, freely given, Odessa constellates a restorative energy that exists for its own sake in a moment that mixes memory and desire in the lives of both women. After the drought that crippled the Strikers' ranch and their marriage, the clue to the memory this moment unlocks for Jace is the beautiful gray-winged hawk she sees outside the bathroom window as she undresses for a shower, having just reclaimed the bedroom she once shared with Will from the dust and cobwebs that marked years of disuse. As birders will recognize, the gray-winged hawk is none other than the male sparrow hawk of Grampa Siquani's love medicine. This straying wife has, indeed, found her way home. Jace's tears reveal the extraordinary depth of her connection to her husband, so long suppressed. To open herself sexually to Will, however, is to open herself to the possibility of rejection all over again. When, after initiating sex with Will, Jace makes the abrupt decision to leave the ranch ahead of the coming storm, she is conscious only of its danger, not yet attuned to its healing potential.

In her own time Jace is able to reintegrate her life, to bring masculine and feminine, Indian and white relationships into a new balance. The feminine connection that brings Jace to emotional awareness does not have the power to effect a change in Odessa's life. Odessa is a cold-blooded murderer. Her moral sense and her sense of empathy, like her closest childhood friend, seem to have vanished mysteriously. Jemmie and her family simply disappeared from the Mescalero reservation one day, never to be heard from again. Odessa's feeling for Jace echoes her emotional investment in this early relationship. Jemmie, Odessa confides to Billy, was "the only purely good person I ever knew" (115). Seeing a photo of the young Jace, Odessa notes how much she resembles her lost friend. It is significant that Jemmie was white, not that Odessa had not been surrounded by whites her whole life. Her parents were moved to San Jose as part of federal American Indian relocation efforts predicated on the expectation that Indian identity would disappear in the assimilation process. This is just what happened in Odessa's family, but living for a year with her grandmother gave Odessa the opportunity to learn something of what her parents had left behind. Before her reimmersion in white culture and her education for genocide had come a positive awareness of American Indian identity balanced by a positive white identity.

To secure a small fortune, Odessa murders five men and, after forcing hostile sex on him, attempts to murder Will Striker. What Odessa seems to want more than money, however, is a stable, respected identity. She is clearly aware of her deracination, describing herself in terms that make her an integral part of the postcolonial New Mexico atomic landscape. She calls herself a radon daughter, a natural poison resulting from the breakup of a traditional way of life (117). Odessa plans to resolve her identity crisis with a formula Western escape south of the border. Once she gets there, Odessa knows exactly who she will be—a rich Yankee among the Indians (117). It is the only identity her cultural alienation has prepared her for.

That Odessa should figure her tribal identity in nuclear terms has particular resonance for a Mescalero Apache. In the 1990s Mescalero sovereignty was closely tied to plans for locating a medium-range storage facility for nuclear waste on reservation lands within a few miles of the Three Rivers Recreation Area, and the tribe strenuously opposed legislation enacted by the State of New Mexico to prohibit construction of an MRS within the state. Owens links Odessa directly to Three Rivers—the closest town, she tells Billy, to her grandmother's home (114). A mutual concern with money also links Odessa with her tribe. Investments in a major ski resort, a timber operation, and a cattle ranch made the Mescaleros one of the nation's wealthiest tribes before the heyday of casino gaming. As Wendell Chino, who served as tribal president from 1964 until his death in 1998, liked to say, "'The Navajos make rugs, the Pueblos make pots and the Mescaleros make money'" (Carter 11).

One element that distinguishes the good guys from the bad guys throughout Owens's novel is the absence of the profit motive. It is not the only distinguishing element, however. Paco Ortega, the Pueblo head of the drug ring, has no interest whatever in money. His sole motive is to avenge five hundred years of racism and colonialism. Ortega is a generous man who takes good care of his operatives, sparing no expense for advanced technology to assure their success over the "narcs." Content to drive a fifteen-year-old pickup, he has never altered his own lifestyle. Ortega lives like his neighbors. He does not want people to talk. And he maintains the utmost respect for traditional spiritual practices and powers. From the contemporary Native perspective, Paco Ortega can talk the talk. He perfectly articulates the truths that have given meaning to the work of contemporary American Indian authors. Echoing Leslie Silko and Scott Momaday, Ortega insists, "I know my relations, all of them. I know the stories that tell me where my people came from, where we are, and where we are going. How many people in America can say that? Isn't that a kind of wealth most of the world yearns for?" (171). Ortega, unfortunately, does not understand the nature of the story any better than Billy Keene does. For Ortega returning the gift is an act of revenge, not an act of generosity, but revenge tragedy is strictly a Euramerican genre. It has no Native precursor. Only Odessa, who desires both revenge and profit, has a stronger motivation for evil than her ex-lover.

Owens's cast of Western characters would be incomplete without the canny "Mexican." The inclusion of Mouse Meléndez, indeed, gives Owens the opportunity to interrogate racial stereotyping from another perspective. The blond Mouse has never been confused or uncomfortable with respect to his own racial identity, though both his friends and his enemies are, including Billy Keene. Mouse is strictly Caucasian and traces his ancestry to Spain, where, he insists, there are lots of blonds (88). On his mother's side, he is a Georgia "cracker." In his first appearance Mouse seems to embody the stereotype of the macho Mexican lover with a knife, and even Billy has to think twice. Mouse's machismo (always undercut by his ridiculous nickname) is also stereotypical biker behavior. In the conflict between nature and nurture, Billy sides finally with nurture. Reconciled to his old friend through an impromptu act of biker generosity, a barbeque in his own backyard, Billy forgives Mouse's knife as "a bad habit he picked up in California" (76).

Ultimately, Mouse comes face to face with his evil twin, the snaky Duane Scales, who remains confused about the racial/cultural interface until the moment he is removed from the action. "You sure are fucking white for a guy named Meléndez," Scales observes antagonistically (179). Paco Ortega's Black Irish/Cajun hit man has never been comfortable with his racial identity. In Ortega's words, he sees himself as "too brown for a white man" (179). That the American Indian in charge should have a white sidekick comically reverses the Western genre tradition, but Ortega's relationship with Duane confuses the issue even further. To achieve his version of western justice, Ortega is perfectly willing to play Tonto to Duane Scales's Lone Ranger. Mouse's honest admission of his whiteness, however, leads ultimately to his demise when he admits to Paco Ortega that his ancestors came to New Mexico with Oñate. These were the very Spaniards responsible for the Acoma massacre, the first of the Indian atrocities Ortega is determined to avenge.

Scales's identity problem is even more complex than Mouse's. The novel's preeminent environmental spokesman, Scales not only wants dope and money, he wants to be more Indian than the Indians, America's environmental poster boys. Ortega has him pegged as one of Custer's Indian scouts, but if his bitter self-characterization is to be believed, Scales is "nothing but a bleeding fucking heart liberal who hates what the white man's done to his goddam red brother" (163). Though his environmental causes change minute by minute, the Mescalero medium-range nuclear-storage facility remains Scales's cause célèbre. He is only too happy to savage the Mescalero decision-making process with antinuclear truisms. It is little wonder that nuclear power makes Scales nervous. Bombs and bullets are closely linked, as Odessa Whitehawk recognizes: "Uranium turns into lead if given enough time to decay. So these bullets are really like tiny atomic bombs. Inside a person, the lead flowers like a mushroom cloud, and that person has his own personal Trinity Site" (118). Duane Scales wants nothing more than ultimate power, the nuclear trigger. He fires the first shot in the power exchange that will end *Nightland*.

Billy Keene's Old West death is ultimately his punishment for theft, though his plan to rebuild the profit-making potential of his ranch seems modest enough. Ortega and his entire gang die, and so, in the end, does his ex-lover Odessa—killed in a classic shootout by a skilled, lucky, and sexually reticent hero (Cawelti, *Six-Gun* 60). Like the formula Western hero that he is, Will Striker shoots only in self-defense. Unlike the typical hero, however, Will displays no tendency to defend a society built on profit. Jay Gurian describes the Western hero finally as "a commercial extension of the drive for private property" (7). When Will brought home his share of the drug loot, he hung it promptly on an old nail in the abandoned well. The money simply disappears. Has Will accidentally effected the ancient deep-well sacrifice practiced by the Cherokees' Maya ancestors? With the disappearance of the money and Jace's return to the ranch comes an abundance of water that could, in and of itself, make the Strikers rich. Even so, Will has no plans to work the ranch; he intends to complete the restoration of the land by giving up ranching for trout fishing, letting his cows go wild and penning up his bulls Satellite and Trinity, those prizes of breeding technology. He will even sell the bulldozer that brought him a small cash flow on the fire lines during his leanest years.

Will's decision parallels a similar one made by his wife. Refusing to profit in any way from an affair with a partner in her law firm, Jace decides to return home and serve the cause of justice as a lawyer in the county public defender's office, a job that has never made an attorney rich. Grampa Siquani's move to the Striker home assures that the story of the West will continue, now as a story of death and survival—of life as a whole. Indeed, the landscape of Owens's New West includes all life, physical and spiritual, the earth "heavy and dark, populated by the dead," held by living roots (216).

In this Nightland, Will has survived, just as his dream suggested—before he was shot by Odessa, Will saw himself as the last man on earth, standing on a hilltop with his wife and children, water rising around them and sounds of dancing across the water. In fact, Will dreamed the archetypal story of Cherokee survivance, a story that Grampa Siquani once told the ghost Arturo (Ugvweyuhi 105–06).

This is the fourth time Owens invokes this story in *Nightland*, a number that in American Indian cultures traditionally signals conclusion. It is not death and dancing bones that hold Will's attention finally, but sunlight on the water, the origin and source of life. And in the water, Will sees his own fleeting image among many others—a vision and a prophecy. With his daughter's pregnancy, Will is about to become a grandfather. In the assurance of mixedblood generational continuity and the continuity of Native story, even the genre Western, albeit now a hybrid, survives, restored to its origins in romance. Thunder in this landscape clearly holds the promise of rain.

WORKS CITED

Carter, Luther J. "The Mescalero Option." *Bulletin of the Atomic Scientists* 50.5 (Sep.–Oct. 1994): 11–13.

Cawelti, John B. *Adventure, Mystery, and Romance: Formula Stories as Art and Popular Culture.* Chicago: U of Chicago P, 1976.

———. *The Six-Gun Mystique.* Bowling Green, Ohio: Popular Press, 1971.

Dugan, Joyce. "Women in Leadership Roles." Address. Southern Illinois University, Carbondale. Mar. 3, 1997.

Gurian, Jay. *Western American Writing: Tradition and Promise.* Deland, Fla.: Everett/Edwards, 1975.

Hail, Raven. "The Cherokees in Texas." *The Raven Speaks* 1.3 (June 7, 1968): unpaginated. Reprinted in *The Raven Speaks: Cherokee Indian Lore in Cherokee and English.* Scottsdale, Ariz.: Raven Hail Books, 1987.

———. "The Seven Directions." *The Raven Speaks* 4.6 (Sep. 7, 1971): unpaginated. Reprinted in *The Raven Speaks: Cherokee Indian Lore in Cherokee and English.* Scottsdale, Ariz.: Raven Hail Books, 1987.

Heatherington, Madelon. "Romance Without Women: The Sterile Fiction of the American West." *Under the Sun: Myth and Literature in Western American Literature.* Troy, N.Y.: Whitston, 1985.

Kilpatrick, Jack F., and Anna G. Kilpatrick. *Friends of Thunder: Folktales of the Oklahoma Cherokee.* Dallas: Southern Methodist UP, 1964.

———. *Run Toward the Nightland: Magic of the Oklahoma Cherokees.* Dallas: Southern Methodist UP, 1967.

Mooney, James. *Myths of the Cherokee.* 1900. New York: Johnson Reprint, 1970.

Owens, Louis. Telephone interview. May 28,1997.

Smith, Benny. Personal interview. Nov. 22, 1996.

Smith, Henry Nash. *Virgin Land: The American West in Symbol and Myth.* Cambridge: Harvard UP, 1950.

Ugvweyuhi. *Journey to Sunrise: Myths and Legends of the Cherokee.* Claremore, Okla.: Egi Press, 1977.

Vizenor, Gerald. "Commutation of Death." *Crossbloods: Bone Courts, Bingo, and Other Reports.* Minneapolis: U of Minnesota P, 1976. 152–55.

Williams, Walter L. *The Spirit and the Flesh: Sexual Diversity in American Indian Culture.* Boston: Beacon, 1986.

CHAPTER SIX

SECULARIZING MYTHOLOGICAL SPACE IN LOUIS OWENS'S *DARK RIVER*

GRETCHEN RONNOW

Some simple assertions can be made about Louis Owens's fifth novel, *Dark River*. It has Native American characters; it has an action-adventure plot. It is structured by myths and ritual; it is about language and storytelling. It is about death. Obviously, however, *Dark River* is a far-from-simple novel. It is graced by violence and the sacred—or, we might say, by the sacraments of violence. It may seem that the overt project of many Native American authors is to mythologize secular space—to show that from an Indian point of view, the so-called mundane world is holy, endowed with sacred mythological attributes. Prototypically, Tayo, in Laguna author Leslie Silko's *Ceremony*, comes to learn: "Everywhere he looked, he saw a world made of [sacred] stories" (100). But, I would assert, *Dark River* depicts the limits of myth. *Dark River* describes the ultimate uselessness of myth in holding a culture together and the inability of myth to contain or to satisfy the individuating Self. But because *Dark River* subverts its own story and fractures any restricting structure, we are able to glimpse the transcendent possibilities—not of myth, but of language.

Of course, one of the main structuring features of the novel is myth, particularly the Apache Hero Twin myth. Sets of twins and doubles proliferate throughout the text. Often one individual of the set is sympathetic and heroic, the other a dark nemesis. There is also in the novel the sense that these various sets of twins, avatars of characters from the "time immemorial," are caught in the cosmic spiritual struggle between dark and light, creation and destruction of which myth is so fond. The beauty of Owens's prose and the ancientness of the myth prefigure the sacrificial quality inherent in "twinning" and death.

In *Violence and the Sacred,* Rene Girard, discussing "monstrous doubles," comments that "religious thought makes no distinction between biological twins and twins of violence engendered by the disintegration of the cultural order" (252). These days we may take it for granted that "culture" and "order" anywhere we look are disintegrating, perhaps never have been integrated. Certainly any monolithic "culture" (for instance, the Apache "culture" of the novel) is a romantic illusion. And long lists could be made of all the twins, doubles, pairs, and mirror images in *Dark River.* Jake, whose surname "Nashoba" means "wolf" in Choctaw, has seen a white wolf, supposedly extinct, while he patrols the river (13). He remembers the two brothers in the stories of his own people, Chahtah and Chikasah, who had been separated by a flooding river and formed separate tribes (23). He feels a special affinity for Jessie, a young man of the little town of Black Mountain, who begins to tell him the Apache Hero Twin stories. Jake says, "A boy without parents and a ranger without a family seemed to go together" (24). Later, Jessie gets himself shot impersonating a wolf but then becomes a wolf "helper spirit"—Jake "Wolf" and Jessie "Wolf." Jake has heard that "in the old days, twins were a bad sign, evidence of promiscuity or worse, even witchcraft. Some said one twin always had to be killed," but others said that was nonsense (44). So when Mrs. Edwards's sister has twins, she settles the matter "by giving her nephews different names pulled from nowhere, Domingo Perez and Shorty Luke," and insists that each boy is always referred to as "the surviving twin" (44).

Metonymically, a number of characters could "double" Jake or mirror him in some way. Xavier Two Bears, the tribal chairman, a physically "big man" as is Jake, is, in some ways, "as foreign to the tribe" as Jake (61). When Jake encounters a group of militia survivalists who have come to the canyon to train, he unexpectedly recognizes Stroud, his captain in Vietnam, whose life Jake had saved, and Nguyen, his Vietnamese counterpart. "Jake felt as though he were in a ridiculous dream, with Vietnam rice paddies and jungles turned into a dry pine forest and his old platoon composed of middle-aged morons. And him the enemy. Charlie in Indian Country, just like they always said" (48). Except here in a weird, surrealistic reversal, Nguyen, literally "Charlie in Indian Country," has moved to the United States, become rich, bought a house on a Phoenix golf course, and here captured Jake, an Indian in "Indian Country," on "sovereign tribal land" (156).

The "evil" twin or the "dangerous" or "destructive" twin is, however, most apparently Lee Jensen, a type that in Stroud's words is "a hell of a lot bloodthirstier than the real" recon rangers or Special Forces guys who had actually been in Vietnam (120). Ultimately, Jensen hunts Jake in the "most deadly of games"—the two men matched in warrior skill and psychological cunning. Their "storied" combat soon echoes the legendary battle between the Apache hero Child of the Water (or Monster Slayer) and Owl Monster, one of the monsters covered in heavy layers of flintlike armor. Jake is wounded by Jensen, and as he rolls down the hill he hears "the crash of a two-legged thing as it plunged down the slope above him, driving itself into the earth heavily with each plunge. It was an alien, metallic, unfamiliar disturbance, and it rushed upon him with the utmost evil" (198). Even earlier in the novel Jake has anticipated this encounter, in a dream aligning himself even more intimately with his "twin." Living as a troubled Vietnam vet, an outsider to the people at Black Mountain, he calls himself the "world's enemy." "'I will kill the world,' he'd said as he rolled to his side and fell into a sickened sleep in which he battled a brother he'd never had, circling in the dark and hearing the clatter of metal as his brother stalked him. In the background a train whistle sounded like the repeated

cries of owls, or owls cried like a distant train" (93). The references
to metal and to brother and to owls echo the same motifs in the
Apache myths.

Throughout the novel Jake continues to have the impression
that "the one who hunted him was made of metal" (215, 259)—as
is Child of the Water's nemesis. But in Jessie's version of the old
story, "the boy with the bow and arrows came down to earth and
slew all the monsters there" (233), and Child of the Water does not
die but becomes one of the Hero Twins. In James L. Haley's version
of the Apache Monster Slayer story, Child of the Water is born to
White-painted Woman, made pregnant by Lightning (in some ver-
sions, the Sun). When he is still a little boy, Child of the Water
wants to "go kill Owl-man Giant and the other monsters" (16). A
duel ensues. "When Child of the Water shot the fourth arrow, Owl-
man Giant had only one flint coat left. You could see his heart beat-
ing under it . . . and the arrow went into his heart [leaving piles of
flint]" (18). During Jake's battle with Jensen, Avrum Goldberg, the
resident anthropologist, and Shorty Luke, stealer of stories, appear,
and they are ultimately the ones with the bow and arrows who finish off the "metal monster," not so much killing him as transforming him into a participant in continuing the unfinished story.
Avrum has the bow and arrows and Shorty has had the dream—
"A metal man, the one whose clothes make noise and who carries
a rifle. A dream of a dark metal shield and spear. . . . In part of the
dream sun and water were fighting" (256).

Avrum is a type of "twin" in that he has become more "Indian"
than the Indians; and more metaphysically, Mrs. Edwards has told
him that on the outside he "would remain a strange clay fired in
Black Mountain soil, but his bones [will remember] a tribal, nomadic
people of mountain, desert, and mesa. Therefore he understood"
(269). Avrum and Shorty have been following the story line down
into the deep canyon where they can imagine Monster Slayer and
"that other one, the twin, all covered in black metal" (257). When
Shorty Luke gets involved in the "cosmic battle" part of the story,
he says, "I'm thinking maybe Spider and the Twins can save it"

(213); but there is no easy correspondence between the identity of the mythological Hero Twins and any set of twins in this novel, nor between the "Monsters" of myth and the "villains" in the story. Nor do we know for sure what "it" needs to be saved by mythological heroes.

Rene Girard writes that in most groups at the center of cultural chaos, "the subject watches the monstrosity that takes shape within him and outside him simultaneously. In his efforts to explain what is happening to him, he attributes the origin of the apparition to some exterior cause. . . . The whole interpretation of the experience is dominated by the sense that the monster is alien to himself" (165). But the reader of Dark River has quickly sensed that the inner natures of monsters and apparitions are quite familiar to Jake and to the other characters. These apparitions are sometimes humorous, sometimes deadly.

The main purpose or function of "monstrous" doubling (at least as Girard sees it) is that one twin or mirror image can be a scape-goat. Jake is, unknowingly, being prepared—particularly by Mrs. Jonathan Edwards—to be the sacrificial victim of this community. He is too foreign, too alien to fit comfortably into their lives. Jake has been the main outsider to the community even as he has lived deep within it for twenty years. Jessie has told him, "You walk into a room and people get all tense" (28). Even his wife, Tali, had made Jake move out of their home. "She'd put him out, but . . . she hadn't thrown him away. He knew she wanted him there in the game warden's little shack where she could watch him" (37). Tali believes Jacob moves through the world "unconscious, connected to nothing." She believes him unprepared "for the world she inhabited." She declares: "Jacob Nashoba didn't belong" (263). Mrs. Edwards con-stantly calls him "the mixedblood outsider" (270) against whom she pits her considerable power: "from the first he'd felt that the old woman was his implacable enemy, that she'd seen into his heart at first glimpse and knew his irremediable guilt" (29). He believes him-self guilty and troubled—an enemy of the people. He believes himself unworthy of wife, home, and happiness. He acquiesces to his exile.

Girard continues, "The transformation of the real into the unreal is part of the process by which [the human community] conceals from [it]self the human origin of [its] own violence, by attributing it to the gods" (161) or to the proprieties of "our story." By displacing the blame for the troubles onto the double, the community can believe itself guiltless, its stories sacrosanct. Some might argue that the notion of a scapegoat or sacrificial victim is rooted in the complex traditions of vengeances and atonements of the Islamic/Judeo/Christian theologies and is alien to Native Americans. But the mechanics of blame seem almost universal; being fearful, humans shun and ostracize each other. In Leslie Silko's *Ceremony*, Night Swan, a woman of power, herself feared and shunned by the community, tells Tayo, a young and desolate man of mixedblood and warrior experience, "They are afraid, Tayo. They feel something happening; they can see something happening around them, and it scares them. Indians or Mexicans or whites—most people are afraid of change. They think that if their children have the same color of skin, the same color of eyes, that nothing is changing. They are fools. They blame us, the ones who look different. That way they don't have to think about what has happened inside themselves" (104). Silko writes powerfully of the seductive temptation of humans to blame troubles and dis-ease on the different Other.

In *Dark River* Owens shows us that each of us is simultaneously monstrous and Monster Slayer, since "the monstrous double is also to be found wherever we encounter an 'I' and an 'Other' caught up in a constant interchange of differences" (Girard 164). Any community composed of mortal individuals carries its own guilt. No one person needs to be singled out or excluded in the name of community vitality. Each member of the Apache community should have believed Shorty Luke about the necessity of continually *changing* the stories: "It's going to take improvisation" (257). Shorty explains that part of the large, even universal story "has drifted beyond this moment like one of those leaves you see in a stream that overtakes another and moves on while the other moves around and around. Sometimes stories do that" (270). Mrs. Edwards and others seem to be trying to keep the story local, private, mythological; yet the human story is always inclusive of all oddities, all disruptions. Jake is not antipathetic to their world.

There are other casualties in these cosmic, mythological battles in the novel, but Jake Nashoba most fully fits the parameters of Girard's proper sacrificial victim—the one whose ritual sacrifice is expected to cleanse the community. Nashoba himself has long had a sense of blood sacrifice. "He thought of the cabin in Mississippi . . . his granma talking about blooded earth as though sacrifice had been made" (42); and again, she drags herself "back toward their cabin, leaving his five-year-old self alone with tree, river, and blood" (52). Also, his own body has bled in Vietnam and once again in this deep canyon.

Girard reminds us that "we should not conclude, however, that the surrogate victim is simply foreign to the community. Rather, he is seen as a 'monstrous double.' He partakes of all possible differences within the community, particularly the difference between within and without, for he passes freely from the interior to the exterior and back again. Thus, the surrogate victim constitutes both a link and a barrier between the community and the sacred" (271). The Apache community in *Dark River* easily designates Jake as the marginal outsider though he "passes freely" in and out of the community, into the sacredness of nature and the river, and into the profane spaces of tribal politics and war's aftermath. Jake could have been a link for community and family members to the sacred, but they criticize him and his seeming lack of tribal affiliation and knowledge of the proper stories. Mrs. Edwards accuses Jake: "Did you forget everything, or don't those Choctaw people you come from have stories?" (42).

The cultural order of this community is disintegrating. In an almost comic proposal, Avrum has tried to get the people to give up their casino, their TV satellite dishes, RVs, commercial hunting, chainsaws and microwaves, condos and Land Cruisers (70–74) and "become a traditional tribe again, living the way everyone lived before the white men came" (71). Everyone flatly rejects his plan, although Jake wonders if "maybe anthropologists were the real Indians anyway. If the whole idea of Indian was just an invention, then it made sense that an actor hired to play Indians . . . would have a lot in common with an anthropologist who studied what his own kind had invented" (92). The ordered world of the Apache (which always existed only in myth) is topsy-turvy once again.

And so Jake, following the unspoken but mutually understood script of the scapegoat/lone wolf, the script of self-blame, decides to leave. As his one last act for family and community, he wants to check on his surrogate daughter, Alison. That effort entangles him with Stroud and Jensen and the militia. Jensen shoots Jake, and he falls "into darkness shrouded by the tangled roots of a great, downed tree . . . the hole left by the massive root wad of the pine" (199). A series of complicated images and activities accrue to this massive and tangled root wad; but by the end of the novel "the earth had opened up, and two enormous mandibles framed by spider legs reached out and seized Jake. In a moment he was gone, dragged into a hole that closed at once" (284). Many of the other characters look into this hole (a hole that is at once literal, literary, physical, and metaphysical) to see and speak to Jake. Jessie, the history major turned vision-quest dealer turned ghost and wolf, even sits "with his feet over the edge of the hole" (279). Lee Jensen also falls into the hole but climbs out (281), and when he is finally captured, his rifle (the iron weapon of the Monster) falls into the hole (284). In 1992, in *Other Destinies: Understanding the American Indian Novel,* Owens wrote that James Welch's *Fools Crow* "is about returning, about going home to an identity, about looking back through the hole in time." And, Owens writes, "the world seen [by going through that hole in time] is one in which man is not an isolated, identityless drifter" (165).

Jake, throughout the novel, has sensed that there is something about the Dark River that connects him to home—especially to the idea of home. He remembers scenes on the river in Mississippi when he was a boy. Once the old grandfather had "unexpectedly, raised his eyes to look directly at where he hid, the eyes so taut that he could feel them go over him like smooth hands. He'd run from the old man then . . . and he'd never gone back to that place. Not because he was afraid of the old man, but because of a feeling so much like love that he feared he would be drawn into that world forever, on the other side of the river" (109). While in the hole he again experiences the feel of hands soothing him: "Hands touched him everywhere at once, busy, delightfully soft hands that seemed to lift and move him" (198); later he feels hands "probing his flesh, molding his bones"— his body as "rolled clay" (214). It is not so much that his physical body is being healed as that he is metaphorically turning into the "clay of the story" that other characters are getting their hands into (269). In this strange, surrealistic, metaphorical "death," Jake finally feels warm, safe, loved, and accepted. From the depths he smiles at Shorty with affection. "He realized that he had never felt so well in his life since his momentary vision in Mississippi so many years before. All anger was gone. He had a feeling that something very good was approaching" (256). Even his wife in the guise of Spider seems to be present and says, "You knew this all the time, didn't you?" (271). The "this" that he always already knew is perhaps that slipping through such a hole in time would bring him home.

At that very moment the old Choctaw man welcomes back his Grandson. "*Halito*. It's been a long time." Jacob turns "toward the smiling old Choctaw man, the flow of a big, dark river in his brown eyes" (271). With the ambiguous reference to "his" brown eyes, we may rest assured that the warm, dark river of knowledge and identity flows in both men. In the last line of the novel the storyteller's voice proclaims, "It is said that Jacob Nashoba went home" (286). Frank Kermode comments in *The Sense of an Ending* that "ends are ends only when they are not negative but frankly transfigure the events in which they were immanent" (175). Jake's role "ends" in the novel, but his own end is not negative. His "end" has transfigured all the events of his life from his childhood in Mississippi, to Vietnam, to the Apache land, and back to the dark river. Certainly, in this novel events, characters, stories, the immanently sacred, and the profane have been transposed and transfigured by the end.

Jake is a fictional creation, but his experience resonates for the reader, for real people in this seemingly postfamily, post-tribal, postmodern world. One of the most widely traveled, displaced, mixed-ancestry, global citizens writing today, Pico Iyer (who, like Jake Nashoba, seems always to feel the need to search for a proper "home"), writes that as the millennium approached, he found himself rereading "a relatively obscure twelfth-century Saxon monk, Hugo of St. Victor: 'The man who finds his homeland sweet is still a tender beginner; he to whom every soil is as his native one is already strong, but he is perfect to whom the entire world is a foreign land'" (77). Paradoxically, as in St. Victor's koan, Jake has never needed to "go home" to be perfect. When Mrs. Edwards tells Tali "Jacob Nashoba was always lost; there was never anything we could do" (253), she may be correct in fact but wrong in implication. Being "lost" or being without the parochialism of "home" may be part of perfection; and certainly if Jake is also Child of the Water, there is nothing mere mortals can do to change his cosmic destiny. Besides, Tali has earlier confronted Mrs. Edwards with the accusation that "You wanted to help him and he wouldn't let you. That's it, isn't it?" [the real cause of Mrs. Edwards's stubborn animosity toward Jake] (219). Mrs. Edwards agrees at the end to help Tali find Jacob, who is down in the canyon. But the two women try to "retrieve" or find Jake in the wrong ways. Mrs. Edwards begins to put words and lines on a paper, to draw a map that she holds out to Tali (254). But "the way" can never be delineated in writing nor known in words. For Jake, trying to find a "sweet homeland," especially a homeland in Mrs. Edwards's world, would make him only a "tender beginner." Early in the novel Jake "lived with a vague yearning to go home, but he couldn't locate that place on all the maps he bought and hoarded. When he'd finally found his way down into the canyon for the first time, he had felt with each downward step a kind of exultation. At the river he had sat with an astonished sense of having arrived somewhere at last. The violence that pushed at his flesh from within disappeared in the canyon" (50–51), and he knows the length of the river, every bend and pool, better than anyone else in the novel, including the people who supposedly belong to that place.

He knows the place—the dark river—by heart and by body, as Neil Harrison describes in a poem about the Elkhorn River: "Parts of this river I know / by heart," by fishing, by hunting, by

> . . . putting
> together pieces of the river . . .
> flowing through the seasons
> on her secret way . . .
> an eternal state of flux.
> You can find her name
> and image on a million maps,
> but she's a mystery a man can only
> learn in part, in those places
> he's come to know by heart (9).

There is something sacred, solid, and inviolable in Jacob Nashoba's being lost in the mysteries.

In *Other Destinies* Owens writes that in the oral tradition, stories are never original and always have the "duty of providing immortality—of preventing the death of a culture" (169). In writing *Dark River* Owens explicitly takes on the issue of whether or not the oral tradition can prevent the death of individuals by turning them into legendary heroes or of cultures by preserving their purported cultural integrity. Stories are powerful, but they are not omnipotent. All these characters, even the villains, the international visitors, get involved in "working the clay" of each others' stories and of the grand story they are all living, which links their present lives to the "time immemorial" myths; but still, many die, the "culture" is as dis-integrated as ever, and the story line is open ended at the conclusion of the novel. Owens also seems to be experimenting with the "delightful possibility," as he calls it in *Other Destinies*, of erasing the author as icon (170). In *Dark River* the narrator, storyteller, author/authorial function become so entangled that they all but disappear. What is ultimately brought to the foreground is the notion that *Dark River* is a written text, not a traditional "oral story."

In his latest book, *I Hear the Train*, Owens, wondering what catastrophe "erased all memories of the mother [his grandmother] from family stories" as some of the Apache characters are trying to erase Jake Nashoba's presence and memory from their midst, goes even further in his critique of story and legend, declaring that "heritage, history, and story are the real crucibles of catastrophe" (96). Owens writes that "the thought of origins does not soothe all of us. . . . The past's residence within language makes it inescapably mere fiction" (97). The group or individual identities to be found in creation stories and their concomitant teleologies are fictions and provide scant comfort. Owens continues, "Despite my most strenuous efforts within language, I can determine nothing of the inexorably absolute past, of origins; the past, with its endless accretions, renders me inauthentic" (97). Jake's efforts in the novel to align heritage, history, and story may be just as painful as those of Owens.

Neither myth nor history can perform, as Levi-Strauss calls it, "the specific task of mediating irreducible opposites" (Crossan 35). Pierre Maranda goes so far as to say that "myth is also and more than anything else the hallucinogenic chant in which mankind harmonizes the vagaries of history" (Crossan 37). Myth and communal stories often demand that the individual be sacrificed for the sake of "meaning" and harmony. But in his seminal work *The Dark Interval*, John Dominic Crossan argues in favor of parable. He writes that "'reality' is the world we create in and by our language and our story so that what is 'out there,' apart from our imagination and without our language, is as unknowable as, say, our fingerprints, had we never been conceived" (25). Yet there is an "out there," and that mystery is sensed in the movement of and at the "edges of language" and at the "limit of story" (30). Testing those edges is what parable is all about (30); testing those edges is what *Dark River* is all about. Parable and *Dark River* "continually and deliberately subvert final words about 'reality' and thereby introduce the possibility of transcendence" (Crossan 105). Jake Nashoba certainly transcends time and space, story and heritage.

Michel Foucault believes that "writing unfolds like a game that inevitably moves beyond its own rules and finally leaves them behind. Thus, the essential basis of this writing is not the exalted emotions related to the act of composition or the insertion of a subject into language. Rather, it is primarily concerned with creating *an opening where the writing subject endlessly disappears*" (116) [emphasis mine]. The image of most of the main characters in *Dark River* slipping at one time or another into the opening in the earth under the great tree—all the while discussing story endings and narrative conclusions—comes immediately to mind. Foucault claims that another theme is even more familiar; "it is the kinship between writing and death. . . . This conception of a spoken or written narrative as a protection against death has been transformed by our culture. Writing is now linked to sacrifice and to the sacrifice of life itself" (117). Jake Nashoba and company and perhaps the readers fall through that "opening where the writing subject endlessly disappears." In Girardian terms Jake and easy meaning have been sacrificed to the complex and conflicting demands of various cultures and of writing. Foucault continues:

> Boundless misfortune, the resounding gift of the gods, marks the point where language begins; but the limit of death opens . . . within language, an infinite space. Before the imminence of death, language rushes forth, but it also starts again, tells of itself, discovers the story of the story and the possibility that this interpenetration might never end . . . [story is born], a murmuring which repeats, recounts, and redoubles itself endlessly. (54–55)

Hence, in this novel shines the relevance of the "sacred, monstrous doubles," whose complicated existences parallel the infinite redoubling of language and interpretation, whose "sacrifice" replicates the death associated with writing. In *Other Destinies* Louis Owens quotes Gerald Vizenor quoting Octavio Paz from "The Monkey

Grammarian": "Writing is a search for meaning that writing itself violently expels. At the end of the search meaning evaporates and reveals to us a reality that literally is meaningless. . . . The word is a disincarnation of the world in search of its meaning; and an incarnation: a destruction of meaning, a return to body" (241). And Roland Barthes says that "writing is the destruction of every voice, of every point of origin. Writing is that neutral, composite, oblique space where our subject slips away, the negative where all identity is lost, starting with the very identity of the body writing" (253). Barthes says that "we now know that a text [is] a multidimensional space in which a variety of writings, none of them original, blend and clash. The text is a tissue of quotations drawn from the innumerable centers of culture" (256). In *Dark River* Owens writes to challenge meaning.

Louis Owens has discovered, as Foucault phrases it, "the related categories of exhaustion, excess, the limit, and transgression—the strange and unyielding form of these irrevocable movements which consume and consummate us" (49). Any creative ability, any culturally cohesive tendency of the oral tradition and oral storytelling dies in writing, yet we have also long abandoned the "logical positivism" of writing. In *Dark River* Owens transgresses all the boundaries of form and content, creating a plenitude of entangled voices and existences. The book compels us with its kaleidoscopic details and chimerical myths; at the same time, it is a book that consumes the world of story yet consummates and confirms something whole and holy about the transcendent Self.

WORKS CITED

Barthes, Roland. "The Death of an Author." *Falling into Theory: Conflicting Views on Reading Literature.* Boston: Bedford/St. Martins, 2000.

Crossan, John Dominic. *The Dark Interval: Towards a Theology of Story.* Sonoma, Calif.: Polebridge, 1988.

Foucault, Michel. *Language, Counter-Memory, Practice.* Ithaca, N.Y.: Cornell UP, 1977.

Girard, Rene. *Violence and the Sacred.* Baltimore: Johns Hopkins UP, 1977.

Haley, James L. *Apaches: A History and Culture Portrait.* Norman: U of Oklahoma P, 1997.

Harrison, Neil. "Elkhorn." *In a River of Wind*. Mankato, Minn.: Bridgeburner's, 2000.

Iyer, Pico. "Citizen Nowhere: The Search for the Self in a Shifting World." *Civilization* (Feb./Mar. 2000): 72–77.

Kermode, Frank. *The Sense of an Ending*. New York: Oxford UP, 1967.

Silko, Leslie. *Ceremony*. New York: Signet, 1977.

CHAPTER SEVEN

LOUIS OWENS'S
REPRESENTATIONS OF
WORKING-CLASS CONSCIOUSNESS

RENNY CHRISTOPHER

Very little has been written about Native Americans and social class[1] and even less about contemporary Native American writers' relationship to social class. Louis Owens is a Native writer of working-class origin whose work can be seen as working-class writing as well as mixedblood writing, and an examination of his work from the critical perspective of working-class studies can illuminate aspects of his writing that have not yet received the attention they warrant.

Owens is a mixedblood Choctaw/Cherokee/Irish writer and also a mixed-class writer. Owens came from the working class and, as a professor of literature, entered the middle class; his writing reflects a working-class, or perhaps better, a mixed-class consciousness in that his works refuse to celebrate the possibility of upward mobility. Working-class writers frequently question the middle-class values that underlie most of canonical American literature—values of individualism, materialism, ambition, and movement. Owens's work fits in a genre of working-class literature that I call "unhappy narratives of upward mobility," which questions or rejects outright all those values in favor of working-class values of community, inter-dependence, and connectedness.[2] He has said that he feels "like I live in the world I grew up in, my parents' world, and that out of that world I deal with this other one. The result is that I feel like a foreigner in the academic world" (personal communication, August 1999). The world of his parents was a working-class one; the university world is often an unwelcoming one for academics from the working class, because of the difference in value systems.[3]

This aspect of Owens's life has been well documented, but not in the context of working-class consciousness. This is not surprising. As Martha C. Knack and Alice Littlefield note in their introduction to *Native Americans and Wage Labor: Ethnohistorical Perspectives,* even scholars studying North American Indian economic life have not paid attention to Native Americans as participants in wage labor, as members of the working class, although for at least a century large numbers of Native American individuals have been wage laborers. Knack and Littlefield cite as a reason for this neglect "[a]nthropo-logical fascinations with the 'traditional,' or compulsions to salvage the 'aboriginal' before it became hopelessly contaminated by the 'modern.'" This infatuation with the past combines with the ten-dency to "study" Native communities as separate from the non-Native and create "theories [that] are too narrow to account for the phenomenon of Indian wage labor, which of historical necessity has existed along the contact zone between Indian and non-Indian com-munities and cultures," (3) the contact zone which forms a focal point in much of Owens's work.

The majority of American Indians are now part of the working class, but they occupy a particularly exploited sector of that class, with "higher turnover of jobs . . . more dependence on temporary or seasonal work, greater dependence on public employment, and below average incomes" (Littlefield and Knack 15). And while she does not address the issue of class directly, Joane Nagel reports that in 1990, only 68.7 percent of Indians were high-school graduates (98). Class is implied in such figures, since most non-high-school graduates are held within the lower levels of working-class economic and social status, and holding a bachelor's degree is usually the minimum entrance requirement into the middle class.

Class oppression is intertwined with racial oppression. Richard Jarvenpa writes that the "development of reservations and reserves has perpetuated racial segregation, administrative paternalism and lower-class status for Indian people" (29), and that "three-quarters of all Indians in the U.S., and over half of all Canadian Indians, have incomes below official poverty levels. Half of all U.S. and Canadian Indians tallied in the labor force are unemployed" (35). At the other end of the social scale, affluent, urban people with Indian ancestry "may not identify themselves as Indians, except under advantageous circumstances, while expressing contempt for and distancing themselves from less affluent Indians in ghettos and on reservations" (36). Between the extremes of poverty and affluence, Jarvenpa notes the existence of a "relatively stable" urban Indian working class.

Jarvenpa also examines cultural movements and adaptations, concluding that "self-determination, with its emphasis upon group rights, stands in opposition to the concept of individual rights embedded in Western law and institutions" (44). This is not far from working-class culture's emphasis upon community, collectivity, interdependence (as opposed to bourgeois culture's emphasis on individualism), suggesting that a Native consciousness, or more specifically a *mixedblood* consciousness, might not be incompatible with a working-class consciousness.

Owens's autobiographical writing places him clearly as a working-class writer, and his fiction consistently expresses not only a mixed-blood Native American perspective but an identifiably working-class perspective as well. His work needs to be viewed in the context of Native American studies but also, simultaneously, in the context of Working Class Studies, in part because Owens himself has noted the existence of a working-class dimension in mixedblood writing. In one instance he points out that Mourning Dove wrote "in a tent after working as a farm laborer all day" (*MM* 39). He has written that the "Native American novel is the quintessential postmodern frontier text, and the problem of identity at the center of virtually every Native American novel is the problem of internalized transculturation" (MM 46). The lines that Owens's own work crosses are not only lines of racial identification but of class experience and consciousness.

In novels such as *Wolfsong, Bone Game,* and *Nightland,* Owens is writing directly about class experience as well as about ethnic experience. Because American culture in general, and literary studies in particular, have very poorly developed vocabularies with which to discuss class experience and the representation of it, it is easy to discuss literary works in terms of race/ethnicity and gender/sexuality, for which we have developed vocabularies that have come not only out of academic discourse but out of social movements and activism. With the birth/rebirth of working-class studies over the past decade or more, a focus on writers' representations of class experience has once again (following the period of class consciousness aroused in the 1930s) become possible. It is important to look at writers of color in terms of their representation of class as well as of race, so that not only white working-class writers count as "classed" (instead of also "raced") and so that writers of color count as "classed" (instead of only "raced"). An incident in *I Hear the Train* illustrates the way in which something that is really a factor of class can be misascribed to race. Describing how his older brother, Gene, ran cross-country races in high school barefoot, Owens writes that "people who knew our family sometimes attributed his barefoot running to the fact that he was 'Indian.' The reality was, of course, that he simply couldn't afford cross-country shoes. The money we made from summer and after-school jobs went for clothes and food, not frivolous things like running shoes" (5–6). A white working-class boy in similar circumstances might also have run barefoot, but people who knew the Owens family saw "Indianness" where they should have seen poverty, thus making race stand in for class, of which there is much less consciousness in the United States than there is of race.

In writing of how he felt about the family's mixedblood identity when he was a child, Owens says that he thought no one but a

Choctaw "could be as beautiful as my father's mother, or as great a hunter as my father, and though in California I was embarrassed by our poverty and bad grammar, I was nonetheless comfortable with who we were" (*MM* 176). What he seems to be expressing here is a complicated matrix of comfort and discomfort related to ethnicity and class: while he is "comfortable" with what he understands about his family's ethnic composition, he is "embarrassed" by the markers of the low-class status they inhabit. In *Mixedblood Messages* he writes of his ability to pass for white: passing "was easy, something I did not really have to think about very much. The hard part was being poor in a small town where people knew everyone. Dirt poor, shit poor, offal poor, embarrassing poor" (196). For the young Owens, ethnicity apparently posed far less of a problem in identity formation than did class. Low-class status, for members of all ethnic groups, is a source of shame in this culture, which blames the poor for their own poverty.

Owens is of particular interest in terms of working-class studies because mixed-class experiences are common and crucial in the discussion of class in America, and Owens is not only a person of mixed blood; he is also a person of mixed-class background, having been born into an impoverished working-class culture and having become, eventually, a college professor. Owens writes that those

> of us who write, teach, and critique Native American literatures, whether we identify as American Indian, Euramerican, both, or neither, face the complex challenge of attempting to mediate without violating, and, above all, to facilitate an awareness that the literature we call Native American is indeed an "other" literature that nonetheless—in keeping with trickster's ubiquitous and uncontainable presence—participates profoundly in the discourse we call American and World literature. (*MM* 56)

One of the ways Owens's work participates in American and World literature is by being part of yet another "other" literature—working-class literature, that is, works by writers of working-class origin who exhibit working-class consciousness in their writing.

Owens writes in *Mixedblood Messages* of the simultaneously alienating and encompassing effects of a mixedblood identity; he does not address class directly, but the passage below comes at the end of a section in which he has carefully documented the extreme poverty of his Mississippi childhood, the place in the lower levels of the working class his family occupied once they moved to California, and his own alienation from them through his education and entry into the white-collar world. He writes,

> I am descended from those people [Choctaws], *but I am not those people,* just as I bear the blood of the Trail of Tears and of an enormous Owens clan that reunites periodically . . . but I am not those people either. The descendant of mixedblood sharecroppers and the dispossessed of two continents, I believe I am the rightful heir of Choctaw and Cherokee storytellers and of Shakespeare and Yeats and Cervantes. Finally, everything converges and the center holds in the margins. This, if we are to go on. (177)

By stressing "sharecroppers" along with "mixedblood," and "dispossessed of two continents"—meaning the Natives forced along the Trail of Tears and all the paths of displacement and genocide as well as the poor of Europe who came to do that displacing because of their own exploitation on that continent—Owens is indicating not only his ethnic ancestry but his working-class ancestry. By making claim as a Choctaw/Cherokee/European mixedblood to Native and European traditions, he is also making claim *as a working-class man* to those traditions. The feeling of not being "of those people" is one that is common to narratives that chronicle upward mobility.

Owens's autobiographical writings, *Mixedblood Messages: Literature, Film, Family, Place* and *I Hear the Train: Inventions and Reflections,* set the class context in which to understand his fictions. He describes a process of writing family history that is common in working-class

literature, when writers try to recover the family histories and lives
of people who have lived outside the web of documentation:

> Uncle August and all the rest are particles scattered, the chaos
> of invasion, coloniality, deracination, and removal embedded
> in their blood and photographs. Like Uncle August, we are all
> between the tracks, framed by a vanishing point but satisfied
> and defiant to the end. . . . on the back of a postcard photo of
> mainstreet Muldrow, Oklahoma, in 1913, also addressed to his
> mother, he writes, "I her the train so Bee good tell I see you."
> I, too, hear the train. Unseen, it rushes along shining tracks
> bracketing Uncle August in memory that arrives out of the
> dark and disappears at the vanishing point of convergence in
> a photograph. My inheritance, it leaves in the air a trace out of
> which I will construct history, mirroring consciousness. . . .
> Like that dollop of sourdough left behind in the bowl to dou-
> ble indefinitely into another loaf, it becomes stories that birth
> others. And, as Vladimir Nabokov knew and showed us so
> brilliantly in his novel *Pale Fire,* we make stories in order to
> find ourselves at home in a chaos made familiar and comforting
> through the stories we make. . . . (*Train* xiii)

Owens demonstrates his mixed-class consciousness as well as
mixedblood consciousness here, putting together the semiliterate
Uncle August and Vladimir Nabokov. Owens quotes Uncle August's
postcard, with original grammar and spelling intact, not to exoticise
or humiliate him but to lovingly preserve him as he was and to bring
him into a highly literary work, filled with literary allusions, in order
to mix that semilegendary, uneducated figure of Owens's Native
and working-class history with his educated and middle-class present. He does so to insist upon and demand the respect and recognition of that heritage—one usually invisible, erased in the world of
letters—just as the very well-educated, professorial, professional
writer Owens will insist that his earlier blue-collar self, a firefighter,
is equally his true self, and perhaps his preferred self.

In *Mixedblood Messages* Owens reprints family photographs and
tells family stories. He writes about the criminals in his family,

including Uncle Bob, who "spent more than half his short life in prison," describing how "more than once we watched Uncle Bob walk away in handcuffs" (137), and tells how he himself was born in prison. He describes the rural poverty of Mississippi, in which he spent his childhood "in a two-room cabin a stone's throw from the Yazoo River" without electricity or plumbing (152). He notes that it is not his "habit to write or talk in public about my family's everyday pathos or to quote various family members, for after all, each of us has a saga of our own to tell. However I think this personal history has some bearing on the subject of mixedblood identity as it is articulated in literature" (147). I would argue that it also has a bearing on his working-class consciousness, and would further note that such reticence about talking (or writing) about family things in public is something that working-class writers suffer across ethnicities.

Revelation of a past that may be unpalatable, inexplicable, or unacceptable to middle-class readers is also a common element of working-class literature, exemplified by Owens's revelations about his criminal uncle and his defiant announcement that he himself was born in prison. (His father was working as a guard, and he was born in the prison infirmary; his mother was incarcerated only in the sense of being married to a man with a particularly ironic and unpleasant blue-collar occupation.) Owens expands on this theme in a chapter of *I Hear the Train* called "My Criminal Youth," in which he describes the curriculum of bicycle theft and breaking-and-entering that he followed under the influence of a cousin when he first moved to California from Mississippi at the age of eight. "California, I saw at once, was made of desirable objects and those who possessed such objects" (77). As he describes it, it is the first time he has lived among more affluent people, "on the periphery of a quasi-middle-class community on the edge of a great city. We were the bottom rung, of course" (78). Again, the feeling of shame imposed on those of lower-class status in this society emerges.

But here theft functions as a metaphor as well as a literal reality of his past, as it sometimes does in working-class literature, especially in descriptions of education, when upwardly mobile working-class students feel that they are stealing what they are not entitled to have. Owens describes a particular incident in which he peers through the living-room window at a family whose bicycle he is about to steal from their front porch. The family is sitting around a television (Owens's family does not have one, and there are too many of them—nine siblings—to sit around it if they did have one). He envies a perceived (and possibly, even probably, false) sense of stability that this middle-class family possesses. "There was a wholeness about the scene, a kind of completeness that I had never imagined in a family before. In my experience families were in constant flux, coming and going, messy and uncontained" (81). He takes off with the bike, and reflecting back upon it, he still feels "the awfulness of the moment in which I broke into that perfect order, violated whatever it was inside the house that I could not understand. . . . At the time I knew it marked a point of departure, like a ticket bought and punched for a journey to a place I didn't even suspect existed" (81–82). And he did indeed embark on a journey, out of the working-class world in material terms even if he never left it in spirit, thus feeling divided along class lines. Working-class writers often describe getting an education as a form of theft, their very presence in the middle class as writers as a form of theft. Owens uses theft as a metaphor in a way similar to that used by white working-class writers such as Jack London and Dorothy Allison.

Owens's brother was the first person in the history of the family to receive a high-school diploma, Owens himself was the second, and he alone went on to college. He writes of his own educational destiny—that he "drifted" into a junior college "and then, to my amazement and the astonishment of the few who paid attention, on to the University of California at Santa Barbara. So that now for more than twenty years I have lived in a world incalculably different from that of everyone else in my family" (*MM* 176). Noting this, Owens describes how contact with his family makes him feel "sometimes like a time traveler beamed into an awkward past" (*Train* 7), a feeling recorded by working-class writers who have left their family of origin and received an education, from Jack London to Agnes Smedley to Anzia Yezierska to Richard Rodriguez.

He also documents his own blue-collar work history. Owens started "by hoeing beans at nine years old and graduating to weeding and thinning sugar beets by the time I was thirteen and fourteen," working side by side with braceros, using the infamous short-handled hoe (19). While working in the fields, he fantasized "about the perfect job. Someday someone will pay you as much money as you can possibly imagine, say three-fifty an hour, to backpack in a mountain wilderness with meadows and streams and snowfields, like the pictures you've seen. But the men and women in the rows beside you don't think like that. They think of their families across the border, babies and kids in school, and they imagine working many years in the fields" (19–20). As is the case with many working-class kids who have later undergone upward mobility, he knows himself to be an outsider all along.

He writes about working at a mushroom farm, describing in detail the conditions of work and talking about the owner's son, who was one of the part-time workers. "Unlike the rest of us, who were not thought to be college material, he knew he would be successful. . . . Our older brothers and friends were already part of a war in a place called Vietnam, a war that had not become ugly yet for most of us, and we looked forward to our turns at such excitement as soon as we graduated" (30). Even while he had dreams of better work and a better life, he knew where his class position placed him in the hierarchy of life chances.

Nonetheless, against the odds, he did go to college (he notes that in 1968, the year he entered the University, his father's income was $3,000 [*Train* 44]), but as is the case with many working-class college graduates, his education did not lead him immediately into a white-collar job. Instead, he worked for the Forest Service first on a trail crew, with a gang of M.A.s and Ph.D.s working for love of the wilderness, next as a wilderness ranger, and then—the job he writes about with the greatest joy—as a member of a "hotshot" firefighting crew. He notes the falsity of media images that portray this work as "miserable" and "dangerous," writing that

> [j]ust off camera are a bunch of men and women having the time of their lives and making good money to boot. . . . it's dangerous, and people have died, including some of my friends, but that's not what it's all about. As a sawyer I was up front, cutting the first swatch of line while a puller stood behind my shoulder pulling away the cut brush and limbs and tossing them to the side for someone else. . . . We could cut a ten-foot line down to mineral earth in minutes, working in controlled mania. We were efficient, good at what we did, young, excited. (58)

What he describes is a blue-collar job that has what few blue-collar jobs have: a chance to use one's skills in a situation allowing a great deal of autonomy and exercise of judgment and a chance for heroism, for a sense of achievement. "And all these many years later, in a different life, I find myself dreaming of dark forests that crownout in racing flames, of small oak trees that explode like comets into the night sky, and of alpine ridges a million miles from the world" (63). In this blue-collar world where the mythology of blue-collar work is really true, where workers can do something well in a sort of journeyman-craft situation with a dash of danger and romance thrown in, Owens seems to have found a satisfaction unrivaled in any white-collar work except, perhaps, writing itself.

As a novelist, Owens has produced some extraordinary works which perform as both mixedblood consciousness and mixed-class consciousness. In *Wolfsong* the Joseph family has a history of working in logging. According to Knack and Littlefield, logging is one of the areas that were sometimes known as "Indian jobs." These "were often unskilled or at best semiskilled jobs. Some involved large-scale resource extraction, such as timbering and harvesting . . . [f]ew, however, involved control of material or financial resources, highly paid skills, or decision-making control over the worker's economic future.

In most cases there was explicit segregation of work crews and supervisory functions by ethnicity" (29). The work crews in Forks, Washington, the setting for *Wolfsong*, are not segregated, perhaps because it is a small and sparsely populated place, the logging companies we see in operation are small, local companies (although there is a reference to Weyerhaeuser working "over the mountain"), and, due to an apparent labor shortage, it is not possible to segregate work crews. It is true, though, that we see no Indian supervisors in the Forks logging industry as Owens portrays it. And although the crews are not segregated at work, one telling scene shows their social segregation: Jimmy silently leaves the Red Dog tavern when Jake Tobin begins making racist remarks (*Wolfsong* 98).

Patricia C. Albers, in "From Legend to Labor: Changing Perspectives on Native American Work," notes how

> popular stereotypes place Native Americans in a double bind when it comes to realizing a sense of personal and/or social identity through their own labor. As an example, when Native Americans manufacture dream-catchers, even on an assembly line, their ethnic identity is validated. When they rebuild an engine block as part of a pattern of reciprocity among kin, or when they do this as a wage laborer in a commercial garage, their ethnic identity is denied. In the first instance their work is associated with a legendary "traditionality" emblematic of the American Indian; in the second their labor occupies a liminal space because it lacks the cultural boundaries that stereotypically associate Native Americans with particular economic activities. Imagemaking of this kind reaches beyond the realm of identity because it influences the very character of the labor Native Americans perform, encouraging them to pursue specific types of jobs while excluding them from others. (249)

The additional layer of difficulty in *Wolfsong* comes from the fact that in logging, the fullblood men of the Joseph family are helping to destroy the natural world. Uncle Jim ultimately becomes a monkey wrencher, taking shots at bulldozers to protect that natural world by preventing the construction of a road through a wilderness area which will provide access to an area where an open-pit copper mine will be dug. The family, as well as all the Native inhabitants of Washington State who are caught up in the logging economy, are trapped in a complicated web. Economic necessity, pride in the quality of their work (Uncle Jim is called one of the best loggers ever, and Tom himself is told by his boss that he could be the best choker setter he ever had), and recognition of capitalism's destruction of not only the natural world but the very resources that provide the jobs which give economic sustenance and identity. The unresolvability of these paradoxes is recognized in the novel's unresolvable ending, which leaves Tom running (or floating, perhaps, if he is dead or dying) into an indeterminate future because there is no place for him either in Forks or at the University of California. Tom's sense of belonging nowhere and with no one echoes Owens's own, described in his autobiographical writings.

Tom is uncomfortable at the university, and the history of forced acculturation through schooling is emphasized by Uncle Jim's memory of boarding school, where "they had cut out the tongues of Indians, sewing in different tongues while the children slept" (5). Uncle Jim only reconciles himself to Tom's going off to the university by promising that he will provide a counter-education when Tom comes back. He says that the university would be bad for Tom's brother Jimmy, "and for a lot of the other kids in the valley, not just Indian kids neither, it wouldn't be too good. But for you it'll be fine. When you come back we'll go for a long walk . . . we'll walk clear over the mountains to Lake Chelan and I'll tell you all the stories . . . and I'll teach you all them things you ain't learned yet" (88). But it is not fine for Tom. At the university he meets intellectually sophisticated, upwardly mobile Native American students and, comparing them to his uncle and brother, thinks of his family as "Indians not Native Americans." This seems to represent for him not only a different stance toward the issue of ethnicity but a class difference (161). Tom says, "They built that campus on top of an old Indian burial ground. Sacred ground. Nobody else seemed to notice it, but I could feel those people there all the time" (65).

But it is not only this that makes Tom uneasy. He is the first kid, white or Indian, from Forks to get a scholarship to any university. He comes from the rural working-class to the urban middle-class university. He has refused the more homey destiny that might have been his—he could have married Karen. "She would have worked while he went to junior college. They would have lived a familiar story" (73). Instead, he has chosen the unfamiliar, and rather than embracing the material values and ethical code required by the university path to upward mobility, he has returned home, feeling like an outsider even there. He also rejects the one path he might have been able to reconcile himself to—that of wilderness ranger. That job has been offered to him more than once, but he chooses instead to "range the wilderness" (207) in his own way, rejecting both a middle-class and a working-class life—either of which might have been available to him—in an attempt to opt out of the entire system.

Of all Owens's novels, *Wolfsong* is the one that focuses most on work itself, with detailed descriptions of labor of a kind that appear rarely in American literature, including a consciousness of the dangers of blue-collar work.

At the bottom of the tower, the yarder's diesel engine farted out noise and fumes, while in a cage above the engine a man grabbed levers and caused a steel cable to run in a wide triangle from the top of the tower back down to the base of the tower. The mainline cable ran up the slope thirty feet from the ground and passed through a block at the tailhold and angled off to a second stump before sliding back down to the tower, and from the mainline hung two choker cables which two men were frantically wrapping around a pair of logs, the men's shiny hardhats bobbing and sinking out of sight in the tangle of fallen trees. Finally the two jumped free, scrambling out of the narrowing vee of the cable triangle that the logger called the jaws of death and leaping behind a stump just as a third figure shrilled three short blasts on a whistle and the man in the cage jerked levers to start the haulback . . . . Tom watched the small men in the unit wrestle with the forest. There was something heroic in those puny figures working to move trees, and something disastrously out of proportion. (138)

When Tom himself takes his brother's place in the logging crew after the fight with Buddy and Jake, his presence disrupts the unity of the workforce, because his coworkers blame him for Jake's injury. They threaten him simply by not working with him as a team, and this could result in his death. A good deal of blue-collar work requires cooperation to insure the safety of all the workers, and thus represents that larger ethic of interdependence which I identify as a core working-class value. When Vern fires him, he says, "A guy's got to be careful if the guys he works with don't look out for him, and some of these boys ain't going to be looking out for you any too much" (153). The logging crew stands as a metaphor for the lack of solidarity among the workers, a solidarity that might be able to oppose the oppression under which they all labor.

Tom remembers stories he has heard of the Wobblies, and specifically of the Everett massacre, in which sheriff's deputies killed five hundred workers. "And so he became aware that they killed everyone, these whites, not only Indians but everyone, each other" (140). The insight that Tom does not quite attain is that they do not kill each other at random; those deputies are in the paradoxical position of being workers hired by the bosses to kill other workers for the benefit of the bosses. Thinking of the workers, Tom recognizes part of the paradox: that these "good, desperate men were the enemy too . . . men who would destroy their mother earth" (140). But the workers, the "good, desperate men," include not only whites but his brother Jimmy as well, and even Tom himself while he is working on the logging crew. He reflects on the job he takes, setting chokers, that it "was a job intent on destroying you, ripping your hands off with jaggers of frayed cable or flaying you with the electric lash of a broken mainline" (141). This job can serve as a metonymy for the exploitation of all blue-collar workers.

Tom's brother Jimmy is focused solely on economic concerns. "With the mill damned near shut down and logging almost dead, people need the jobs that mine'll bring in," he says (32). Even J. D. Hill, the big businessman in town, has some regard for the destruction being wreaked. "I feel a little bad about cutting that road into the wilderness area. But it's going to happen whether we like it or not, and I'm going to make sure that the multinational company doesn't just come in here and take everything. I'm going to see to it that some of that money stays in the valley" (67). In his own inadequate and collaborationist way, Hill is trying to do good for his community, but he, like everyone else, is caught in the web of capitalism, and there is no way out. This "no way out" is voiced repeatedly by Jimmy, the most defeated character in the novel. He says Uncle Jim "never saw that we have to live here, the way it is right now" (112). Tom, though, knows that Jimmy's real economic outlook will not save him or anyone else. When Jimmy insists that their uncle's monkey wrenching was pointless, Tom counters, "instead you want to help them dig a big fucking hole in the middle of the last country around here that isn't clearcut. So a few people can go another ten or twenty years swilling beer and buying four-wheel drives" (120).

The way the working class is valued by the bosses is made clear in a scene in which a representative of Honeycutt Copper comes to sell the idea of the mine at a town meeting. "He was proud of the fact that he didn't have a racist bone in his body, but still the word 'logger' kept reminding him of the word 'nigger.' Logger-nigger, nogger-ligger" (115). And in this is perhaps one clue to a way out. If workers could recognize their true interests—preservation and sustainability—across race lines, perhaps together they could fight the classist, racist, profit-maddened bosses. But as ever, racial conflicts divide working-class people. Jake, Buddy, and two others jump Tom and Jimmy, because Buddy knows or suspects that Tom has been seeing Karen again. Jake says, "We don't want woods niggers bothering white girls" (131). Juxtaposed with the Honeycutt Copper representative's conflation of all loggers—that is, all workers—with "niggers," Jake's characterization of Indians as "woods niggers" pointedly shows the bosses' divide-and-conquer strategy. And indeed, as a result of the broken arm Jake sustains in the fight, his own class status is reduced from that of proud logger to that of disabled security guard, over which he is bitter and from which he finds no way out.

Grider, the white ranger who tries to talk Tom into becoming a ranger himself, talks about what is necessary in saving the wilderness. He says, "you . . . have to figure it's all your country now, just like it's all mine. White and Indian don't matter any more" (173). What matters to Grider is saving the wilderness, saving the earth. Thus Owens gives a piece of the truth to Uncle Jimmy, a fullblood, uneducated Stehemish, and another piece of the truth to Grider, the white, college-educated ranger. Ab Masingale, an old logger, also has a piece of the truth. He notes that the valley is mostly clear-cut and crisscrossed by roads, and the game is gone, and "it's a crying shame. And it was fellas like me that done it . . . and you all know it ain't gonna stop. There ain't no way it can stop" (185). Buddy objects that maybe the old loggers did all that, but they had to make a living. Ab, then, has no way out to offer except to note that Buddy's generation is going to be stuck with the results: "Hell, someday a man won't be able to breathe any more" (185). Tom already cannot breathe, and so he tries to go for the walk all the way to Canada that his uncle promised him when he returned from the university. But his uncle is dead, and Tom does not make it. As someone who has crossed class lines through his education, he cannot find a place for himself in the world. The novel gives pieces of truth to various characters, but Tom cannot bring those pieces together for himself, from either a race-based or a class-based perspective.

Nightland also expresses an oppositional working-class consciousness that rejects bourgeois values as destructive. This consciousness is allied with the indigenous consciousness represented in the novel by the figure of Siquani, the possibly four-hundred-year-old grandfather who converses with ghosts and who reads the signs to know that evil is coming. Siquani represents one pole in the novel, a consciousness opposed on ethnic cultural grounds to the avariciousness and destructiveness of white bourgeois culture, but other characters—notably Will, the mixedblood protagonist, and his white wife,

Jace—are characters who move to a less assimilationist stance in regard to bourgeois culture through the course of the novel. While Will's turning away from that culture is partially influenced by his Native roots—he has always respected Siquani's ways, although he does not completely share them—Will is a mixedblood working-class man, and part of his rejection of bourgeois values derives from his rootedness in alternative, pan-ethnic working-class values. For Jace, a member of the white world by heritage (although, like Will's and Billy's mothers, set somewhat in opposition to it by her marriage to an Indian), her return from bourgeois ambition to rejoin her husband in more humble surroundings than those she has sought in the city represents a return to working-class values.

Will and his friend from childhood, Billy, are economic refugees. Their parents fled Oklahoma along with the other dustbowl refugees to seek a better living in New Mexico, but now that land, too, has dried up, and despite the fact that Will still owns his parents' ranch free and clear, he can barely make a living from it. Will and Billy, though they are both mixedbloods raised in working-class circumstances, have different relationships to the core bourgeois values of acquisition and upward mobility; Billy embraces them recklessly, which ultimately leads to his death, while Will regards them with caution and suspicion. Billy has always rejected Siquani's worldview: "Now don't start in with Cherokee superstition. I get enough of that from Grampa," he says to Will (11). Billy is destroyed not only because he rejects Native tradition but because he adopts materialist, bourgeois values, buying a fancy new truck with money that he is supposed to be keeping secret.

Will's equilibrium is thrown off by the acquisition of the drug money. When he returns home with his half, "the home he'd been born and grown up in seemed suddenly distant and strange, a dark stone set down in the night" (31). Will has not succumbed to materialist values; he "could buy a new truck, but that wouldn't make much of a dent [in the found money] and besides, the idea didn't appeal to him. He could rebuild the Chevy instead. He didn't need a new house. He didn't want a television or new clothes" (79).

Odessa, like Billy, is corrupted by materialist, bourgeois values. "I have a Ph.D. in genocide," she says. "When I was young and innocent I thought I could get a white education and fight back. But I was stupid. Now . . . I'm going to have the American dream. Almost a million dollars" (303). Higher education in America is not only white but also middle-class—higher education is usually the gateway to the middle class, and in the course of higher education, values such as individualism and acquisitiveness are inculcated into students. For Odessa, the combination of a white education and a bourgeois education has corrupted her so that she is going to be an imperialist herself—she plans to go to South America—making her no better than those she blames for displacing her people.

When Will checks the hiding place of the money at the end of the novel, the money has vanished; there is water in the well instead, in which Will sees a crowd of faces reflected. The temptation—which Will was not very tempted by—toward the material values that destroyed Billy and Odessa is removed from Will's world, seemingly removed by the spirits of the land, and replaced by water in the well, symbolizing a healing of the land. But the faces in the water also suggest community, which is a working-class value as well.

Analyzing the class positioning and attitudes of a writer such as Louis Owens can help uncover dimensions of his work that do not emerge through other analytical approaches. Bringing writings such as his into working-class studies and literary theory can also help expand that theory to encompass a more complex and therefore more useful vision of the working class, working-class literary production, and the intersections of race/ethnicity and class. As Patricia Albers writes in her conclusion to the volume *Native Americans and Wage Labor*, studies need to focus on situations that allow Native peoples "to construct an identity as wage workers without destroying basic cultural values." She further notes that in the "study of relationships among capitalism, wage labor, and ethnicity, the lived-in experiences of the workers must take center stage because it is at the point of their labor that ethnic heritage intersects with capitalism and the workplace" (258–59). By reading autobiographical and fictional works of writers such as Owens who write out of both a Native/mixedblood consciousness and a working-class consciousness, the dimensions of understanding that Albers calls for within sociology and anthropology can be further enlarged. Both working-class autobiography and fiction can be regarded as a form of testimony, and that testimony can help unlock the usually hidden dimension, the frequently silent term of the trinity of race, class, and gender: class.

NOTES

1. For the few studies that have been done, see Russel Lawrence Barsh, "Plains Indian Agrarianism and Class Conflict," *Great Plains Quarterly* 7.2 (1987): 83–90; Thomas Biolsi, *Organizing the Lakota: The Political Economy of the New Deal on the Pine Ridge and Rosebud Reservations* (Tucson: U of Arizona P, 1992); Thomas C. Brockman, "Correlation of Social Class and Education on the Flathead Indian Reservation, Montana," *Rocky Mountain Social Science Journal* 8.2 (1971): 11–17; Renny Christopher and Carolyn Whitson, "Towards a Theory of Working-Class Literature," *Thought & Action* 15.1 (1999); Sandra L. Faimann-Silva, *Chocktaws at the Crossroads: The Political Economy of Class and Culture in the Oklahoma Timber Region* (Lincoln: U of Nebraska P, 1997); Alice Littlefield and Martha C. Knack, eds., *Native Americans and Wage Labor*; Castle McLaughlin, "Nation, Tribe, and Class: The Dynamics of Agrarian Transformation on the Fort Berthold Reservation," *American Indian Culture and Research Journal* 22.3 (1998): 101–38; John H. Moore, ed., *The Political Economy of North American Indians* (Norman: U of Oklahoma P, 1993); Joane Nagel, *American Indian Ethnic Renewal*; and Paul C. Rosier, "'The Real Indians, Who Constitute the Real Tribe': Class, Ethnicity, and Ira Politics on the Blackfeet Reservation," *Journal of American Ethnic History* 18.4 (1999): 3–39.

2. See Renny Christopher, "Rags to Riches to Suicide, Unhappy Narratives of Upward Mobility: Martin Eden, Bread Givers, Delia's Song, Hunger of Memory," *College Literature* 29.4 (2002).

3. See C. L. Barney Dews and Carolyn Leste Lawe, *This Fine Place So Far from Home: Academics from the Working Class* (Philadelphia UP, 1995); and Michelle M. Tocarczyk and Elizabeth A. Fay, *Working-Class Women in the Academy: Laborers in the Knowledge Factory* (Amherst: U of Massachusetts P, 1993).

WORKS CITED

Albers, Patricia C. "From Legend to Labor: Changing Perspectives on Native American Work." *Native Americans and Wage Labor.* Ed. Alice Littlefield and Martha C. Knack. Norman: U of Oklahoma P, 1996.

Jarvenpa, Richard. "The Political Economy and Political Ethnicity of American Indian Adaptations and Identities." *Ethnic and Racial Studies* 8.1 (1985): 29–49.

Littlefield, Alice, and Martha C. Knack, eds. *Native Americans and Wage Labor*. Norman: U of Oklahoma P, 1996.

Nagel, Joane. *American Indian Ethnic Renewal: Red Power and the Resurgence of Identity and Culture*. New York: Oxford UP, 1997.

CHAPTER EIGHT

WOLFSONG AND PACIFIC REFRAINS

JOHN PURDY

There is one obvious conclusion that must be drawn from even the hastiest survey of Louis Owens's canon: it is broad in its scope. At the center of his work one finds his fiction, while orbiting this narrative core one also finds an impressive body of non-fiction—autobiography, literary criticism, and social/cultural critique. But the scope goes beyond genres. The wide diversity of his fiction, for instance, is readily apparent. However, when trying to chart its parameters, one evokes the types of conventional classifications that Owens's work so often resists. One could note the variety of characters, settings, issues, and so on, that his novels encompass, but this also seems too restrictive of his canon's expansive nature. Owens likes to experiment, to push the parameters and potentials of language in order to intersect and intercept readers' imaginations, including the expectations they have been conditioned to construct when they read "Native American literature."

For instance, one can consider the differences between his first novel, *Wolfsong*, and his later fiction. It would be relatively easy to mark the former, "debut" work as a fairly conventional piece—in its narrative style and subject matter at least—reflective of issues and discourse current to its time and to view the later *Dark River* as a popular mystery "potboiler," but to do so misses their intriguing depths and nuances. Owens pieces together contemporary materials into clever stories that resemble stories with recognizable story conventions and orientations, yet he subtly reconfigures them to reveal a reality of contemporary America that is lost in the portrayals others, including Hollywood, market. In a way, he is like the Badger in Silko's *Storyteller:*

> Words like bones
> Scattered all over the place. . . .
> Old Skeleton Fixer spoke to the bones
> Because things don't die
> They fall to pieces maybe,
> Get scattered or separate,
> But Old Man Badger can tell
> How they once fit together. (242–43)

Wolfsong is a novel that "tells" about fitting together in old ways; it is about resurrection and survival. It is also a good example of Owens's talent, for it is a deceptively simple read.

Moving chronologically through the story of Jim Joseph's death and the subsequent return of his nephew to continue his resistance to a proposed mining operation in a pristine wilderness area, it at first seems to avoid the complex investigation of the mythological that one finds in *The Sharpest Sight* or the intricate probing of evil psyches of *Bone Game,* for example. However, I would argue that it is equally complex and that it represents a uniquely productive access point for a discussion of Owens's canon. This is not simply because it was his first novel but also because it demonstrates Owens's comprehension of and commentary on contemporary Native American literatures, as well as a number of the controversial issues with which our society contends. It also reveals how he marks his own terrain in current literary production.

But there is a complicating factor in any attempt to explore the novel's complexities, and that is the reader—in this case, me. Let me tell you a story. In 1993 I was able to entice Louis to my campus to meet with a group of teachers from around the country who were participating in my National Endowment for the Humanities seminar on four first novels by American Indian writers. This was shortly after the publication of *Wolfsong* and the year after his expansive and insightful collection of essays, *Other Destinies: Understanding the American Indian Novel*, was published. As we moved into a discussion of some of his readings of the novels in that collection and therefore in our seminar, I had to comment upon the unfortunate editing of the manuscript in some places, for instance where he discussed my own work on D'Arcy McNickle's *The Surrounded*, particularly where the editor did not catch a misspelling, letting "arguing ingenuously" remain when Owens had so obviously intended "arguing ingeniously." What ensued from that moment of conflicting readings highlighted by humor, and what continues to ensue, is an open exchange of ideas about texts—supposedly the ideal basic to literary criticism itself. What follows, then, is an exploration of *Wolfsong* that foregrounds our mutual contributions to the novel: what Owens brings to its construction but also what a reader versed in American literature and the setting of the novel contributes. I shared with him the original draft of this essay, which was a fairly conventional "reading" of the novel. He responded to it, and from there I have revised it with the hope of weaving our two strands into a critical discussion that will demonstrate the complexities of the novel.

Owens, of course, is both reader and author, as *Other Destinies* and his essays and books on other authors signify. When I asked him in an interview in 1998 about the ways that his literary critical studies work in conjunction with his fiction, he was quick to respond: "I think . . . inevitably they will interact. They have to. The mind works as a whole, so, to say while writing a piece of fiction that the ideas from reading and writing criticism don't work in somehow would be dishonest. It may not be conscious, but it has to have some effect. Gerald Vizenor is perhaps the best at making it obvious, at blurring the line between the two in the minds of his readers" ("Clear Waters" 8).

Wolfsong reflects this conjoining, but I am not suggesting that the novel is derivative. Instead, it presents a refinement, a personally productive extension and response to critical discourse about Native literatures and peoples current with its writing and with sociological debates about economics and environment. I would argue that this extension can be seen, in the novel, to derive from the fortuitous collaboration between lived and reflective experience—from both physical and scholarly activity. After all, this is what some of the characters in the novel represent—different pathways to knowing. To explore this idea I intend to focus upon several places where the novel provides what Greg Sarris calls for in *Keeping Slug Woman Alive: A Holistic Approach to American Indian Texts:* a dialogue between reader and text.

> Dialogue in the most general sense is understood as conversation between two or more people, people talking back and forth with one another. M. M. Bakhtin sees dialogue as an essential characteristic of the novel, which for Bakhtin is comprised of a diversity of voices. . . . Thus, a unit or system of language, say the novel, can be seen as a representative of dialogue and interaction between a number of languages and voices. But as David Bleich notes about the novel, and I would add all other units of language activity, it is not just a *representation* of interaction but also the *occasion* for interaction (418). A reader's intermingling internal voices hold dialogue with the intermingling voices of the novel. (4)

As I read *Wolfsong,* I find many "intermingling voices," including those of McNickle, Silko, Vizenor, Momaday, and Welch, to name a few. These voices situate the novel within a network of authors and ideas shaped by my reading of their texts.

As critics have noted time and time again, each of these authors, like so many others, is intimately concerned with change—with loss, of course, but also with how to accommodate sometimes sweeping alterations in individuals, cultures, places—and therefore with survival. This concern has been paramount in the literary texts of the present generation of writers, and it is at the heart of *Wolfsong*. It makes sense, then, that one would find resonance when looking at them together. Out of this overarching human angst comes all else: issues of identity, history, economics, racism. To his credit, Owens's dramatic portrayal of these issues is made vivid by the lived experience of people who face change on a daily basis, and he does not solely draw the easy lines of binaries to sound their ideologies nor their anxieties. He complicates the simplistic either/or logic of such debates.

But first let me set the stage, since it, too, is an active participant in this drama. Much of the novel derives from Owens's experiences in the Northwest.

> The first novel I wrote was *Wolfsong*. I began it in my attic room in the Forest Service bunkhouse in Darrington, Washington one fall after the snows came and almost everyone else had left for the year. I wanted really to write a novel about the wilderness area itself, the Glacier Peak Wilderness, making the place the real protagonist of the novel and the characters ways of giving the trees and mountains and streams and glaciers a voice. (Purdy, "Clear Waters" 6)

The novel is, indeed, a narrative of this place and the peoples who have interacted in/with it over a long period of time. The narrative's descriptive details carry that collective voice to us, just as the events carry the human drama that is enacted with the wilderness as a chorus, the strophe and antistrophe—yet another literary refrain.

While working for the Forest Service in the Mount Baker/Snoqualmie National Forest, which includes the Glacier Peak Wilderness Area, Owens encountered the myriad personalities—and their revealing contradictions—who inhabit this landscape on the "American frontier" after the heyday of Manifest Destiny and during the death throes of the Industrial Revolution. His eye for detail is astute. I live near Darrington, Washington, and can say that Owens's depiction of the forces that have changed this place over the last two centuries foregrounds all the underlying assumptions upon which current issues, such as extractive economies, are based.

There are certainly autobiographical/historical elements in the
novel, including the main conflict in the fictional community of Forks,
and these elements adhere to the character of the protagonist.

> Tom Joseph was modeled very loosely upon a fellow I worked
> with. His family were Suiattle and lived near the ranger sta-
> tion in Darrington. I placed Tom Joseph's house where his
> family's house was. However, Tom Joseph is an entirely fic-
> tional character, with more of me in him than anyone else. I
> suppose one could say that I split my own character into Tom
> and the wilderness ranger who tries to help him. I was the
> wilderness ranger there, yet I think Tom's character is proba-
> bly much closer to my own. I know all that country well, hiked
> all those trails, climbed Glacier Peak by the route Tom takes, by
> myself once and with friends once. And finally, I was very dis-
> turbed to discover a copper company's plans to put an open
> pit mine at Image Lake. (Personal correspondence, 12 May
> 2001. All future references to personal correspondence will be
> cited by date only.)

The issue of conservation in our country has been an ongoing and
emotional one for generations. The focus currently, as always, is
change: Should the community continue as it has or evolve in another
direction? Owens personalizes the issue through his characters and
their interaction, drawing upon those people from his own experience who must answer this question in "the real world" of contemporary economic survival.

The construction of Owens's fictional characters also resonates for
a reader conversant in the works of other Native writers. Characters
in the novel have autobiographical analogs, but they also evoke a
mingling of fictional voices. The character of McBride is a good
example. McBride evolved from one of Owens's personal acquain-
tances, a Native American activist: "The physical description and the
personality . . . including the green eyes" all derive from him (2
August 2001). However, it is difficult to read the description of this
character without evoking the shadow of D'Arcy McNickle, one of
the novelists Owens has written about quite often and to whom he

devotes a chapter in *Other Destinies*. Interestingly, scholars quite often discuss the way that the story of the main character in McNickle's first novel, Archilde in *The Surrounded*, is so closely patterned after McNickle's own life. Likewise, Archilde's story is about change and his search for identity, as is Tom Joseph's in *Wolfsong*. There are other similarities between *The Surrounded* and *Wolfsong* as well.

When McBride visits the Josephs late in the novel, the one descriptive detail about his physical appearance that is repeated is those green eyes. Such a detail, though, evokes Silko's *Ceremony*, in which green eyes mark the "mixedblood," including Tayo. The idea of mixed ancestry and self-identity is raised again by *Wolfsong*'s narrator a page later. "He [Tom] thought about the fact that McBride had been through a lot of ceremonies that he knew nothing about and how funny that was. He was the fullblood, but McBride, who'd grown up on the old Flathead reservation, seemed more Indian in some ways with his seven-eighths white ancestry" (183). McNickle is called forth again by the location of his childhood and the blood quantum most often attributed to him.

Owens's character, when considered in relation to McNickle and his canon, extends the discourse about identity politics that is presented in the novel. The character McBride represents a locus, of sorts, wherein an added level of understanding is offered for an initiated audience through the evocation of critical debates about the author McNickle: his ancestry, his accomplishments, his own fictional constructions and contributions. Within the novel, McBride inhabits one place on a rainbow of characters who are defined—by some—by race but who also resist or revise that definition and the criteria upon which identity is established, much as McNickle's life exemplifies. There are many other characters on that rainbow. Tom's brother, Jimmy, is also "fullblood," but he very actively tries to identify, economically and philosophically, with "white"—with those who wish to continue the extractive economies of the heyday of logging in the valley. His life is made easier by doing.

Tom's story echoes Archilde's in other, structural ways. He, too, returns home after a year in the wide world, walking down the lane to his family's home to find his mother—eyes weary—sitting out-side her house. This motif had almost reached the status of a con-vention by 1987, when Bill Bevis termed it "homing-in." Owens frames the event, however, and thereby provides contexts and sub-texts for the story that is about to unfold. McNickle's novel begins with a homecoming, then builds to a conflict and resolution of sorts (and this is where our readings of the novel originally diverged); *Wolfsong* begins with the conflict—Jim Joseph's stand against the road building—and then opens the frame to follow Tom Joseph on his long way home, an extension of the earlier texts' convention of homecoming that also foregrounds the central characters and issues, "giving the trees and mountains and streams and glaciers a voice."

For instance, when I read the descriptive passage focused on the front yard of the Joseph house, I am reminded of McNickle's descrip-tion of Archilde's uncle's home, old Modeste's camp, but in Owens's narrative landscape the vegetation becomes representative of a recur-rent refrain throughout the novel—irrepressible plant life reclaiming the place and thus providing a "voice" of resistance for the moun-tains and forests against human incursions. The reader can find a subtext to the descriptive detail throughout the novel that adds yet another layer of complication: a space promoting further dialogue.

There are other home yards described that deserve scrutiny, as can be seen in one of the first local characters Owens introduces as Tom makes his way home: "Old John," who is quickly renamed "Mad John" due to the community's reactions to his behavior. As Owens notes, such characters are a lived reality in some communi-ties. "Many characters in the novel are based on people I knew when I worked up there, some based quite closely on those people. . . . You see, you cannot make up things that fine. I gathered many such sto-ries from logger friends in the town, really wonderful people with huge hearts and a love for the place. Of course, I could only use a minute fraction of such stories in the novel" (12 May 2001). When he responded to my draft discussion of this character, Owens extended his use of local characters to include him: "Mad John was a very real person in and around Darrington. He didn't really have the rusting tractor with the sign about Jesus in the blackberry patch, however; I saw that tractor and sign somewhere to the north of Darrington, maybe around Rockport" (2 August 2001).

John is a preacher, we are told, one who has visions indiscernible to most of the valley's people—he "sees" demons in the wilderness. One cannot help but think of John "Big Bluff" Tosamah in N. Scott Momaday's novel, *House Made of Dawn*, who also is given to preaching through parable, but also their Christian antecedent, the visionary John the Baptist. At once, this character evokes the age-old presentation of European cosmological orientations transplanted to the "New World" wherein the wilderness is equated with the lack of heavenly order and therefore the devil. This is easy enough to identify, a recognizable convention; however, in the opening chapter the narrator has Jim Joseph also see shapes and shadows in the wilderness, but he reacts to them from a very different orientation. He talks to them and then dances with them. The underlying suggestion is intriguing. In this fictional landscape, despite dramatic change, spirits still dwell.

Moreover, read from this orientation and based on a long acquaintance with place, Mad John's behavior has an added element of irony, for this reader at least, that is likewise tied to the descriptive detail of the landscape. Tom and Amel pass his house and see Mad John hacking the blackberry vines that encroach upon it and threaten to eradicate it over time. The description of the yard foreshadows that of Tom's own home a few pages later, with notable, significant differences. The blackberry has a wide distribution in the Northwest, but like the immigrants themselves, it is a hybrid. *Rubus ursinus* is the only indigenous blackberry. It is no longer as common as it once was, since others—the Evergreen and Himalayan—were introduced by the Americans, who used *Rubus ursinus* for selective crossbreeding. The hybrids found a ready environment in which they thrived far beyond the farmers' fields and altered the place forever. Their pleasurable flavor has resulted in a changed valley since the advent of the Europeans. Philosophically, Mad John is hacking his metaphoric cousin.

But Tom also remembers John from years gone by, when John would storm into the Josephs' yard, with its own derelict vehicles and extensive undergrowth much like John's but Modeste's as well. Tom and his brother would then flee to take refuge in the vines of the salmonberry, an indigenous, seasonal berry. His mother, however, would only laugh at Mad John's loud pronouncements and offer him coffee. Like the Josephs, this local character lives on the margins and has a relationship with the locale that most others cannot comprehend.

Characters who complicate the essentialist ideals of racial binaries abound. In other words, Owens once again adopts a convention of racial distinction as constructed in other books but then extends that convention in a way that challenges its underlying assumptions. He does not simply present the "Stehemish" as eco-warrior stereotypes, nor as the only ones who can come to know and appreciate place. Ranger Grider is but one further example. Like Tom, he has hiked the trails and knows the mountains, and also like Tom, he wonders about what has changed, what has been lost and could be lost in the future, due to the ongoing colonial history of the valley. He, too, thinks back to the generations of Stehemish of the past. When Tom shares some cultural history about Dakobed with the ranger, their exchange provides a lesson about loss and reclamation that Tom is beginning to learn:

> He looked at Grider. "My tribe used to call her Dakobed."
> "Why do you say 'used to'? Don't you still call her that?"
> Tom looked at the ranger with surprise and thought for a moment about the question.
> "It means something like mother or the source, doesn't it?" Grider asked.
> Tom nodded. "I thought you just started here this summer."
> "That's right. I worked on the Bob Marshall before this."
> "So how do you know things like that?"
> Grider smiled. "I read books. I went to college like you."
> (167)

The emphasis on the verb tense derives from debates about representations of Indian history and cultural survivance from the era, but it is raised by the non-Stehemish character. Moreover, the accumulation of knowledge from all available sources can complement lived experience, as it does here, and the two need not be antithetical, nor racially restrictive.[1]

Owens extends the possibility, but this is not to suggest that Tom and Grider reflect a contemporary reenactment of Natty Bumppo and Chingachgook. While those conventional narrative antecedents certainly reside in the shadows for readers, Owens's characters subvert them, refocusing readers' attention on the shared—or not shared—values the characters' behavior epitomizes. How do they stand on the issue of the mine, and therefore reveal their concept of self in relationship with their world? It is Grider, after all, who offers a legal solution to the mine conflict: the Endangered Species Act would protect the falcons who nest near Image Lake. Owens's fascination with another American literary genius, John Steinbeck, about whom he has written critical studies, makes a great deal of sense in this context, for his values reflect those of someone like Grider.

> I'm interested in perhaps writing another book about John Steinbeck, believe it or not, as a very early ecologist. I think that's an aspect of Steinbeck that has never been appreciated enough. . . . I think it's because his worldview is very close to what you might find in those [Native] communities, and what Steinbeck is arguing in his writing is that we have to be responsible for what he terms the whole thing, knowable and unknowable, in a very deep way. (Purdy "Clear Waters," 17–18)

There are other refrains in the novel that provide an antistrophe of our readings of other authors—for instance, the central ecological conflict: the mine. The mining of uranium at Laguna Pueblo became a divisive issue for the people there, too, and the mine itself is a central point of reference in the land and therefore the work of Leslie

Marmon Silko. In her fist novel, *Ceremony*, the final confrontation between the character who represents a positive force for the communal future (Tayo) and those who represent destruction and evil (Emo and his crew) takes place at the mine site; in *Wolfsong*, Tom Joseph blows up the water tower at the mine site, killing J. D. Hill, the developer/industrialist who would destroy Image Lake and its surroundings. A reader versed in Silko's canon might say "evil is dead for now," but not in ways that Tayo conceives.

Tayo's inaction is a deliberate and enlightened decision. Tom's actions, however, have inadvertent consequences, "the kind of unanticipated violence that usually accompanies trickster acts. In fact, there is a coyote story of a destructive flood up in the Northwest that lurks at the base of the incident in the novel, that unleashing of dangerous waters" (2 August 2001). The element of chance—but a chance that is everything but random and indifferent—can be found in other works by Native authors as well, but here Owens found complementary resonance with authors who may not be easily evoked if one reads the novel simply as a work of some essentialist idea of "Indian literature."

> Candidly speaking, I was also nodding there to Eliot and a perverse sort of freeing of waters that stands in contrast to the cycle of water that is a motif running through the novel. I think the Fisher King story illuminates both a deep sense of humanity's relatedness to the natural world and an equal sense (a guilty sense) that Western man has desecrated that world and that relationship. The familiar coyote story is why the ravens comment on the event of the water tank destruction and [Hill's] death. To act is to open the world up to unintended violence; there's no exception to the rule. To act is to risk things. Tom acts. (2 August 2001)

Both Tayo's and Archilde's actions/inactions, and therefore stories, reach a cusp in their respective conflicts: Tayo hides in the rocks above the mine and recognizes the story patterns that have shaped his own, and Archilde anticipates and then watches as Elise shoots Sheriff Quigley, who has come to the roadless mountains, interestingly enough, to arrest him for the murder of a game warden. The motif, the conventional refrain, is quite familiar in *Wolfsong*; however, here the protagonist, also recognizing the influences that have shaped his own character, "lights out for the territory." In fact, I cannot read the conclusion of *Wolfsong* without feeling a further slight twinge of recognition and wonder: Does Tom Joseph's standoff on that mountain ridge resonate with the conclusion of James Welch's *The Death of Jim Loney*? If so, the conclusions of the two novels reflect a further similarity and ambiguity when considered together. Loney, who throughout the novel is continually described in terms of the wolf, seemingly transcends the restrictive, racist world as he is shot and falls, transforming into the mysterious bird he has seen time and time again in his vision.[2] Tom's acceptance of the Wolf power, however, provides him with the strength and will to survive, even if it means exile. The potential for both action that thwarts the influence of people like J. D. Hill *and* survival is heartening. A future is assured.

I asked Owens if he had thought of a sequel to the novel, and if so, what Tom Joseph would be doing today.

I've been urged a number of times to write a sequel, and I've considered it. I see the novel as an incomplete circle. Tom has left home and gone south to Santa Barbara, moving south and west. He's now left home again, this time moving north and east. When the circle is completed, he should be back in his home valley. A sequel would have to take place in Forks, in that valley. However, the sequel I've imagined features Tom as an extremely old man, in the last months of his life, maybe eighty or older. He has never married. Jimmy has died long before, and the family ends with Tom. (This is not a Vanishing American story.) I imagine Tom as someone who has made peace with his anger and with the world, who has come back because he could not live apart from those rivers and those mountains where the stories of his people live. I think he must be wise but of what sort would that wisdom be? What has he learned? That is what the book must be about. I've had so many things I've wanted and needed to write about that I've never undertaken that sequel. It might still happen. (12 May 2001)

The motif of "an extremely old man" reflecting back on his life can be found in the movie *Little Big Man*, to which Owens makes reference in *Other Destinies* during a discussion of Indian identity and Michael Dorris's novel *Yellow Raft on Blue Water*. In the proposed sequel as elsewhere, though, the nature of that reflection would no doubt be markedly different: the resonance would transform.

For readers who have a background in contemporary Native literatures, then, the quiet refrains, the intermingling of voices from other authors are numerous in the novel; from Karen's dream of bears (as in Silko, Momaday, and Vizenor) to Jim Joseph's memory of boarding school, where tongues were cut out and replaced with new ones, the literary web extends as Owens's novel and reader intersect with them. This can be seen in its resonance with Welch's own first novel, *Winter in the Blood*. One of its most comic scenes is the burial of the unnamed protagonist's grandmother, who has been painted up by the town's mortician and placed in a gaudy coffin that is too large for the grave. It is not a good fit in any sense of the word, as the protagonist recognizes. The antistrophe is enacted with Jim Joseph's funeral, in a coastal rain forest that has its own character. Although the hearse (and its driver) must be coaxed over the muddy road to the "Indian" cemetery, the coffin slides into its welcoming grave: "As they lowered the coffin the roots brushed the sides lovingly" (52). Later, after his mother's funeral, though, Tom Joseph has his own revelation of old ways and transplanted customs; he rips each headstone—his father's, mother's, and uncle's—from its place and tosses them into the river. The graves and their inhabitants disappear back into the land.

Or one might consider the following description of Tom's climb in the mountains: "When he breathed, the air had lost its cutting edge, and the day came streaming together where he stood. In a land of rain such a day was a gift, a thing to be prayed for. He wished he knew such a prayer, something in the old language, but he was inarticulate before such beauty, his tongue a heavy, dead thing" (93).

I cannot encounter the word "inarticulate" here without its evoking *House Made of Dawn*, where Abel's own homecoming is a failure due to his loss of language:

> Had he been able to say it, anything of his own language— even the commonplace formula of greeting "Where are you going"—which had no being beyond sound, no visible substance, would once again shown him whole to himself; but he was dumb. Not dumb—silence was the older and better part of custom still—but *inarticulate*. (Emphasis in the original, 58)

But the *Wolfsong* passage resonates as well with Tayo's dawn song as he prepares for his own climb into the mountains, up Mount Taylor, when he searches for the spotted cattle in *Ceremony*, a journey that will result in the return of the rains and terminate the drought that has plagued the land since Tayo's own homecoming, likewise a failure to this point. Both would pray, in a sense, to the sun. Tayo's journey up the mountain is successful due to the intervention of a being long thought to be extinct, like the wolf in Owens's novel—the mountain lion. A reading of Silko's novel closely complements and compliments a reading of *Wolfsong* in a number of other interesting ways.

Like Tayo's father, Tom Joseph's father is obscure, and it is his uncle who ho raises him, bringing him to a degree of understanding, at least, of the ancient ways of life in the valley. Tom's mother most closely resembles Tayo's Auntie, whose melding of tradition and Christianity is clearly evoked in the image of her Bible with its eagle-feather bookmark (76). Like Tayo, Tom faces the loss of the knowledge—provided by stories—that previous generations possessed about their relationship with their land, and this loss places the future in doubt. How does one maintain the delicate balance necessary to keep the world alive and vital, if the stories of that maintenance are lost? As Momaday once said, oral literature is only one generation removed from extinction, and this is an underlying concern of both novels. It is a realization about change that Tom Joseph has faced for quite some time:

> He'd come to the wilderness first as a boy, stepping in the bootprints of his uncle, and the wilderness had been an enormous, boundless world of meadows and waterfalls, silver lakes, granite and ice. But as he'd grown, the wilderness had shrunk, and he'd come, finally, to know the smallness, the delicacy of the place, a fragment of what had once been, with everything connected so carefully like the strands of a spider's web across a path at sunrise. (82)

One hears Old Ku'oosh's words to Tayo in *Ceremony:*

> "But you know, grandson, this world is fragile."
> The word he chose to express "fragile" was filled with the intricacies of a continuing process, and with the strength inherent in spider webs woven across paths through sand hills where early in the morning the sun becomes entangled in each filament of the web. (35)

The echoes of refrains are myriad. Both Tayo and Tom come to realize that they have retained more of the past than they originally believed, and each comes, with help, to a vision of the future that hinges upon his acceptance of an identity that is referential to that past.

And here a discussion of the similarities should cease. While there is a benefit to looking at the novel's relatives and thus recognizing its location in relationship to them, to make comparisons such as these one too often seeks the minutiae of common denominators and by doing so reduces texts to generalizations, to the conventions that Owens's works resist. The "Stehemish" are not Pueblo, nor Gros Ventre, nor the equally fictionalized "Little Elk" of McNickle's last novel. Their histories, cultures, and environments—both physical and social as well as fictional—are dramatically different, and thus the beneficial influence of Owens's firsthand intimacy with the Northwest, and with the economies and lifestyles that inhere in this land. Much like the blackberry, the conventions of literature transplanted to this landscape are responsive to the local and the indigenous. Elsewhere—in essays and subsequently in *Other Destinies*—borrowing from a quotation from McNickle, Owens refers to this difference as a variation of "the map of the mind," an idea alluded to in *Wolfsong*.[3] We might also consider the varying maps of the mind between the "mingling voices" in dialogue during the *"occasion* for interaction," the reading of the novel.

I would argue that it is the "voice" of the place and its lifeways that provides further, complicated layers of reading, and that this is itself an extension of the various intertextual resonances one finds in the novel. The physical *presence* of this land transforms its fictional chorus. I have touched on this above, as I explored the characters and my reading of them in light of characters from other books. However, it is in the language itself that one of Owens's talents reveals itself: his ability to deploy the metaphoric potential of descriptive detail, wherein the familiar is made visible in a new light. To illustrate this, I would like to examine a fairly lengthy passage from early in the novel in which the Joseph family travels to the cemetery to bury Jim Joseph. While it is immensely evocative of place, of "local" color, the description carries much more with it.

The family travels to the cemetery in Gordon's new Buick, and with them comes the preacher, who agrees with Gordon's assessment of Jim Joseph's mental state: "crazy as a coon" (45). As the preacher ponders this, he looks out the window:

> In a yard beside the road he saw a white dog lunging at the end of its chain, snarling at the car with a mouth as red as blood. The dog's coat shone with rain, and its feet were braced in two inches of mud. On the ridge of the framed house behind the dog, two ravens watched with cocked heads.
>
> The three vehicles left the asphalt and rattled along a Forest Service road, the tires kicking small rocks up to ping against the pickup and Buick. Jenny's husband slowed to get out of range of the pickup tires, cursing softly when the first pebble rang from the car's bumper. The Buick's wide, heavy wipers

swept clean swaths across the windshield, and the rain beaded on the waxed hood.

After half an hour along the straight gravel road between narrow lines of tall, dark second-growth, the hearse slowed and turned to the right on a wide path of mud and clay hacked from a wall of vine maple and alder and vines. (46)

Is there more here than a simple setting of the stage and a localizing of the characters?

> I can say that I wanted to accomplish at least a couple of things there. I wanted to invoke a sense of human-constructed boundary and control: yard, framed house, dog chain. And I wanted to open the scene with a symbol that couldn't be nailed down very easily, a symbol that threatened to break its chain and get at the reader. And then I wanted the reader to have a sense of easing uneasily into a kind of vegetative world, as if the reader is in a sense being buried, with much difficulty, in the scene. It should echo the opening scene of the novel, with the immersion of Jim Joseph in the wilderness itself. To demarcate the places where we are buried is to reinforce the false and dangerous boundaries. Tom reacts to this intuitively when he tries to eradicate the grave markers. Graves frame the dead, gravestones chain us to particular time and place. (2 August 2001)

In other words, given these impulses, the scene carries many of the novel's central concerns, and Owens's playful response—"gravestones chain us"—can resonate with our own initial reactions to the scene.

The image of control is obvious, from the carving of lots and private property from the vegetative world to the chain itself, all of which provides the suggestive stage that the two crows watch so intently. Moreover, the pervasive wetness that might provide some of the "un-ease" for readers versed in rainy funerals gives us at once the local and the universal. This is all very familiar: I've seen that house and dog, or ones so very much like it. Vine maple, alder, vines, crows, and Forest Service gravel roads with the ping of rocks on undercarriages echoing in the background. There is a comfort to the Buick's ease, the sweep of those wipers as the rain falls outside while we are buried safely within its shell. Yet at once pragmatic and fiscally responsible—damaged cars require repair, and one that is well maintained lasts longer—Gordon's caution speaks volumes of the pervasive, the invisible, the utilitarian economics of our society and day. This one Indian character—from "down river" in the terms of derision of the locals—conveys it all. The machine he drives and the intricate mechanisms and institutions that lurk behind it control his actions and determine our lives, our futures, unless we act otherwise.

Wolfsong may be "second growth," coming on the heels of generations of authors and texts that preceded its publication, but it certainly has its own originality in the complicated and myriad voices with which it speaks. It may bear some resemblance to those earlier texts, as any book on similar subjects and with similar concerns may resonate with certain refrains, but it also extends those subjects and concerns into a landscape that alters them, wraps them in vines, and roots them in a figurative language that transforms readers' worlds. "Forest Service" will never read the same as it did before this novel was written.

NOTES

1. The possibility that scholarship may provide lost knowledge has been raised earlier: "It occurred to him [Tom] that there must be books that would tell him about his ancestors."

2. For further discussion of this, see my essay, "Bha'a and *The Death of Jim Loney*."

3. Tom Joseph recognizes this at the town meeting to discuss the mine proposal, as he surveys the people who attend. (See page 121.)

WORKS CITED

Bevis, William. "Native American Novels: Homing In." *Recovering the Word: Essays on Native American Literature*. Ed. Brian Swann and Arnold Krupat. Berkeley: U of California P, 1987.

McNickle, D'Arcy. *The Surrounded*. Albuquerque: U of New Mexico P, 1977.

———. *Wind from an Enemy Sky*. New York: Harper and Row, 1979.

Momaday, N. Scott. *House Made of Dawn*. New York: Harper and Row, 1968.

Purdy, John. "Bha'a and *The Death of Jim Loney*." *Studies in American Indian Literatures* 11.1 (winter 1987): 17–25. Reprinted in *Studies in American Indian Literatures: Series 1 and 2* (compendium issue), 1977–92.

———. "Clear Waters: A Conversation with Louis Owens." *Studies in American Indian Literatures* 10.2 (summer 1998): 6–22.

Sarris, Greg. *Keeping Slug Woman Alive: A Holistic Approach to American Indian Texts*. Berkeley: U of California P, 1993.

Silko, Leslie Marmon. *Ceremony*. New York: Viking, 1977.

———. *Storyteller*. New York: Arcade, 1981.

Welch, James. *The Death of Jim Loney*. New York: Harper and Row, 1979.

———. *Winter in the Blood*. New York: Harper and Row, 1974.

CHAPTER NINE

NOT THE CALL OF THE WILD

The Idea of Wilderness in Louis Owens's
Wolfsong *and* Mixedblood Messages

DAVID BRANDE

L ouis Owens's *Mixedblood Messages*, in addition to contributing
to Native American literary criticism, develops Owens's treatment of what are inextricably interconnected issues: the survival of indigenous tribal social forms, the preservation of intact
ecosystems, and the complicated tensions between dominant Euramerican environmental practices and ideologies, on one hand, and
indigenous tribal ways of inhabiting and representing the landscape, on the other. In his fiction and criticism Owens addresses the
difficulties that arise when these sets of questions are broached
simultaneously—as, I think he would argue, they must be. My
intention here is primarily to explore Owens's treatment of the idea
of "wilderness" in *Mixedblood Messages* and his first novel, *Wolfsong*.
I argue that these two texts locate a particular Euramerican notion
of "wilderness" within the long history of territorial and cultural
colonization on this continent, characterizing it as an idealist and
ahistorical category that does not denote the pristine opposite of
Euramerican environmental depredation but rather constitutes a
compensatory fantasy of that dominant culture—a fantasy that
erases the historical presence of Native peoples. Owens's response

to this notion is informed by his dual commitments to Native American cultural politics and to environmental preservation and is complicated by his self-conscious approach to what, in *Mixedblood Messages*, he calls the "frontier" between the Native and the Euramerican. Therefore, in addition to contextualizing the notion of wilderness, Owens's work also addresses fundamental and controversial questions about Native identity and (heterogeneous and dynamic) tribal orientations toward nonhuman nature. That is, alongside Owens's critique of the idea of wilderness is a discussion of the epistemological and political status of Native representations of Native attitudes toward the land. This discussion, explicit in *Mixedblood Messages*, is implicit in *Wolfsong* but no less powerful; indeed, the novel complicates the questions surrounding Native claims to a fundamentally different and more sustainable relationship with nonhuman nature by squarely facing the cultural and psychic consequences of colonization: the pervasive and insidious nature of Euramerican stereotypes of Native Americans and the difficulty of separating these stereotypes from that which they misrepresent. Nonetheless, I argue that in both texts Owens stages a kind of Native "standpoint epistemology" of the environment, based on long-term tenure in particular ecosystems, that both undercuts the dominant-culture idea of "wilderness" and counters recent skeptical attacks on any claims on behalf of specifically tribal orientations to the land.

For readers not familiar with the plot of *Wolfsong*, a short summary of the narrative will establish the geographical, economic, and cultural context of the protagonist's trajectory—a trajectory that both traces the effects of dominant-culture environmental thought and practice (including the notion of wilderness) and, finally, outlines a trickster narrative that is no less powerful for its subtlety and irony. In *Wolfsong* a young man, Tom Joseph, descended from a fictional Salish tribe, comes home after a year at UC Santa Barbara to an economically depressed logging town in the North Cascades to attend the burial of his uncle. At home he becomes as distressed as his uncle was about a copper mine under development in a nearby "wilderness" area. (This is historically accurate in that Kennicot Copper—

"Honeycutt," in the novel—owns mineral rights in the Glacier Peak Wilderness and can develop them when it chooses.) The uncle, before his death, has hidden himself in the mountains, putting bullet holes in the D8 caterpillars cutting the road into the mine site—not, presumably, because he hopes to stop the mine but to express his intractable resistance to it. The title of *Wolfsong* refers to the uncle's spirit-helper, which he "wills" to his nephew before his death and which draws Tom to follow his uncle in somehow resisting the mine. Consciously, Tom simply wants to return home to his native valley, where he feels closer to the mystery of his own cultural and familial origins—seemingly distant origins, given the virtual disappearance of his tribe from the valley and the early death of his father. The economics of life in the valley are harsh, though, with the mine and its road building quickly becoming the only game in town—one Tom finds unacceptable given the degree to which he has internalized his uncle's values with regard to the land. There seems to be little Tom can do to stop the mine, and he finds it impossible to resettle in the valley, to coexist with the ex-loggers and soon-to-be ex-loggers with whom he grew up. Tom's sometimes violent conflicts with valley residents only sharpen the necessity for him to win some understanding of his identity in relation to his ancestral and geographic origins. Finally, after the death of his mother, Tom blows up a water tank at the mine site, unintentionally killing a man. The conclusion of the story represents Tom's escape from the men who are tracking him after the killing and the beginning of his flight to Canada, where, it is implied, he will find sanctuary with a small intertribal community he has visited earlier in the story.

The description of Tom's escape strongly suggests that he has gained the assistance of his uncle's spirit-helper, the wolf, and it suggests his association with the trickster, who, in oral tradition, will always return to exhibit forms of instructive mischief. From this point of view the story's final word, "END," which could be read as a despairing commentary on the novel's various losses, is instead an ironic signifier of the survival of the tribal subject and tribal lifeways.[1] The influence on Owens of Gerald Vizenor's trickster

narratives and self-consciously postmodernist criticism, which
Owens discusses throughout *Mixedblood Messages,* underscores the
interpretation of this "conclusion" as the mark of an ironic tribal
counternarrative to the myth of the vanishing Indian.

If Tom's character takes part in the trickster in anything like
Vizenor's terms, however, it means that he is less a "protagonist"
than an ongoing act of signification of tribal values and survival.[2]
As Owens remarks in *Mixedblood Messages,* in his mind "the true
protagonist of *Wolfsong* is the so-called wilderness itself, a place I
felt and still feel that I knew as well as anyone alive" (22). (Owens
worked for the Forest Service in the Glacier Peak—or Dakobed—
area for several years.) If his anthropomorphizing of wilderness is a
familiar-enough trope to readers of environmental literature, however, his "so-called" introduces less familiar and less comfortable
issues. To call attention to the linguistic and therefore sociohistorical
nature of the signifier "wilderness" risks appearing—depending on
one's audience—either to state the obvious or to give aid and comfort to the forces of brown rapacity and environmental destruction
and to descend into the dark mazes of academic skepticism. But as
Roderick Nash argues in the first line of *Wilderness and the American
Mind,* "'Wilderness' has a deceptive concreteness at first glance."
And as Max Oelschlaeger remarks, arguing for the ontogenetic
nature of language and thus the necessity of thinking through the
signification of wilderness, language studies "are fundamental to
exposing and then overcoming the presuppositions which entrench
the distinction between nature and culture" (273). This exposition
and overcoming is, I believe, Owens's point; one of the most important aspects of Owens's work generally is the care and sophistica-
tion with which he represents the thorough imbrication—the indi-
visibility—of what we call culture and what we call nature. *Wolfsong,*
in its treatment of conflicts over wilderness preservation and resource
extraction, firmly situates the symbolic forms of culture (including the
idea of wilderness) within *more* or *less* sustainable ways of making
a living within particular ecosystems.

Early in the novel, Owens explicitly calls into question the onto-
logical status of "wilderness" and indicates the cultural and sociopolitical context of this notion. On one of his trips into the high Cascades
around Dakobed, Tom has his brother Jimmy—who is invested in
assimilation and resource extraction as his survival strategies—drop
him off at a trailhead that has become a road head, the beginning of
the new road into the mine site, the road project itself an opportunity to log old-growth cedar. The narrator tells us that "[t]he mountains had been taken from Indian people by white invaders and had
been taken from the invaders by the invaders' government and
made an official wilderness area by government act" (80). Here
Owens forcefully situates the idea of wilderness within the context
of historical conflict over land and the authoritative legal discourse
of the dominant culture: "wilderness" as a product of the Wilderness Act, an *effect* of culture rather than its antecedent or Hegelian (or
Turnerian) antithesis. As fundamentally important as this place is
to Tom's identity, its status as "wilderness" is conventional and artifactual, and wilderness as artifact is contrasted on the same page
with "the raw scent of burning cedar" from a pile of stumps, from
the desecration of beings that the coastal Salish have historically
regarded as sacred. This contrast between the institutional under-
pinnings of "wilderness," on one hand, and the raw sensory input
of burning cedar, on the other, points to what are, at base, epistemological differences—differences between what counts for knowledge in oral and literate cultures. This is consistent with Owens's
remark in *Mixedblood Messages* calling attention to the ways "Native
Americans are beginning . . . to demand that non-Indian readers
acknowledge different epistemologies" (4). I would stress that epistemological differences are necessarily cultural and sociopolitical
differences, that epistemology is rooted in the social, in the ways in
which people organize their labor and structure their relations with
their environment. Oelschlaeger makes this point when he argues
that "science is inextricably entangled with the culture that sustains
it," although he then goes on to make the somewhat confusing

remark that "[o]nly a few intellects of our century have grasped this crucially important fact" (292). He mentions Einstein and Leopold in this connection but makes no reference to the many scholars engaged in the sociology and anthropology of science or in ethnobotany, no reference to the challenges posed to Euramerican scientific, juridical, and political epistemologies by tribal peoples and lifeways—a challenge kept alive over five centuries of colonialism, genocide, and ecocide.

The designated wilderness area, then, as such, is an artifact of a literate, institutional culture with specific epistemological assumptions—with its own assumptions about how best to know the world and its underlying assumption that the land is a stock of resources to be either efficiently exploited or set apart from industrial resource extraction (in an aestheticist and capitalist version of the sacred, in which natural beauty is reserved and invested over the long term). On the other hand, Tom's experience of "the raw scent of burning cedar," like so much of the novel, invites readers to entertain the possibility of a different approach to nonhuman nature, an approach that is at once more directly physical and more frankly metaphysical. That is, Tom is driven to experience physical contact with a landscape that is metaphysically significant:

> He stared at the white mountain, the center, the great mother [the Salish *Dakobed* roughly translates as "Great Mother"], and tried to feel what it had meant to his tribe. They had woven it over thousands of years into their stories, telling themselves who they were and would always be in relation to the beautiful peak. Through their relationship with the mountain, they knew they were significant, a people to be reckoned with upon the earth. (92)

Rather than seeing the mountain as an inert feature of the geography—an economically valuable feature, given its mineral deposits and timber—Tom attempts to recreate the sense of reciprocity his tribe had felt in relation to it. Millennia of physical proximity to the mountain had allowed for the sedimentation, the stratification, of a cultural identity achieved through an oral tradition that is predicated on the mountain's presence and that establishes and celebrates the mountain's metaphysical role in the life of the tribe.[3] Tom struggles to call up the "blood memory" that would tie him to this place, the sense of belonging and rootedness that was the effect, fundamentally, of the oral stories and indigenous epistemology of his tribal ancestors, and which is different from the epistemology of the literate, institutional culture that creates "wilderness."

In *Mixedblood Messages* Owens claims in all seriousness that what is at stake in the clash between these two epistemologies is nothing less than the future of all life. He meditates on the two names of Glacier Peak/Dakobed as expressions of these two epistemologies and explores their practical and ecological implications:

> At the center of the Glacier Peak Wilderness . . . is the vastly beautiful mountain named on maps, most unimaginatively, Glacier Peak. We look at the peak and see glaciers, and the text of the mountain is laid bare. There are other names for the peak, however, one of which is Dakobed . . . The local Indian people, the Suiattle, look at Dakobed and see the place from which they came, the place where they were born, the mother earth. Their stories tell them they are related in an ancient and crucial way to this magnificent peak. There is an . . . invaluable message in this knowledge, for whereas a society may well mine the heart out of something called a natural resource, one does not violate one's mother. The future of that wilderness and, of course, the future of all life depends upon whose stories we listen to. (211)

Naming, this passage suggests, is a compressed form of narrative, in which cultural values and culturally specific epistemologies condense into place-names expressing underlying assumptions about the relations between humans and nonhuman nature. The name "Glacier Peak" is not merely unimaginative; it is generic, reflecting a lack of long, intimate contact with the land. "Dakobed," on the other hand, is the linguistic expression of millennia of physical proximity; more importantly, the name itself is a normative, constraining act, an instance of performative language that establishes a particular form of relationship between human and nonhuman ("one does not violate one's mother"), a relationship that is more sustainable than the relationship between "natural resource" and scientific-industrial society.[4] In the novel, then, Owens dramatizes Tom's yearning for participation in an epistemological order that has been thoroughly displaced from the valley, and in Mixedblood Messages he indicates what he takes to be at stake in that displacement—namely, every-thing. In both texts the signifier "wilderness" is a central part of the symbolic field on which these fundamentally different epistemolo-gies clash. And while Tom and his uncle both wish the physical char-acter of the designated wilderness area to be preserved against resource extraction, and in this their interests coincide with those of the white environmentalists who make a brief appearance in the story, the designation of wilderness brings with it peculiar assump-tions about the relationship between people and nonhuman nature, assumptions having consequences for indigenous people.

Owens dramatizes those assumptions and their consequences in an autobiographical story in the short chapter "Burning the Shelter" in Mixedblood Messages, describing an experience from his employ-ment as a seasonal ranger with the Forest Service in the area in which Wolfsong is set. The story bears directly on Native presences in and perspectives on what the dominant culture calls wilderness. Sent into Glacier Peak Wilderness to take part in a Forest Service plan to remove all human-made objects from the area, Owens has the task of destroying a very old and partially collapsed shelter in a meadow high on the mountain. He writes that after five days of hard labor in bad weather he felt "very smug . . . about returning the White Pass meadow to its 'original' state" (215). On his way down the mountain, however, he stops to talk to two elderly Salish women on their way up to the shelter, and he learns to his discomfort that the structure he has just proudly destroyed was built by their father. As one of them says, "We been coming up here each year since we was little. . . . A long time ago, this was all our land . . . all Indi'n land everywhere you can see. Our people had houses up in these mountains, for gathering berries every year" (215). The conclusions Owens draws from this experience are worth quoting:

> Gradually, almost painfully, I began to understand that what I called "wilderness" was an absurdity, nothing more than a figment of the European imagination. An "absolute fake." Before the European invasion, there was no wilderness in North America; there was only the fertile continent where people lived in a hard-learned balance with the natural world. In embracing a philosophy that saw the White Pass shelter—and all traces of humanity—as a shameful stain upon the "pure" wilderness, I had succumbed to a five-hundred-year-old pattern of deadly thinking that separates us from the natural world. (216)

While he goes on to emphasize that this in no way means that what is today called wilderness does not need safeguarding, Owens seems clearly, here, to ground his own point of view in the practical, "hard-learned" insights of Native people, in a Native-standpoint epistemology of the environment. And Owens links the institution of wilderness to colonization when he says of the women, "[t]hey forgave me without saying it—my ignorance and my part in the long pattern of loss that they knew so well" (216). "Wilderness," then, overwrites tribal history and erases the presence of tribal people from the discourse and consciousness of the dominant culture.

"Wilderness," in the novel, also signifies Euramerica's alienation from and ambivalence toward nonhuman nature, the "pattern of deadly thinking" most economically staged in the character of an old logger who "loved nature and was deadly efficient at stripping it bare" (150). And, as Susan Bernardin argues, "Even the 'Sahara Clubbers,' who come to protest the mining and who, according to Tom, tend to romanticize Indians and wilderness share with those who demonize the land a sense of the land as 'other'" (86). In this, the story clearly implies that the modern Euramerican wilderness ethic is related to that which it generally casts as its opposite, suggesting that the ideology of wilderness is symptomatic of a larger conflict internal to the dominant culture—that the idea of wilderness is itself merely one aspect of a larger story about a culture that does not know how to live sustainably with nonhuman nature. On one hand, one finds unrestrained and unsustainable intervention in natural ecosystems, and on the other, a compensatory preservationist ethos that, while useful as a political counterweight, is nonetheless an attempt to purify nature of human involvement. That *Wolfsong* questions the preservationist impulse is clear from Jim Joseph's sarcastic remarks about white fly fishermen, those well-heeled emblems of ecologically sensitive participation in the outdoors. As part of his nephew's education, Joseph indicates the conflict between the practices of putatively enlightened white sportsmen and those of ancient subsistence economies:

> "These white people are funny," he [said] over his shoulder as they walked. "They want us to shoot old, tough bucks instead of young does. They don't want us to catch fish with nets because they want to stand out in the streams in rubber pants and catch them with chicken feathers. We eat the fish, but they stuff them and put them on walls. I've seen that, Tommy, fish on walls. Even just fish heads sometimes, with their mouths open like grizzly bears. It made me laugh." (36)

The tension between sport and sustenance is obvious in this passage, with its implications for the connections between white privilege and various environmental philosophies. What gives the passage its satirical sting is the implication that this kind of sport—as "low impact" as fly-fishing might wish to be—both alienates the participant from a direct experience of the world and infantilizes him/her: the fly fisher does not eat his/her catch but mounts or releases it, does not get wet but wears "rubber pants" (over Orvis diapers, perhaps). The artifice and restraint that lend fly-fishing, a "wilderness" pursuit, its occasionally self-righteous caché are, here, the evidence of its removal of itself from the trophic systems that make up the living body of the world.

The maintenance of boundaries (whether rubber or symbolic) between the *natural* and the *cultural*, in the service either of resource extraction or of "wilderness" preservation, is, Owens argues, at the root of Euramerican ideology and environmental destruction. Responding to arguments over the historical environmental practices of indigenous Americans, Owens indicates the persistent nature/culture dichotomy at the core of the dominant culture, a dichotomy that forecloses the possibility of either a sustainable living or a good understanding of indigenous peoples:

> According to one study, "little or no natural landscape" existed in southern California at the time the Spanish first arrived there. The author of the study assumes, of course, that humanity is not a "natural" part of the landscape; though herbivores grazing and thus altering the landscape is natural, human interaction with and imprint upon the same landscape is unnatural. This displacement of humanity from nature points to perhaps the most profound cause of humankind's destructive relationship with our environment. (224)

The context of this passage is, again, discussion of the environmental practices of indigenous Americans, the political implications of which I touch on below, but what is immediately pertinent is the connection Owens goes on to make between this displacement of humanity from nature and the notion of wilderness. After summarizing a description of indigenous land-use practices in what is now California, he writes, "They had not marked portions of it off as untouchable 'wilderness,' thus leaving the rest to be despoiled; rather, they had developed a sophisticated, holistic understanding of the ecosystems they inhabited and applied that understanding successfully" (224–25). Here, too, Owens appeals to historical indigenous practices as sustainable alternatives to dominant-culture ideas about both "natural resources" and "wilderness."

Given the widespread disappearance of sustainable land-use practices and the ensuing reliance of the vast majority of people on large-scale industrial systems, it is perhaps simple justice that Owens refrains from demonizing the loggers and other characters in *Wolfsong* who are eager to cut timber and mine copper out of the designated wilderness area. These characters are less evil than they are simply at a loss to imagine any alternatives to the ways of life to which they have been acculturated and which seem literally compulsive. One of the valley's old-timers reflects on what has been lost and the seeming inevitability of the causes:

> "What I'm getting at is that once this whole valley and all these mountains was the finest danged country a man could lay eyes on. And now most of it's been clearcut and got roads through it and most of the game's gone, and it's a crying shame. And it was fellas like me that done it, me and Floyd and Sam and the rest of you yahoos that made them roads and cut them trees and shot ever last grizzly and wolf below Canada. And you all know it ain't going to stop. There ain't no way it can stop. Now they're digging that open-pit mine up there, and pretty soon there'll be another reason to go a little further. Pretty soon there won't be nothing left." (185)

Tom's brother Jimmy, a logger, speaks from the point of view of the white newcomers who earned a living as long as there was timber to cut and who now see the mine as the only way for them to live and work in the valley. Jimmy says to Tom, "You go off to college and then you want to come back here and wander around that so-called wilderness pretending you're an honest-to-goodness indian talking about mother earth. That's great, but who's going to buy the porkchops you take on your backpack trips?" (120). In these lines Owens has Jimmy speak the same "so-called" the narrator speaks earlier in the story, as if, for all its fatal ignorance, the "resource extraction" mentality in the story does, at least, recognize that a living comes from the land—even if it refuses to consider the long-term effects of its modes of operation. Earlier, Jimmy says to Tom, "[Uncle Jim] didn't understand that Indian don't matter no more. What matters is that we're people and we have to live here, with other people like J.D. and all the rest. Hell, I don't even know what Indian means, and neither do you. All I know is there won't be any logging here pretty soon, and then what'll we do?" To which Tom responds,

"We'll do something else . . . Our people lived here a thousand years without logging. Even if everybody has to leave, every one of us, that's better than an open-pit mine" (112). And this, of course, is the choice Tom makes at the end of the novel, enacting his own tribal migration north to a community across the Canadian border.

Jimmy's comments about "honest-to-goodness" Indians and knowing what Indian means, though, ratchet up the intensity of the conflict, undercutting Tom's search for his origins and his stubborn belief that if the land was sacred to their uncle it ought to be sacred to them as well (33). For Jimmy, Indian identity is an anachronism and a losing proposition. In response to Tom's childhood talk of the wolf spirit, Jimmy had laughed and suggested that Tom focus on chainsaws and carburetors (35). For Tom, however, the question of the mine and the question of his own origins are inextricably bound up; his search for his cultural origins is one and the same as his search for his geographical origins—a desperate position for him to be in, while his geography of home undergoes the latest wave in a long, large-scale industrial assault: "He'd tried to imagine what it would've been like to have been a real Indian, before the whites came and began to cut the trees—and pay Indians to cut the trees—and everything changed" (37). It would seem, here, that for the young Tom Joseph, being a "real" Indian is incompatible with industrial resource extraction, but in apparent contradiction, he thinks of his brother the logger as genuinely "Indian" (161). In any case, for Tom identity is in large part a function of one's relation to the land, and this is, in a sense, not very different from the crew boss Vern Reese's sympathetic comment to Tom that Tom would never be a "real log-ger" because his "heart just ain't in it" (152). For characters on all sides of the resource-extraction issues, one's perspective on the world (one's epistemology, if you will) is conditioned by the specific nature of one's practical engagement with the landscape.

If this is the case, though, and timber has been king in the valley for a century and Tom's people have all but disappeared, Jimmy's remark that he "[doesn't] know what Indian means, and neither do you" would seem to have some force. Tom is in such confusion, after all, because, his mother tells him, "[t]here were things [Uncle Jim] couldn't teach you because they were lost to him just like they are lost to me and the others . . . [t]hings you would have to know now to stay in this valley" (77). This, then, is the underlying question Owens raises about the authenticity of Native cultures after European contact and colonization: What kind of regard should be paid to putatively Native epistemologies at the end of the twentieth century? More specifically, if "wilderness" is an artifact of Euramerican legal, aesthetic, literary, and political discourses, what is the epistemological and political status of Native claims to knowledge about Native occupancy of the land? In a passage from the novel immediately following the narrator's description of the wilderness area as legislative act, Tom remembers his Uncle Jim ruminating over the meaning of this piece of U.S. legislation:

> "This is a good thing they did," Uncle Jim had said, "because now maybe they won't cut all the trees and build roads. But if you think about it, it's pretty funny. When our people lived here long ago, before the white folks came, there wasn't any wilderness and there wasn't any wild animals. There was only the mountains and river, two-leggeds and four-leggeds and underwater people and all the rest. It took white people to make the country and the animals wild. Now they got to make a law saying it's wild so's they can protect it from themselves." (80–81)

This pronouncement would be taken purely at face value by the romantic whites at Tom's university, who wear climbing boots to class and want Indians to have names like Sonny Sixkiller (126). But the frequency with which Owens has Tom confront white stereotypes of Indians suggests that Owens wants us to consider whether "the ecological Indian" is not another of those stereotypes.

Lee Schweninger, in a footnote to "Landscape and Cultural Identity in Louis Owens' *Wolfsong*," suggests that if "the ecological Indian" is, in fact, a white imposition, this would not matter since some Indians make this a satisfying aspect of their identity.

He writes, "[i]n this context, it finally matters little where American Indians actually stand or stood in relation to the land. Owens himself recognizes that he writes with an environmental perspective" (108). But whatever Schweninger's intentions, this claim runs the risk of marginalizing tribal self-definitions whenever those self-definitions might compete with a dominant-culture perspective that calls itself "environmental"; that is, an "environmental" perspective, in this view, trumps a "tribal" perspective. In this, Schweninger reflects the skepticism of writers such as Calvin Martin, Sam Gill, and more recently Shepard Krech, with regard to these figures' efforts to debunk romanticized notions about Native religious/environmental practices. I would suggest, though, that it is hard to imagine a context in which it would not matter where Native Americans actually stand or stood in relation to the land. As David Rich Lewis, whom Schweninger references, argues, "Land (its loss, location, and resource wealth or poverty), exploitation of land, and changing Indian needs, attitudes, and religious demands define the issues facing modern Indians and their environments" (424). While assuming that tribal cultures are, like all cultures, dynamic, Lewis links changing tribal attitudes and religious demands directly to specific, material forms of land tenure and use. Intertwined questions of history and authenticity are central to ongoing controversies over tribal lands and resources, such as tribal hunting and fishing rights, supposedly guaranteed by treaty. Whether the context is controversy over treaty rights or an analysis of a text by a mixedblood author with commitments to both Native cultural politics and environmental protection, the question of Native "authenticity" will not go away, precisely because it is the discursive and symbolic ground on which the history of Native land tenure *matters* with regard to the future of Native land tenure.

In a chapter from *Mixedblood Messages* provocatively titled "'Everywhere There Was Life': How Native Americans Can Save the World," Owens responds directly to recent challenges to the idea of the ecological Indian. He writes:

It has long been fashionable for Euramericans and Native Americans alike . . . to speak and write of American Indians as something like genetically predetermined environmentalists. . . . In the past few years, however, a group of brave and daring revisionist cultural historians have sought to show this environmentalist image for what they think it is: historically and culturally inaccurate romanticism. (220)

Owens, here, suggests both the conventionality of the Indian as ecological icon and a certain bad faith on the part of the iconoclasts. *Mixedblood Messages* deals largely with the vicissitudes of Native American identity at the ambiguous and dynamic symbolic "frontier" between the Native and the Euramerican, reflecting a certain acceptance of the play of signifiers along this frontier, acknowledging the degree to which "the American Indian in the world consciousness has become not only a static artifact but more importantly . . . a contested space, a place of signification to be emptied out and reinhabited by Euramerica" (5). Owens reserves his sarcasm, however, for dominant-culture writers invested in the subversion of any claims that indigenous people were or are any different in their approaches to the natural world than a modern industrial subject. Owens leans in this section of his argument on Vine Deloria's *Red Earth, White Lies* to suggest the political, cultural, and environmental context of these iconoclastic responses to the notion of the ecological Indian. He quotes Deloria:

"Some people are offended by the idea that many people believe . . . Indians were more concerned and thoughtful ecologists than modern industrial users. Advocating the extinction theory is a good way to support continued despoliation of the environment by suggesting that at no time were human beings careful of the lands upon which they lived." (229)

Owens rests his case for the differences between indigenous and industrial cultures not on any essentialist notion of Indianness but on the varying ecological impacts of different cultures:

Being in a position, I think, to accept the fact that the original Americans, like all human beings throughout time, did indeed impact their environments, and that in fact the whole concept of "wilderness"—that space defined in the U.S. Wilderness Act of 1964 as being forever "untrammeled by man"—is a romantic European notion, we have to recognize nonetheless that Native Americans managed to live on this continent for many thousands of years without destroying it, poisoning it, or making it uninhabitable. In just five hundred years, Western man has come close to accomplishing that apocalypse. (225)

Owens appeals, here—without recourse to static, fetishized images of noble hunter-gatherers—to the long, complex history of developed and developing Native epistemologies, perspectives developed over millennia of trial and error and survival, perspectives to which the dominant culture would, apparently, do well to pay attention. The chapter's subtitle, "How Native Americans Can Save the World," is, for all its self-parody, a serious reference to the necessity of preserving indigenous cultures—not out of a dominant-culture noblesse oblige but out of the recognition that these cultures are, in fact, different from modern industrial culture precisely in the degree of indispensable knowledge they have about local ecosystems. For Owens, it is clear, an "environmental perspective" is always also a perspective on the actual relationships between specific groups of human beings and particular ecosystems. In this, his work reflects a sophisticated blend of insights from tribal cultures, "deep" and social ecologies, and struggles for environmental justice.

These insights are reflected in Owens's fiction from the beginning. The narrative trajectory of *Wolfsong* reflects—if rather subtly—a distinctly non-Western and nonindustrial worldview. While the incautious or uninformed reader is likely to read Tom's act of sabotage and homicide and his escape as the desperate end to a desperate story, Tom's affiliation to the trickster, demonstrated by Lalonde, suggests a very different significance for the story as a whole. It implies a mythic view of the world, in which history is not an arrow but a circle, in which the trickster dies and comes back again, and in which tribal values and lifeways continue. The wolf in *Wolfsong* is neither the "lone wolf" of Euramerican cultural mythology nor the embodiment of raw, uncivilized Nature—as in the case of Buck, Jack London's quasi-Nietzschean *Überhund;* it signifies, rather, a "spirit-helper," a system of reciprocal exchange between human and non-human nature. Tom's actions and his flight at the story's "END" represent his internalization and enactment of the tribal epistemology taught him by his uncle, this system of reciprocal exchange necessary to a sustainable living in the world. From this perspective, the opposition between pork chops and mother earth is dangerous nonsense, symptomatic of the Euramerican separation of nature and culture—a separation that the idea of wilderness only, Owens argues, reinforces. As Owens suggests in both his fiction and his essays, "wilderness" is, from a tribal perspective, less Euramerican civilization's *other* than a compensatory and fatally ahistorical fantasy *of* that civilization.

NOTES

1. See LaLonde, p. 40, for a similar reading of the novel's conclusion and, more generally, a treatment of Tom's relationship to the trickster.

2. See Vizenor, "Trickster Discourse."

3. In using these geological metaphors, I do not mean to imply that a cultural identity of this type is static, rather that it evolves over a relatively long period of time.

4. For discussions of the normative effects of indigenous storytelling, see Basso, in particular, and Abram and Brande.

WORKS CITED

Abram, David. *The Spell of the Sensuous.* New York: Vintage, 1996.

Basso, Keith H. *Wisdom Sits in Places: Landscape and Language Among the Western Apache.* Albuquerque: U of New Mexico P, 1996.

Bernardin, Susan. "Wilderness Conditions: Ranging for Place and Identity in Louis Owens' *Wolfsong." Studies in American Indian Literatures* 10.2 (1998): 79–93.

Brande, David. "Money, Memory and Territory in Craig Lesley's *Winterkill."* Forthcoming in *Western American Literature.*

Deloria, Vine. "Comfortable Fictions and the Struggle for Turf: An Essay Review of The Invented Indian: Cultural Fictions and Government Policies." *Natives and Academics: Researching and Writing about American Indians.* Ed. Devon A. Mihesuah. Lincoln: U of Nebraska P, 1998. 65–83.

———. *Red Earth, White Lies: Native Americans and the Myth of Scientific Fact.* New York: Scribners, 1995.

LaLonde, Chris. "Trickster, Trickster Discourse, and Identity in Louis Owens' *Wolfsong.*" *Studies in American Indian Literatures* 7.1 (1995): 27–42.

Lewis, David Rich. "Native Americans and the Environment: A Survey of Twentieth-Century Issues." *American Indian Quarterly* 19.3 (1995): 423–50.

Nash, Roderick. *Wilderness and the American Mind.* New Haven: Yale UP, 1982.

Oelschlaeger, Max. *The Idea of Wilderness: From Prehistory to the Age of Ecology.* New Haven: Yale UP, 1991.

———. "Wilderness, Civilization, and Language." *The Wilderness Condition: Essays on Environment and Civilization.* Ed. Max Oelschlaeger. Washington, D.C.: Island Press, 1992. 271–308.

Schweninger, Lee. "Landscape and Cultural Identity in Louis Owens's *Wolfsong.*" *Studies in American Indian Literatures* 10.2 (1998): 94–110.

Vizenor, Gerald. "Trickster Discourse: Comic Holotropes and Language Games." *Narrative Chance: Postmodern Discourse on Native American Indian Literatures.* Ed. Gerald Vizenor. Albuquerque: U of New Mexico P, 1989. 187–211.

CHAPTER TEN

THE LUDIC VIOLENCE OF
LOUIS OWENS'S
THE SHARPEST SIGHT

PAUL BEEKMAN TAYLOR

As he shatters the frame of his house with a sledgehammer, Jessard Deal chants solemnly to himself, his vast gods, and the universe: "We begin with the world around us, and we gradually move centripetally, toward the center. When we get there, we smash that too. But that's always last" (*SS* 149). His words and act have symbolic purport. The world that he is in the act of destroying is in small his house, in larger the Euramerican world of values that includes, he would believe, the world of the indigenous Chicano and Indian inhabitants of his area, and in largest himself at the bull's-eye center. The sledgehammer is not enough to do the job properly. It needs the collaboration of language, for without his spoken words there is no intervention of meaning into the arbitrary din of destruction. Like the Indian above his Tiptoe Inn bar, frozen in the circle of his paddle ripples, Deal would destroy his house to escape physical and psychological enclosures. After he retreats into the even smaller circle of his back-room office with hammer and books, the spring of his violent psychopathic personality is wound even tighter until, after the verbal and physical violation of Diana above Amarga Bay, the spring latch of his life gives way beside a billiard table. Jessard is an exemplary player of games of physical and verbal violence.

Violence of gesture and language can be either tightly or loosely rule bound, either distinct or coordinate; or, as Nietzsche suggested in *Beyond Good and Evil,* either "Apollonian" or "Dionysian." The former is measured, moderate, anticompetitive, and exercised to maintain life. Luther and Onatima exemplify Apollonian violence in their loosely rule-bound respect for natural balance. It coordinates energies to benefit the commonweal by balancing accounts, while Dionysian violence is a feature of group against group, where balance is neither possible nor sought. It serves domination. Jessard Deal reflects the distinct Dionysian struggle.

I favor the term *ludic,* from the Latin *ludens,* for game-codified violence that serves a collective cultural function and both *imperialistic* and *ideological* for violence of speech and gesture that gains by dominating an individual or group. The former marks balance, the latter interest weighted for one side against another. *Ludus,* or game, is Apollonian when its ritual form establishes and maintains social and psychological equilibrium; it is Dionysian in function where game and sport requires a winner. Ludic violence is progressive, while ideological and imperialistic violence is arbitrary, manifesting an exclusive power either to dominate others by enslavement or to eliminate them by usurping their rights to life. Domination can be for public and political purpose or for private, economic and moral advantage. Public assent to usurp the right of life of others is justified by economic greed as well as by racial and religious insecurity. Private violence against others is incited often by the sort of psychotic personality or paranoia exhibited by Jessard Deal, Paul Kantner in Owens's *Bone Game,* and Lee Jensen in *Dark River.* On the other hand, in the ludic arena of North American Indian culture, as in the billiard games in Deal's Tiptoe Inn, to win is to kill "symbolically."

Language remains a decisive instrument in the ordered combat between violator and violated in "Euramerican" culture. Luther explains to Cole his people's duel convention, whose terms, when explained by a Choctaw to an Anglo challenger, gain victory without a fight (96). The Indian game of lacrosse ("little war-brother") was conventionally accompanied by exchanges of insults by the competing teams. Both in game and in earnest, honor is won or lost in verbal combats. In short, speech is a form of violence and violence is a form of speech. Conversely, a wound is not just a distinct event or unfortunate social circumstance. It is a glyph, a linguistic mark on a bodily locus of resistance and creativity where social conflicts are played out.

Though ludic ideals can be traced from the Olympic Games of ancient Greece through chivalric combat in lists to duels of honor, they are observable throughout the history of Indian game in the Americas. Historically, many Indian tribes played games of the arrow, raced their horses, and staged simulated war games among themselves. The Cherokee, Choctaw, and Creek game of lacrosse was performed as a war game against other tribes to invoke community pride by displaying skills that could be applied to the battlefield. Traditional game meant more to the Cherokee than senseless war, though war is game and game is war. In *The Sharpest Sight* the billiard table in the Tiptoe Inn is a comparable green field of battle upon which lies, finally, the mutilated body of Dan Nemi. In contrast, the one-on-one basketball contest in the same novel between Mundo and Cole is a game that measures power while paying mutual respect. Sport, like ceremonial ritual, mediates between positive and negative violence.

Referring to attitudes in such combats, Owens states that "'Indian' ways of viewing the world are almost always in direct conflict with the dominant *ideologemes* of Euramerica" (*OD* 8). Euramerican appeal to Cartesian and Hegelian divisions of mankind into masters and servants authorizes an overlay of one culture by another and the destruction of ethnic identity. So, the American Indian appears in the passive position of the anonymous and stateless gladiator of the Roman Coliseum whose death was a brief distraction for an audience there to be reminded of the deaths of great Romans who died for the state.

For most traditional American Indians, a natural death after a long and useful life is a good death because it provides tribal continuity.

Gerald Vizenor cites George Bataille to the effect that "Death actually discloses the imposture of reality . . . because death is the great affirmer" (*Manifest Manners* 16). Indian acceptance of death is denial of death. The Hopi say that "what we have buried in the earth is only the stalk. The breath has gone elsewhere and lives on" (Courlander 101).

In *The Sharpest Sight* El Viejo and the Mondragon sisters pursue postmortem quests to activate ethnic germs. For many American Indians in Owens's novels, no matter their tribal affiliations, death is a passageway between lives, not a termination of being. According to Patricia Galloway, the Choctaw believe that when the "psychical elements of the person do not disperse properly, or they do so at a wrong time or in a wrong place," death is bad (278). Attis McCurtain and Jenna Nemi are victims of imperialistic violence, but they hold onto a disturbed form of "life" after the destruction of their bodies. Death due to institutional violence is especially bad, because a death not understood pollutes the social entity.

For most American Indian tribes, traditional belief holds that life of the spirit is not terminated by the body's death, and one has no reason to fear death as long as the spirit survives in dignity. The temper of spirits of the dead is ludic, as El Viejo demonstrates in his conversations with Mundo Morales. Attis's war sickness cannot be healed by Euramerican institutional medicine, and he cannot be reset in harmony with the earth until his brother buries him ceremonially. For the euramerican, Indian ceremony smacks of witchcraft; for the Indian, the violence of the white *is* witchcraft.

The animal life of bear, deer, buzzards, ravens, and owls in the novels of Owens are faithful collaborators with the Indian in countering negative violence. Owens's American Indians are sensitive more to the life that inhabits their landscape than to the wealth into which plant above and mineral below can be converted. Attis can sense tigers and spirits of the dead in the jungles of Vietnam, though his mates cannot. Mundo sees a black mountain lion on the bridge near Amarga, and the mythic panther *koi* stalks the bayou country of Mississippi, terrifying the FBI agents who cannot believe that such beasts still exist there. In all of these cases, real or imagined wildlife wreaks a sort of natural vengeance against the violence of those lacking proper respect for it. The earth and all its disenfranchised residents conspire to recover the land, its inhabitants, and its story. The physical landscape is inextricably bound to a transcendental zone of value that is often elaborated in vision, dream, and postmortem existence.

Luther Cole and Onatima recall Choctaw lore of violence that contrasts with imposed Euramerican cultural ideals. Dan Nemi, Diane Nemi, and Jessard Deal exemplify wasteful aspects of violence, while the fistfights in Deal's Tiptoe Inn are idle sham sport. The American Indian's positive violence of ritual ceremony redresses the negative violence of oppressors in all of Owens's novels, but the ultimate decisive arm of resistance is the fictional style with which Owens inscribes their story. A major feature of that style is its conjoining of Euramerican traditional myths of violence and convergence with Indian tribal mythic lore. Noteworthy is Owens's conjoining of cultural myths of sacrifice that involve twins, brothers, or warrior pairs, one of whom dies, making the other a "last survivor." Attis and Cole reflect typologically the Thunder Boys of Cherokee and Winnebago myth, in which two friends sacrifice their lives for the welfare of their community. In the Underworld they suffer ordeals until they reach the lodge of Earthmaker, who lets them return to the world. In Levi-Stauss's terms, the story means that one dies before his time because he has sacrificed himself as a debt to society. "If one renounces life and seeks death then one increases the full life of his fellow-tribesmen, and secures for oneself a state composed of an indefinite series of half-lives and half-deaths. . . . An altruistic loss of life means life regained" for all those "to whom the sacrifice was consecrated" (Levi-Strauss, 201–2). In effect, death can assure social benefit if the warrior endures violence for the sake of a common good. In *The Sharpest Sight* Attis is a conventional warrior figure who fought in Vietnam, where his spirit suffered from imperialistic violence against both life and land. His death by the riverside starts the process of the rebirth of Jenna—that is, the transfer of her spirit—in her surviving sister Diana, and Attis's brother Cole is a surviving brother who stands to inherit the life Attis forfeits. To reclaim that force, however, he must find Attis's body, bundle its bones in proper Choctaw ritual fashion, and return them to his place of origin, where his spirit finds refuge.

While Choctaw traditional lore plays a major role in this story, Owens represents the ideological violence of the novel in a typological reflection of an analogous European myth. The enemies of the McCurtains—Dan Nemi and his family—take their name from a forest and village on the edge of a lake in the Alban hills near Rome. In the forest is a grove sacred to the goddess Diana Nemorensis, known as Artemis in an earlier Greek version, where a priest known as Rex Nemorensis ritually sacrificed strangers to the vestal virgin. In the Greek myth Artemis loved Hippolytus, who was killed by the sea God Poseidon on orders from jealous Aphrodite. Artemis rescued him from Hades ("the hidden place") and concealed him from the gods under the name Virbius ("one who lived twice"). In the Roman extension of the story, the priest of Nemi performed the ritual of vestal fire by the edge of the lake known as Diana's Mirror, feeding the flames with the wood of a sacred oak.

Correspondences between the events associated with the mythic grove and Owens's Amarga are obvious, and details such as Hoey's fire of ceremonial cure for Diana Nemi recall the vestal fire. Attis's story is of the same mythic strain. Attis is the name of the Phrygian counterpart of the Syrian Adonais, who, according to Hesiod, was born of a tree. The Asiatic fertility goddess Cybele fell in love with Attis (her son) when she saw him hunting in her forest, then drove him mad because he loved a nymph. In his frenzy he castrated himself and bled to death under a pine tree as self-sacrifice to Aphrodite. After death he metamorphosed into that tree and was honored as a tree spirit and god of vegetation. Like the Cherokee myth of the origin of corn, Navajo myths of Changing Woman, and Keresan myths of Thought Woman, the Mediterranean myth explains the death that serves to assure seasonal resurrection of vegetable life.

Cole's brother is a sacrificial victim of imperialist violence. His spirit has been castrated in the forests of Vietnam, where he fought for destroyers rather than healers. Luther reminds Cole that the tragic archetype of the Indian fighting for the Euramerican is the Choctaw General Pushmataha, who won the Battle of New Orleans for Andrew Jackson (20, 68), the only battle the United States won during the War of 1812, though it was fought after the war ended. Pushmataha's reward for his service, Luther reckons, was being left without a "pot to piss in," a sarcastic allusion to the white man's usurpation of Choctaw birthright less than two decades later. Attis's "reward" for his service to the Anglo a century and a half later is loss of a natural spiritual and moral equilibrium.

Reflecting his Greek counterpart, Hippolytus, who was cursed by a father who devoted him to destruction and left in the world of the dead by the goddess Diana, who cannot save him, Attis is murdered on a riverside by Diana, who justifies her crime as vengeance for his killing of her sister Jenna.

Into this mix of myth Owens inserts Jessard Deal, a Paul Bunyan–like folklore figure of whose genealogy and history we know little beyond his confessional allusion to a period of enclosure in prison where he found free movement in English poetry. Deal is both a survivor and a reflection of Attis, who had liked him (81). He is a self-proclaimed "redskin" (102) and, like Luther and Onatima, a reader in search of knowledge of his essence. Like them he has discovered and unleashed the violence and the balm of words (209). Just before he rapes Diana, he prepares her for his violence with the instruction that "pain and poetry make up the real language of truth" (235). Convinced of the inherent, innate evil of men, he is an incarnation of the Choctaw *Nalusachito*, the soul-eater. Deal speaks into being the imperialistic violence that Attis waged reluctantly.

Deal plays warrior and Indian trickster as he indulges in his own carefully orchestrated game. If Attis fought unwittingly for the wrong side, Deal unwittingly aids the right. Both die violent deaths that serve to balance blood accounts. Deal's murder of Dan Nemi and his own death by Hoey's hand are consonant with the rehabilitation of Attis after death ("Hoey" echoes Choctaw *hojo*, "hunter").

Ultimately, story itself is a last survivor, and its ludic violence wins the combat—not just the combat *in* the novel, but the combat *of* the novel. Ludic violence balances the oppressive ideological over-weight of the literary "invention" of the Indian. Story is the Ameri-can Indian's decisive arm in resisting an Anglo dissemination of a history that justifies his violence against landscape and its indige-nous population for his own greed. Like Luther, Owens styles words as ceremony with power to reset nature's proper balance (109). In the myths of recurrence embedded in Owens's fiction, oral inquisi-tion probes and surgically repairs a wasteland. Story is the phar-macopoeia, or vulnerary of cure, and both defense and offense against destruction. Owens's story is "logokinetic"; that is, it has the power to move things. As Jessard Deal in his lyric effusions demon-strates, language acts have resonance in the real world. Word deprived of meaning is but noise.

Because oral story, like words spoken in a ritual, is bound to time and place, story is born anew with every telling. While it can easily resist erosion by repetition, appropriating the Anglo print territory, to speak over it is a daunting task. Anglos "try to write us to death," says Luther, and Onatima observes that Euramericans display a romance with death in their literature and would write the Indian into dying for them (216). To survive being inscribed within a Euramerican text of death, the Indian storyteller must neutralize alien violent intent by deconstructing and reconstructing the Indian of Euramerican story. To speak over the violence of that story, Owens uses Euramerican language and literary forms to shape a particular style that mixes attitudes toward the uses of violence, mythological archetypes, and story structures.

I call that style "conjunctural," because it conjoins indigenous and alien cultural materials with a language containing both English and Choctaw linguistic features as well as themes. The characters in *The Sharpest Sight,* as well as in Owens's other novels, are also conjunc-tural, moving across borders of racial and cultural identities. An implication in Owens's literary strategy is that we, like Mundo Morales, are unaware of our own mixedbreed cultural matrices, if not blood strains, and remain so until we are shaken rudely into consciousness of them.

Owens suggests what W. B. Yeats, Ezra Pound, and T. S. Eliot emphasize in their poetry: that mythological archetypes of ludic violence give birth to and nourish civilizations. He is a trickster storyteller whose mix of structure and style erases borders of racial and cultural dialectic, for the trickster is a liberator,[1] and Owens's fiction rescues the mixed cultural knowledge and wisdom of the dead. The trickster ghosts of the Mondragon sisters and El Viejo guide those who can hear and follow them. Tricksters of their sort are comic and, like the heroes of archetypal comedy, resolve confusion into a reconciliation of values. The trickster Owens is "devolutionary," rolling back Euramerican evolutionary technology toward an essential and nonhierarchic collaboration between residents on shared land.

Luther, Hoey, and Cole transgress Anglo territory as they move over trails the Anglo has shuffled and smudged on Indian terrain. Similarly, Owens reconnoiters and violates the smug sanctuary of the established literary territory. Like Jessard Deal, Owens destroys a house with words. Unlike Jessard, he does not retreat into an inner sanctum with book and hammer but rebuilds on the purged site a new literary form that declares an open house for his reader.

NOTES

1. In "Tribal Discourses: Comic Holotypes and Language Games," Gerald Vizenor calls the trickster a semiotic sign for "social antagonism" who "summons agonistic imagination in a narrative" and unties the Anglo's imposed "hypotragedy" of Indian as vanishing breed.

WORKS CITED

Courlander, Harold. *The Fourth World of the Hopi*. Albuquerque: U of New Mexico P, 1987.

Galloway, Patricia. *Choctaw Genesis 1500–1700*. Lincoln and London: U of Nebraska P, 1995.

Lévi-Strauss, Claude. *Structural Anthropology*. Vol. 2. London: Allen Lane, 1977.

Vizenor, Gerald. *Manifest Manners: Postindian Warriors of Survivance*. Middletown, Conn.: Wesleyan UP, 1994.

————. "Tribal Discourses: Comic Holotypes and Language Games." *Narrative Chance: Postmodern Discourse on Native American Indian Literatures*. Ed. Gerald Vizenor. Albuquerque: U of New Mexico P.

CHAPTER ELEVEN

"You Got to Fish
Ever Goddamn Day"

The Importance of Hunting and Fishing
Through I Hear the Train

JESSE PETERS

The parking lot is crowded with SUVs, campers, and beat-up Chevy pickup trucks. We've managed to save a parking space beside the Jeep by spreading out all our gear, and now we sit in two lounge chairs drinking beer behind sunglasses and wide-brimmed hats. Every now and then, a driver starts to pull into the space, sees us, and then drives away with an almost audible scowl.

"They may not even be coming," Hossein says as he pulls on his waders. He is visibly anxious and keeps looking over at the trail to the river.

"They're coming." I pop open another beer.

"But you know how Louis is. Probably got pissed at all the traffic on the way up here and turned around and went home."

I start putting on my gear too, and, by the time I finish, Hossein already has his rod together and is picking out a fly. I hand him another beer. "What you think they're going to hit today?"

"I don't fucking know. Something black." He takes the beer and grins.

Louis Owens with rainbow trout, San Juan River, New Mexico, summer, 2000. Photograph taken by and courtesy of Jesse Peters.

After I get my rod together, I open my own fly box. "Think I'll start with a royal wulff. Can't go wrong with that. It's all in the cast anyway. Hell, I could probably catch one with a naked hook."

Hossein lets out a full-force laugh. "You couldn't catch one with a stick of damn dynamite. You got to use an old attractor pattern in fast water, and then you got to close your eyes and hope for the best. Just lift your rod tip when you feel something pulling on your line."

I grin. "Maybe I'll let you reel in a twenty incher when I catch one. Just so you know what it feels like."

He laughs so hard I think he might come out of his own body. Then he takes a long drink. "Damn, it is hot as hell in these waders. Thought these things were supposed to breathe. And where are those bastards anyway? Let's go. We can put a note on the windshield and tell them to meet us at the beaver dam." He gets up and starts throwing his duffel bags in the Jeep.

"We should wait on them. They're not that late really."

"One more beer and then I'm gone. I'm telling you, Louis probably went home."

I finish tying on the wulff and clip off the extra line. "I doubt it."

• • •

In a discussion of belief, Charles Sanders Peirce says, "Doubt is an uneasy and dissatisfied state from which we struggle to free ourselves and pass into the state of belief; while the latter is a calm and satisfactory state which we do not wish to avoid, or to change to a belief in anything else. On the contrary, we cling tenaciously, not merely to believing, but to believing just what we do believe" (149). It seems then that belief (whether it takes the form of ideology, definition, and/or narrative), once it is constructed and an individual grounds himself in that linguistic moment, provides a comfort zone that most would not want to leave. However, there is value in the doubt that forces us to seek the comfort of belief. Peirce explains that "both doubt and belief have positive effects on us, though very different ones. Belief does not make us act at once, but puts us into such a condition that we shall behave in a certain way, when the occasion arises. Doubt has not the least effect of this sort, but stimulates us to action until it is destroyed" (149–50). The inherent struggle between belief and doubt is at the heart of Louis Owens's latest work, *I Hear the Train*, but Owens's objective here is not to emphasize the importance of creating and maintaining a belief but rather to stress the inherent power in the motion that doubt creates. "With the doubt, therefore, the struggle begins, and with the cessation of doubt it ends" (Peirce 150), but when that struggle dies so does the self because the self, if it is to resist stagnation, stereotype, and restrictive definition, must necessarily feed off the doubt. As the subtitle of Owens's book suggests, we must remain in a constant state of reflection, invention, and refraction as we try desperately to understand ourselves. *I Hear the Train* models this process by taking the reader, who, like the author, is constantly searching for meaning, through a labyrinth of photo-graphs, stories, and essays. Owens himself tells us in the preface, "Together, I believe they form a pattern, one turn and twist of the labyrinth leading to another. At the center, of course, is the hybrid monster of self, the ultimate cannibal to which all stories lead" (10). In order to find the self we must hunt the self, and throughout the book, Owens uses the metaphors of hunting and fishing to articulate the human need to stalk, create, and perhaps even destroy the world through words.

Owens is very conscious of the fact that he is crafting stories, and he is also aware that the act of crafting narrative and sharing those narratives is a way of moving towards belief, a way of crafting the world—both the world of self and the world of other selves. As he says in the preface to the book, "We make stories in order to find ourselves at home in chaos made familiar and comforting through the stories we make, searching frantically for patterns in the flux of randomly recorded events, a world in which endings stalk us and we can only keep inventing ways to both explain and forestall clo-sure" (9). After all, it is closure that stops all change, motion, and growth, and the concept of a definition of self creates an artificial space, stops motion, fixes stereotypes, and cuts off the creative breath. At the moment when we believe that we understand our-selves and are able to tell our stories, hunting stops and the self becomes stagnant. *I Hear the Train* explains that the notion of fixed belief cannot, and indeed should not, be maintained if the self is to grow and thrive. At times playing the role of trickster and at times drawing on postmodern philosophy, Owens challenges us to resist metanarratives and constantly to reexamine our positions both in the world and in the stories that we create about that world.

• • •

We see the red Landcruiser coming down the hill and it continues through the parking lot straight for us. All the gear has been put up, and we are sitting in our chairs, beer in one hand and rod in the other. The Landcruiser slides to a stop inches away from our knees.

Both doors swing open and Louis and Aaron get out already dressed for the river: boots, waders, fly vests, sunglasses, the whole deal. Hossein and I each open a beer and hold it up. Louis walks up and takes the beer from my hand and Aaron takes the one from Hossein.

Hossein starts laughing. "Where in the hell have ya'll been? I thought you were fishermen."

Louis shakes his head. "That goddamn traffic. Looks like half the world is coming up here to fish. Look at all these cars. Looks like a mall parking lot at Christmas."

"Ya'll must really be dedicated to drive three hours with no air-conditioning in full gear," I say.

Aaron laughs in his low way and wipes the sweat off his head. "Louis had to stop at that last gas station before the turnoff so we could suit up. He knew Hossein would be raring to go. But really I think he was hoping you guys would be late so we would be first on the river."

Hossein gets up and starts folding his chair. "Late? It's only half a mile from the campsite."

"Yeah, but I know you like your beauty rest." Louis walks to the back of the Landcruiser and returns with two rod tubes. He hands one to Aaron.

I decide I better get up and get this chair in the Jeep before I get left behind. "Where you want to go first? Beaver dam?"

"Somewhere away from all these people," Louis says. "The best fish are always in the back channels anyway."

Hossein is standing in front of the vehicles with his arms crossed, holding his rod. "Anytime ya'll get ready we can hunt us up some fish. Or maybe we should just go home."

By now everyone is almost ready. I notice that Aaron still has his same ancient rod and reel. "You still fishing with that shit? Why don't you just tie a rope to a baseball bat?"

He walks over to Hossein and starts waving the rod around as if he is testing the feel of a handmade graphite rod. The old metal rod hardly moves at all. "It's not the tool. It's what you do with it that counts."

Louis slams the Landcruiser door and stuffs the keys under the bumper. Hossein starts for the river with the rest of us waddling behind. He turns back and shouts, "Don't forget your creel, Louis!"

"Don't forget your ass!"

"Finally," I say as I bring up the rear. "I'm ready to burn this river up."

• • •

In *I Hear the Train* the numerous references to Nabakov's novel *Pale Fire*, along with the persistent metaphor of the labyrinth, emphasize the fact that Owens is working from within an understanding of the postmodern condition and draws upon those philosophies as he emphasizes the positive power of the constant recreation of the self through language. Self-reflection and questioning are at the heart of the postmodern goal of resisting metanarratives or "what Vizenor has called 'terminal creeds': those monologic utterances that seek to violate the dialogic of trickster space, to fix opposites and impose static definitions upon the world" (Owens, *MM* 55). Whereas the modern writers believed that there were answers and solutions to the fragmentation and deracination they saw in the world around them, the postmodernists have embraced the questions and tensions and believe that the truth/solution, whatever it may be, is merely a construction that exists in a constant state of flux. David Harvey, drawing on the ideas of Terry Eagleton and comments from the editors of the journal *PRECIS*, has explained the differences between modernism and postmodernism as such:

> "Generally perceived as positivistic, technocentric, and rationalistic, universal modernism has been identified with the belief in linear progress, absolute truths, the rational planning of ideal social orders, and the standardization of knowledge and production." Postmodernism, by way of contrast, privileges "heterogeneity and difference as liberative forces in the redefinition of cultural discourse." Fragmentation, indeterminacy, and intense distrust of all universal or "totalizing"

discourses (to use a favoured phrase) are the hallmark of post-modern thought. (9)

Thus, in a postmodern world, we create ourselves through the construction of narratives that are neither steadfast nor universal. Therefore, it seems logical that the labyrinth, with its confusing routes and paths, along with the mirror, which allows us to analyze our own gaze, replaced the cross as a metaphor for understanding the self. Prescriptive sacrifice and universal morality gave way to the importance of the search itself, and many learned to embrace perpetual motion and constant re-creation and reevaluation.

This search for self is clear in the postmodern novel *Pale Fire,* as Kinbote creates his own narrative, simultaneously outside of and within the text of another. He is driven by the need to find meaning by constantly writing and rewriting his own narrative, and Owens himself is driven by this same need, a need that we all share: "As Nabakov's mad reader/editor Kinbote demonstrates so superbly in the novel *Pale Fire,* we all want to read ourselves into and back out of every text and will go to great extremes to ensure that possibility" (Owens, *Train* 211). Perhaps the drive to see ourselves in the stories around us reflects an inherent need of humans to construct notions of self that we can be comfortable with, that we can believe in and point to when we are asked, who are you? We want the comfort of belief, and the doubts we harbor about ourselves and the worlds we create through language maintain the productive cycle of regeneration of the self. But the questions become how do we find these narratives of self, and where do we look for them?

• • •

"Just take a minute and compose yourself," I say to Louis. "I don't have the time or money to bail your ass out of the local jail."

Two guys who looked like they'd just walked out of an Orvis catalog had just walked through the hole we were fishing. They didn't say a word to us, either. Louis looks like his head is going to explode. "Somebody ought to kick their asses. Idiots. Did you hear that guy with the mirror sunglasses tell the other one that there weren't any fish in the channels?"

I smile. "Yeah."

"Hey, buddy! What the hell do you think we're doing here? Watching TV?" he screams after them. We can still see them, but they don't turn around, and then they disappear around a bend. "This river is like a shopping mall with catalog models everywhere you turn. It's getting so you can't fish for the fishermen." He starts winding in his line.

I start winding mine in too. "Those guys will just go over to the deep water, sink a streamer, and wait for those balls of pink yarn to move. That's the only way they will catch anything."

"Guys like that don't know how to fish."

"No."

"Let's go see if we can find Aaron and Hossein."

"OK."

"I bet they're in that wide flat above the beaver dam. Lots of fish there. Hard to catch, but definitely lots of fish there."

"If we can't catch them, nobody can," I say as we start to walk upstream.

• • •

In *Mixedblood Messages* Louis Owens explains the difference between two notions of reality, the frontier and the territory. He says, "Whereas frontier is always unstable, multidirectional, hybridized, characterized by heteroglossia, and indeterminate, territory is clearly mapped, fully imagined as a place of containment, invented to control and subdue the dangerous potentialities of imagined Indians" (26). Frontier, then, is the place of possibility, of change and growth, a space that defies artificially constructed borders and limitations. In contrast, the territory is a stagnant, defined space in which the dangerous potentialities of "imagined Indians" and, more importantly, of imagining Indians, is stifled and contained. Frontier is fertile; territory is caustic and nonproductive. This philosophy is one of the threads that weaves together the literary career of Owens, and, in *I Hear the Train,* he explains that the self must take root, develop, and continue to grow in the "unstable, multidirectional, hybridized" fields of the frontier. He invites us to do nothing less than examine the events of his life, to try and discover the patterns he sees in the worlds in which he exists. And in doing so, we look through new lenses and ultimately form new patterns for ourselves; we learn new strategies for navigating the complex realities we must necessarily inhabit. Those strategies are dependent upon the realization that we are all, in one way or another, hunting for stories. And it is within frontier space that these stories take shape.

In "Finding Gene," Owens explains why we must necessarily hunt in our lives. In this essay he explains his hunt for the brother that disappeared for decades. This search had taken many forms, but most importantly, it took the shape of a story, a story that eventually was the key to the reunion of the two brothers. As Owens says early in the essay, "I'd begun to wonder what had actually happened and what my imagination had simply formed into history and truth. Without Gene I had no touchstone to truth, no way of verifying memories. I know that we invent what we need to be true, imagining and rewriting until there is some kind of text that gives us back a self" (4). It was the quest to remake the past, and thus the present, by placing that past in the context of story that led Owens to write his second novel, *The Sharpest Sight.* According to Owens, "I also based a major character in that novel on my brother Gene, who had come back from three tours in Vietnam with such pain that he became one of the psychological casualties who disappeared into the Ozark Mountains of Arkansas" (*MM* 182). Eventually, Gene sees a copy of the novel, buys it, and reads it. It is Gene, because of the power of story and the need to find the self, who at long last seeks and finds his brother.

As we see, these two brothers are actually very similar even though they have led different lives; the context might be slightly different, but they both have always had, and continue to have, the drive to hunt. And just as it is Gene who eventually finds

Louis, it is Gene who reminds Louis of the importance of the hunt itself.

One of the first things that Owens tells us Gene does when they are finally reunited in Arkansas is to show him his collection of guns: "He unlocked a big closet and began to bring out guns" (7). These guns trigger memories of the past for Owens, of time spent with his brother and his father in the woods, of parts of himself that he had not thought about in a long time. As he explains: "I hefted and aimed down barrels at peep sights and into darkened scopes, lifted and lined up pistols, spoke softly in terms of admiration and awe, conscious even at the time that guns had become, on this strange day in Arkansas, the petit madeleines of our own remembrance of things past, and even thinking of it in with that absurd, stuffed-shirt Proustian term" (8). But Gene's sharing of his gun collection does more for Owens than simply forcing him to think of his childhood or illuminating the complex self that applies Proustian terms to the experience of holding pistols and peering down barrels.

As Gene tells his brother about a deer he had been stalking for several years, Owens has a realization about the nature of the hunt: "I finally realized, he had never actually killed a deer. It was the hunting that counted, the knowledge that he could think and feel like them, ease into their world, be the deer for a privileged time once each year just before winter set in. I remembered the feeling from the old life we'd shared" (8). For someone like Gene, who had been a part of far too much killing during his three tours of Vietnam, taking the deer's life was not the point at all. The hunt itself is the important experience because it allows one to enter into other worlds and experiences, to become something "other" if only, as Owens describes it, "for a privileged time." And actually, as Owens reveals later in the book, what the hunter is actually stalking, whether it be a memory, a deer, or a brother, is the ever illusive self hiding at the center of the maze of experience. As Owens describes what he experiences and learns during these few days in Arkansas, he is also providing a guide through which we can view all his literary works. On the way home he decides to send his brother "the beaded rifle scabbard a Creek friend had made for me, for Gene was the hunter in the family" (15). But it becomes clear in other places in *I Hear the Train* that Owens is certainly a hunter in his own right.

• • •

When we get to the beaver-dam hole, we notice that the river there has changed since last year. The beavers have reinforced the dam, and the places where water used to spill over with speed and force are now just slow trickles. Clearly, there is not enough oxygen or food here for big trout.

"Sure has changed," Louis says as he steps up and over the dam.

I follow. I've known Louis for years now. He was one of my professors in college, but the classroom was not where our friendship was made. When I think about it, it seems only natural that we should be friends. Although it was in different parts of the country, we both grew up hunting and fishing in the rural landscapes we first called home. He picked beets. I picked okra. We both like to read. We both found out, as soon as we stepped into a college classroom, that almost everyone else thought we talked funny. Our bond is deeper than the ones people usually make in the university. He once told me that the trouble with academia was that there were too many people in it who had never done anything else. I knew just what he meant.

Today is a good day to fish, I think. And somehow we always pair up together on the river.

"Come here for a minute." Louis has stopped on the bank and is kneeling down. I go over and kneel beside him. I take a drink from my canteen and offer it to him.

He takes a long drink, wipes his mouth, and points into the tall, thick grass. "Look at that."

Stretched between two stalks is a spiderweb about a foot across. In the middle sits a black spider with a bright yellow mark on its back. "Man, spiderwebs are amazing," I say.

"Spiders are the best hunters, you know." When he is in the right mood, Louis tells me things.

I think about this for a minute. "But don't they just sit there and wait for something to fly into the web and get trapped?"

"That is only part of it. The easy part. The spider must decide where to build the web, and to do that he must think like the insects he will catch. Why build a web where there are no flies? Or why build a web where the wind will tear it down?"

"I guess the bank of this river is a good place then."

"It's where I'd build one." He blows slightly on the web, and the spider moves quickly, but then just as quickly it settles down and braces itself against a possible stronger breeze.

I take another drink of water. "You know, I did see on the Discovery channel one time where they took a spider into space. Put it in a weightless environment. The amazing thing was that it still built a perfectly symmetrical web even though it had no idea which way was up or down."

Louis stands up. "See. Only the best hunters can make a trap even when they are disoriented." He smiles at me as I stand up.

• • •

Perhaps the clearest articulation of how Owens sees hunting as a metaphor for living, and by that I mean not just existing, but living in a good way, is found in "The Hunter's Dance." This essay begins with Owens describing a scene he once witnessed while on the Black River, a battle between a coyote and a doe over the life of her fawn. Ultimately, Owens decides to intervene, to become part of the story. He knew that he "should do nothing, told [himself] sternly to just turn away" (40). However, as he reflects, he realizes that "perhaps it was just an inexcusable human weakness, blindness, or selfishness that converted everything into personal significance" (41) and forced him to alter the course of events, to place his indelible stamp on the reality of the moment. Regardless of the motivation, his choice to take part in this "dance" leads him to ponder the relationships between humans and the worlds in which they inhabit. Most importantly, his experiences on this river for the better part of a week cause him to reevaluate the role of hunting in his life as well as in the lives of us all.

On the way back home, he ponders:

> In long retrospect, I ask other questions. What kind of god
> would decree that on my way back from the river I should
> stop in Alpine for a hamburger made of the ground flesh of a
> cow raised for that purpose, hormone fed and fattened in
> muddy feedlots, crowded into stockyards with eyes gouged
> out by jostling horns, and finally lined into slaughterhouse fac-
> tories to be killed with the sound and smells of myriad other
> deaths in its ears and nostrils? For five days I had camped on
> the river, catching trout every day and releasing most, but each
> day selecting two or three fish to kill and cook for dinner. What
> god gave those trout lives into my hands? What kind of angry
> god has put so many lives at the disposal of others, the multi-
> tudinous rabbits mere grain for the predators? Is there a code
> to govern such infinite and necessary deaths, values by which
> we live and make die? (44)

I quote this at length because here we see a thought process that
leads Owens to an epiphany about the way that he believes people
should live. What exactly is it that makes a life valuable? And how
is it that we so easily forget that value, that some of us casually buy
ground beef and prepackaged chicken? Perhaps the answer to his
last question in the passage above is yes, there is a code, and it is a
code that only the hunter knows. As he later says, "But somewhere
along the generations, the thing that signaled a man's ability to provide, and that man's kinship with the natural world, had become
merely a trophy, a meaningless signifier of destruction" (47). And
this destruction is not simply of the animals killed for trophies (and
indeed a finely cooked steak consumed in a fancy restaurant is a trophy of sorts) but of the self as well. It is a destruction that stems from
the lack of understanding and respect for the worlds we inhabit and
create, from an ease of existence, from a lack of doubt.

Owens tells us that he "grew up hunting" (44), and he still longs
for those experiences; "But still, I have a running argument with my
wife and daughters. If we are not to be vegetarians, I argue, we should
raise chickens so that we don't have to buy chickens or eggs from a

store. Perhaps I should take up deer hunting again, I suggest, maybe elk or antelope as well. We are irresponsible, I argue, letting others do the killing for us" (49). But his reasoning goes far deeper than just the guilt associated with contributing to the meat industry. The bottom line here, as his brother Gene has reminded him, is that hunting, in the proper way, demands responsibility and self-knowledge. Finally, he explains that "such death must be sacramental, a matter of mutual knowledge and profound respect. How else may the owl or bobcat find the rabbit except by way of the most complete knowledge possible, and what is knowledge if not respect? What is such complete knowledge and respect but a kind of love?" (49–50). We can find none of the things that we seek without knowledge, and we can gain no knowledge without seeking it. This is what the hunter knows; this is why Owens believes that we create stories— to find knowledge and self, the two of which are inseparable.

• • •

There is something in his eyes, and I know that he has told me what he wanted me to know. I think about how much he has taught me over the years. There were lots of academic things, like how and why some writers work against stereotypes, why Steinbeck's ecological theories were ahead of their time, why Frost is a dark poet. But there were other things too. I remember the day we first tied flies together, both of us fumbling with tiny hooks and uncooperative thread. Then I remember the first time we went to the river, just the two of us. He showed me how to cast, which flies worked where, the best way to release the fish.

Up the river, we can see Hossein and Aaron in the flat. They both have fish on. We leave the web behind and start to walk towards them. Louis is slowly pulling line out of his reel.

"Hey, did I ever thank you for teaching me how to fly fish?" I ask his back.

At first I think he does not hear, that the wind has blown my words into the river. But then he says low so that I barely hear it, "Someone had to."

• • •

But the successful hunter/writer must understand the hunt. It is not for mere trophy or sport, and it is a risky endeavor in which there is a thin line between the hunter and the hunted. According to Gerald Vizenor, "Telling a story is as "dangerous" as hunting—dangerous because your life depends on seeing and catching something. It's dangerous because it's an encounter with the unknown—something generally understood, but specifically unknown that may come together, alive or present in the telling or the hunting. To hunt, to tell stories, to write is dangerous. It's also survivance" (McCaffery and Marshall 54).

I Hear the Train is a self-reflexive work in which we see the hunter engaged in the necessary and dangerous hunt for self. In "The Syllogistic Mixedblood" Owens speaks directly to this fact when discussing his musings over old family photographs. He says, "There are fibers out of which a thread might be woven, bits of family story, old photographs with scribbling on the backs, but no coherent narrative. . . . In the end is only the maze and the monster of hybrid potential at its center. I remain in the labyrinth, puzzled, hearing the approach of my own footsteps" (97). This notion is precisely what sets Owens apart from so many of his contemporaries. He understands that hybridization, aside from being an inescapable part of life, is the space of potential. The strength of the mixedblood lies in the fact "that mixedbloods cannot be known—and they know full well that they cannot be known, that the camera will obscure them except within their own vision" (100). He rejects the ease of essentialism and stereotype and instead chooses the creation of narrative, the act that gives self and life meaning, over and over again. Owens hunts with words to make the unknown known, and through all this he realizes that there are no absolutes and that the hunt must go on forever.

Perhaps this point is made best in "Yazoo Dusk," a story about a young man, Cole Bailey, returned home to ask his uncle advice on love. The story opens with Columbus Bailey's words of advice: "You got to fish ever goddamn day" (160). In light of all the other talk of hunting and fishing through *I Hear the Train*, these words become the guiding code for living well.

Cole Bailey reinforces the value of these words by explaining that "Columbus Bailey didn't go nowhere to see people, but people come to see him. He had things they wanted. The old man was *alikchi*. He knew the kinds of medicines people needed" (163–64). And what Cole needs, as we all do, is to search constantly for the answers we seek, to keep casting our lines into the waters around us, hoping to catch something and then release it so that we can catch something else. Cole tells us that "Uncle Col never just answered a question, you see" (164), and neither does Owens.

In all of Louis Owens's work, we are able to see the philosophies he has most recently articulated in *I Hear the Train*. In *Other Destinies* he writes, "The consciousness shared in all of these works [by contemporary Native American writers] is that of the individual attempting to reimagine an identity, to articulate a self" (22). And of his own work, he has said: "Every work is a different gamble and exploration. Every work teaches me a great deal. . . . Stories that carry us from the muddy waters of the Yazoo River to a tent in California and a glacial world of sheerest blue and frozen light. What is this thing that so compels us to thus organize and articulate the world?" (*MM* 183). Whether it is searching for the bones of a dead brother, saving a granddaughter at the bottom of a canyon, discovering the identity of a serial killer, or fighting for the preservation of wilderness, each of his works revolves around a hunt that always represents a rejection of stagnation and closure and a challenge to take the risks necessary as we search for self within the stories around and inside us. In his fiction he shows "Indians" authentically embedded in hybridized, transcultural worlds. Owens teaches us that in a complex world, personal identity is a complicated issue, especially for marginalized or mixedblood peoples faced with stereotypes maintained within the dominant culture. He constructs characters who risk losing the self within the varied voices and experiences that inform them and consciously acknowledge the complex dynamics of the worlds in which they exist and function while simultaneously rejecting the simulations of dominance, an act that speaks to the uncertainty and fluidity of identity. These characters often find both danger and strength in uncertainty, in an elusive but not unattainable confidence, and his novels refuse to give white audiences—or Native audiences, for that matter—either the romantic Indian other they often crave or the comfortable closure they may be used to.

If nothing else, Owens teaches us that meaning is tenuous, liminality is powerful, and sometimes the greatest confidence comes from the greatest uncertainty. As Philip Deloria states so eloquently,

> Liminality is like the light at dawn or dusk, when one can speak of neither daylight nor darkness but only of something in between. Liminality implies change—the world will either get brighter or will sink into night—but if one were plopped down, without any context, at the exact moment of dusk or dawn, it would be hard to discern whether day or night was approaching. Liminality is a frozen moment of unpredictable potential in the midst of a process of change, and it is in that sense that it has been used to describe the in-betweeness found in rite of passage rituals. Evocative, creative, and often frightening, it is critical to an individual's (or a society's) final reemergence as something new. (35)

And the hunt, which for Owens would necessarily occur in the hybridized space of the frontier, forces the hunter to embrace liminality and the creative power it demands. In "Soul-Catcher" he writes, "His father had taught him to hunt in the desert hills and to say a few phrases lake *Chahta isht ia* and *Chahta yakni* in the old language. These words had remained only sounds. . . . But the hunting had been real, a testing of desire and reflex he had felt all the way through" (201). The hunt is a test, and a risky one at that, but ultimately, Owens explains, it is worth the risk and the uncertainty that comes with it. As William Penn says, "doubt and wonder are comic, not tragic. Doubt and wonder mean that the argument is not over the ownership of the past but over the processes of the future informed by the changed and changing past" (110). After all, frontier space has never been about certainty, and if one truly wants to understand who he or she is, then that person must be willing to explore, to hunt, not just between the lines, but beyond them. Owens says it best: "He who loves this world is, in heart, a tracker and hunter, can be nothing else" (50).

• • •

It is almost dark, and Aaron has already taken his rig down. He has done pretty well today despite the shitty rod. Now he is sitting on the bank in his quiet, tranquil way, watching the rest of us fish.

Hossein is casting to a fish over and over, putting the Adams right over its nose. I can see his lips moving every now and then. He talks to fish. And it works too; I've seen him convince more than a few.

I've had an okay day, catching some nice ones, but not as many as I would have liked. But now I am tired and hungry and thinking about the beer at the truck. I clip off my fly, reel up my line, and take my rod apart. I am just walking over to the bank to sit with Aaron when Louis hooks one. From the way his rod is bent over, I know it is a big one. He is standing in the flat and has hooked this fish in the still, dark water just above the dam. The fish that hang around there are big and very hard to catch.

He fights the fish, and we are his audience. Even Hossein has taken down his gear and joined us on the bank. Every few minutes he yells over to Louis, "Keep that rod tip up!"

The dance before us is an interesting one. Louis gets the fish close, and then it runs away again, making his reel whine. He holds the rod high and winds when the fish gets tired. Sometimes he starts to walk while reeling, and Aaron calls out, "Stand your ground." We all laugh, remembering the story Hossein told us about the time an old fisherman gave him that advice.

The battle is beautiful. The sun has fallen behind the land, and a dirty orange glow blazes across the sky above Louis. The water itself is almost black and looks perfectly still. Then the trout jumps and fishtails across the surface. Louis keeps the line tight but is careful not to apply too much tension. In about ten minutes, after the fish is tired, he gets it close enough to net.

Louis wades over to us with his catch, smiling.

"I guess the old man can still fish," Hossein says.

Aaron looks into the net. "Look at the color. Flame red. Amazing."

I remember once, on another trip, Louis had said he might like to keep one of these big rainbows to take home. Something about showing it to his girls and smoking it on the grill. "I bet that one is twenty-one inches for sure. You ought to keep it. We're going back to the truck anyway."

Hossein puts the butt of his rod beside the tail of the fish now freed from the net, lying on the grass gasping for water. The moving mouth of the fish is past the twenty-inch mark carved into Hossein's rod. "Twenty-two. Definitely legal."

Louis says nothing. He picks up the fish, wades out a little way, and kneels in the water. He puts the fish under the water and gently rocks it back and forth.

Louis's audience stands up, and we gather our gear. "You sure you don't want to keep that one?" I ask.

I see a red flash between Louis's hands as the big trout darts away. He stands up and joins us as we start the walk back to the truck.

"Maybe tomorrow."

• • •

WORKS CITED

Deloria, Philip J. *Playing Indian*. New Haven: Yale UP, 1998.

Harvey, David. *The Condition of Postmodernity*. Cambridge: Basil Blackwell, 1989.

McCaffery, Larry, and Tom Marshall. "Head Water: An Interview with Gerald Vizenor." *Chicago Review* 39 (1993): 50–54.

Peirce, Charles Sanders. *Peirce on Signs: Writings on Semiotic*. Ed. James Hoopes. Chapel Hill: U of North Carolina P, 1991.

Penn, William S. *As We Are Now: Mixblood Essays on Race and Identity*. Berkeley: U of California P, 1997.

BIBLIOGRAPHY OF THE
WORKS OF LOUIS OWENS

BOOKS

(and Tom Colonnese) *American Indian Novelists: An Annotated Critical Bibliography.* New York: Garland Press, 1985.

John Steinbeck's Re-Vision of America. Athens: U of Georgia P, 1985.

The Grapes of Wrath: Trouble in the Promised Land. New York: G. K. Hall, 1989.

Wolfsong: A Novel. New York: West End Press, 1991.

(ed.) *American Literary Scholarship: An Annual, 1990.* Durham, N.C.: Duke UP, 1992.

Other Destinies: Understanding the American Indian Novel. Norman: U of Oklahoma P, 1992.

The Sharpest Sight: A Novel. Norman: U of Oklahoma P, 1992.

Bone Game: A Novel. Norman: U of Oklahoma P, 1994.

Nightland: A Novel. New York: Dutton Signet, 1996.

Mixedblood Messages: Literature, Film, Family, Place. Norman: U of Oklahoma P, 1998.

Dark River: A Novel. Norman: U of Oklahoma P, 1999.

I Hear the Train: Inventions, Reflections, Refractions. Norman: U of Oklahoma P, 2001.

ARTICLES AND CHAPTERS

"Paulding's 'The Dumb Girl': A Source of *The Scarlet Letter.*" *Nathaniel Hawthorne Journal* (1974): 140–49.

"James Kirke Paulding and the Foundations of American Realism." *Bulletin of the New York Public Library* 79.1 (1975): 40–50.

"Steinbeck's 'Flight': Into the Jaws of Death." *Steinbeck Quarterly* 10.3–4 (1977): 103–08.

"Steinbeck's 'Mystical Outcrying': *To a God Unknown* and *The Log from the Sea of Cortez.*" *San Jose Studies* 6.2 (1979): 21–32.

"The Threshold of War: Steinbeck's Quest in *Once There Was a War.*" *Steinbeck Quarterly* 13.3–4 (1980): 80–86.

"*The Wayward Bus:* A Triumph of Nature." *San Jose Studies* 6.1 (1980): 45–53.

"Camelot East of Eden: John Steinbeck's *Tortilla Flat*." *Arizona Quarterly* 38.3 (1982): 203–16.

"Steinbeck's 'The Murder': Illusions of Chivalry." *Steinbeck Quarterly* 17.1–2 (1984): 10–14.

"Fiction: The 1930s to the 1950s." *American Literary Scholarship: An Annual, 1983.* Durham, N.C.: Duke UP, 1985. 255–86.

"John Steinbeck's *The Pastures of Heaven*: Illusions of Eden." *Arizona Quarterly* 41.3 (1985): 197–214.

"The Map of the Mind: D'Arcy McNickle and the American Indian Novel." *Western American Literature* 19.4 (1985): 275–83.

"Fiction: The 1930s to the 1950s." *American Literary Scholarship: An Annual, 1984.* Durham, N.C.: Duke UP, 1986. 267–92.

Preface to *The New Native American Novel: Works in Progress.* Albuquerque: U of New Mexico P, 1986. vii–viii.

"Acts of Recovery: The American Indian Novel in the '80s." *Western American Literature* 22.1 (1987): 53–57.

"Fiction: The 1930s to the 1960s." *American Literary Scholarship: An Annual, 1985.* Durham, N.C.: Duke UP, 1987. 253–75.

"James Kirke Paulding." *American Literary Critics and Scholars, 1800–1850.* Ed. John W. Rathburn and Monica M. Grecu. Detroit: Gale Research Co., 1987. Vol. 59 of *Dictionary of Literary Biography.* 242–49.

"John Steinbeck." *Book of Days.* Ann Arbor: Pierian P, 1987. 91–93.

"*Of Mice and Men*: The Dream of Commitment." *John Steinbeck: Modern Critical Views.* Ed. Harold Bloom. New York: Chelsea House, 1987. 145–50.

"Sangres Mezcladas" (Native American Fiction). Special U.S.A. Fiction Issue of *Quimera* 70/71 (Nov. 1987): 20–24.

"Winter in Paris: John Steinbeck's *Pippin IV*." *Steinbeck Quarterly* 20:1–2 (1987): 18–25.

Afterword. *Wind From An Enemy Sky.* By D'Arcy McNickle. Albuquerque: U of New Mexico P, 1988. 257–65.

"Between Two Fires: Native American Novels Today." *World & I* 3 (Oct. 1988): 358–65.

"The Culpable Joads: Desentimentalizing *The Grapes of Wrath*." *Critical Essays on Steinbeck's* The Grapes of Wrath. Ed. John Ditsky. Boston: G. K. Hall, 1989. 108–15.

(and Hector Torres) "Dialogic Structure and Levels of Discourse in *The Grapes of Wrath*." *Arizona Quarterly* 4.4 (winter 1989): 75–94.

"Ecstatic Strategies: Gerald Vizenor's Darkness in *Saint Louis Bearheart*." *Narrative Chance: Postmodern Discourse on Native American Indian Literatures.* Ed. Gerald Vizenor. Albuquerque: U of New Mexico P, 1989. 141–54.

"*The Grapes of Wrath*: Looking Back." *U.S.A. Today* (May 1989): 92–94.

"John Steinbeck." Updated entry in *Concise Dictionary of American Literary Biography: The Age of Maturity, 1929–1941.* Detroit: Gale Research, 1989. 280–309.

"The Red Road to Nowhere: D'Arcy McNickle's *The Surrounded* and 'The Hungry Generations.'" *American Indian Quarterly* 13 (1989): 239–48.

"The Story of a Writing: Narrative Structure in *East of Eden.*" *Rediscovering Steinbeck—Revisionist Views of His Art, Politics and Intellect.* Ed. Cliff Lewis and Carroll Britch. Lewiston, N.Y.: Edwin Mellen P, 1989. 58–76.

"Where the Road Divides: D'Arcy McNickle's *The Surrounded.*" *Native American Literatures.* Ed. Laura Coltelli. Pisa, Italy: Servizio Editoriale U Vicolor Della Croce Rossa, 1989. 133–41.

"Acts of Imagination: N. Scott Momaday's *The Ancient Child.*" *World & I* 5 (March 1990): 434–44.

Afterword. *Bearheart: The Heirship Chronicles.* By Gerald Vizenor. Minneapolis: U of Minnesota P, 1990. 247–54.

"Critics and Common Denominators: Steinbeck's *Sweet Thursday.*" *The Short Novels of John Steinbeck.* Ed. Jackson Benson. Durham, N.C.: Duke UP, 1990. 195–203.

"Earthboy's Return: James Welch's Act of Recovery in *Winter in the Blood.*" *Wicazo Sa Review* 6.2 (fall 1990): 27–37.

"A Garden of My Land: Landscape and Dreamscape in John Steinbeck's Fiction." *Steinbeck Quarterly* 22.3–4 (summer/fall 1990): 78–88.

"'Grampa Killed Indians, Pa Killed Snakes': Steinbeck and the American Indian." *MELUS* 15.2 (summer 1988, pub. 1990): 85–92.

Interview with N. Scott Momaday. *This Is About Vision: Interviews with Southwestern Writers.* Ed. John F. Crawford, William Victor Balassi, and Annie O. Eysturoy. Albuquerque: U of New Mexico P, 1990. 59–69.

"The Mirror and the Vamp: Invention, Reflection, and Bad, Bad Cathy Trask in *East of Eden.*" *Writing the American Classics.* Ed. James Barbour and Tom Quirk. Chapel Hill: U of North Carolina P, 1990. 235–57.

"Steinbeck's Deep Dissembler: *The Short Reign of Pippin IV.*" *The Short Novels of John Steinbeck: Critical Essays with a Checklist to Steinbeck Criticism.* Ed. Jackson J. Benson. Durham, N.C.: Duke UP, 1990. 249–56.

"Bottom and Upland: The Balanced Man in Steinbeck's 'The Harness.'" *Steinbeck's Short Stories in The Long Valley: Essays in Criticism.* Ed. by Tetsumaro Hayashi. Muncie, Ind.: Ball State UP, 1991. 44–48.

"'From the Inside Out': Identity and Authenticity in James Welch's *Fools Crow.*" *The Cresset* (Nov. 1991): 5–10.

Headnotes for Paula Gunn Allen, Simon Ortiz, Lawson Inada, and Robert Hayden sections. *Prentice Hall Anthology of American Literature.* Ed. Emory Elliott, A. Walton Litz. Englewood Cliffs, N.J.: Prentice Hall, 1991.

"The Little Bit of a Story: Steinbeck's 'The Vigilante.'" *Steinbeck's Short Stories in The Long Valley: Essays in Criticism.* Ed. Tetsumaro Hayashi. Muncie, Ind.: Steinbeck Society, 1991. 49–55.

"No Other Destiny: James Welch's *The Death of Jim Loney.*" *Northeast Indian Quarterly* 6 (fall 1991): 49–53.

"Grapes Goes Marching On." *Resources for American Literary Study* 18.2 (1992): 165–70.

"He Had Never Danced with His People: Cultural Survival in John Joseph Mathews's *Sundown.*" *Native American Literatures.* Ed. Laura Coltelli. Pisa, Italy: Servizio Editoriale U Vicolor Della Croce Rossa, 1992. 27–38.

"East of Eden" and *"The Grapes of Wrath." A New Study Guide to Steinbeck's Major Works, with Critical Explications.* Ed. Tetsumaro Hayashi. Methuchen, N.J., and London: Scarecrow P, 1993. 66–89, 90–114.

Editor, Special Focus Issue of *Native American Literature. American Book Review* 14.5 (Jan. 1993).

"'Grinning Aboriginal Demons': Gerald Vizenor's *Bearheart* and the Indian's Escape from Gothic." *Frontier Gothic.* Ed. David Mogen, Scott P. Sanders, and Joanne Karpinski. Rutherford, N.J.: Fairleigh Dickinson UP, 1993. 71–83.

"Patterns of Reality and Barrels of Worms: From *Western Flyer* to Rocinante in Steinbeck's Nonfiction." *The Steinbeck Question: New Essays in Criticism.* Ed. Donald R. Noble. Troy, N.Y.: Whitston Publishing, 1993. 171–83.

"Writing 'in Costume': The Missing Voices of *In Dubious Battle." John Steinbeck: The Years of Greatness.* Ed. Tetsumaro Hayashi. Tuscaloosa: U of Alabama P, 1993. 77–94.

"D'une disparition a l'autre," *Revue d'études Palestiennes* 55.3 (spring 1995): 45–52.

"Mixedblood Geography: Hybridization in Native American Literature." *Histoire et Anthropologie: Revue de Sciences Humaines* 10 (1995): 37–45.

"The Song Is Very Short: Native American Literature and Literary Theory." *Weber Studies* 12.3 (fall 1995): 51–62.

Editor's Preface (Guest Editor). Special Vizenor *Issue of Studies in American Indian Literature* 9.1 (Jan. 1997): 1–2.

"California as a False Eden." *Readings on* The Grapes of Wrath. Literary Companion Series. Ed. Bonnie Szumski. San Diego: Greenhaven P, 1999. 66–75.

Editor's Preface (Guest Editor). Special Personal Narrative Issue of *Weber Studies* 10.2 (winter 1999): 7.

"The Role of the Mountains in *The Pearl." Readings on* The Pearl. Literary Companion Series. Ed. Jill Karson. San Diego: Greenhaven P, 1999. 101–10.

"Where Things Can Happen: California and Writing." *Western American Literature* 34.2 (summer 1999): 150–55.

"The Chrysanthemums: Waiting for Rain." *Short Story Criticism.* Ed. Anja Barnard. Vol. 37. Detroit: The Gale Group, 2000.

"Courting the Stone Age: Native Authenticity in Gerald Vizenor's *Ishi and the Wood Ducks." Multilingua: Journal of Cross-Cultural and Interlanguage Communication* 18.2–3 (1999): 135–47. Reprinted in *Loosening the Seams: Interpretations of Gerald Vizenor.* Ed. A. Robert Lee. Bowling Green, Ind.: Bowling Green State U Popular P, 2000. 233–45.

"Disturbed by Something Deeper": The Native Art of John Joseph Mathews." *Western American Literature* 35.2 (summer 2000): 163–73.

"Mixedbloods and Multiple Narratives: Louise Erdrich's *Love Medicine*." *Louise Erdrich's* Love Medicine: *A Casebook*. Ed. Hertha Sweet Wong. New York: Oxford UP, 2000.

"As If an Indian Were Really an Indian: Native American Voices and Postcolonial Theory." *Native American Representations: First Encounters, Distorted Images, and Literary Appropriations*. Ed. Gretchen Bataille. Chapel Hill: U of North Carolina P, 2001. 63–66.

"Part and Whole: Dangerous Bifurcations." *Native American Literature: Boundaries and Sovereignties*. Ed. Kathryn W. Shanley. Special Issue of Paradoxa 15 (2001): 286–87.

"The Syllogistic Mixedblood: How Roland Barthes Saved Me from the *indians*." *Mixing Race, Mixing Culture: Inter-American Literary Dialogues*. Ed. Monica Kaup and Deborah Rosenthal. Austin: U of Texas P, 2002.

"Their Shadows Before Them: Photographing Indians." *Trading Gazes: Euro-American Women Photographers Among Native North Americans*. Ed. Susan Bernardin, Melody Graulich, Lisa MacFarlane, and Nicole Tonkovich. New Brunswick, N.J.: Rutgers UP, 2003.

SELECTED FICTION, ESSAYS, AND INTERVIEWS

"Nalusachito." Short story. *South Dakota Review* 22.3 (1984): 55–62.

"The Dancing Poodle of Arles." Short story. *Jeopardy* 21 (spring 1985): 7–15.

"Winter Rain." Short story. *Asylum* 1.1 (1985): 1–6.

"The Sharpest Sight." Novel excerpt. *The New Native American Novel: Works in Progress*. Ed. Mary Daugherty Bartlett. Albuquerque: U of New Mexico P, 1986. 65–77.

"Tenure in the Land: N. Scott Momaday." *America West* 1.4 (1986): 20–25.

"A Faceted Complexity." Short story. *Jeopardy* 23 (spring 1987): 63–67.

"Mythic Miles." *America West* 1.11 (1987): 18–23.

"The Sharpest Sight." Novel excerpt. Best New Mexico Writers Issue. *Albuquerque Living* 6.1 (Jan. 1988): 42–44.

"Shelter." Short story. *CUBE Literary Magazine* 1.2 (1988): 23–25.

"Water Witch." *California Childhood: Recollections and Stories of the Golden State*. Ed. Gary Soto. Berkeley: Creative Arts Books, 1988. 83–90.

"Episodes from *The Sharpest Sight*: Work in Progress." *Wicazo Sa Review* 6.2 (fall 1990): 7–14.

"Rainshadows." *Guide to the Arts*. Ashland, Oreg. (Feb. 1991): 18, 36.

"Into the Territory: The Invention of John Wayne." *Icarus* 10 (spring 1993): 95–108.

"The American Indian Wilderness." *The American Nature Writing Newsletter* 6.2 (fall 1994): 7–8.

Introduction to Leslie Silko's "The Man to Send Rain Clouds." *You've Got to Read This: Contemporary American Writers Introduce Stories That Held Them in Awe*. Ed. Ron Hansen and and Jim Shepard. New York: HarperCollins, 1994. 481–88.

"Sous le regard indiene." Interview with Louis Owens. *Le Monde, Temps Libre* Dec. 10, 1994: 5.

"Motion of Fire and Form: Autobiographical Reflections." *Native American Literature: A Brief Introduction and Anthology.* Ed. Gerald Vizenor. HarperCollins, 1995. 83–93.

"The Stand." *Native American Literature.* Ed. Gerald Vizenor. New York: HarperCollins, 1995. 189–92.

"Finding Gene." *Weber Studies* 10.2 (winter 1999): 106–15.

"Shared Blood." *Dark Night Field Notes* 15 (fall 1999): 29–33.

"Blessed Sunshine." Excerpt from novel in progress. *Nothing But the Truth: An Anthology of Native American Literature.* Ed. John Purdy and Jim Ruppert. New York: Prentice Hall, 2000. 126–32.

"Fiction." Introduction to Native American Fiction. *Nothing But the Truth: An Anthology of Native American Literature.* Ed. John Purdy and Jim Ruppert. New York: Prentice Hall, 2000. 190–93.

"Yazoo Dusk." Excerpt from novel in progress. *The Ones Who Stayed Behind: An Anthology of Southeastern Indian Writings.* Ed. Geary Hobson and Janet McAdams. Athens: U of Georgia P, 2000.

In addition to the above stories and essays, Owens published more than thirty nonfiction essays in various nonrefereed national publications as well as numerous reviews.

Contributors

Susan Bernardin is Assistant Professor of English at SUNY College at Oneonta.

David Brande is Assistant Professor of Humanities in the University Honors Program at Portland State University.

Renny Christopher is Associate Professor of English at California State University, Channel Islands.

Neil Harrison teaches English and Creative Writing at Northeast Community College, Norfolk, Nebraska.

Linda Lizut Helstern is a member of the English faculty at the University of Texas-Pan American.

Jacquelyn Kilpatrick is Professor of English at California State University, Channel Islands.

A. Robert Lee, formerly of the University of Kent at Canterbury, United Kingdom, is Professor of American Literature at Nihon University, Tokyo.

Jesse Peters is Assistant Professor of English and American Indian Studies at the University of North Carolina at Pembroke.

Elvira Pulitano is Assistant Professor (Assistante Docteur) in the Emergent Literatures Program at the University of Geneva, Switzerland.

John Purdy is Professor of English at Western Washington University and a former editor of *American Indian Literatures*.

Gretchen Ronnow teaches at Wayne State College.

Paul Beekman Taylor is Professor of Medieval English Language and Literature at the University of Geneva, Switzerland.

INDEX